DATE DUE

NO 14 05			
OE 7 05			
FE - 1 '10			

DEMCO 38-296

Fashion & Merchandising Fads

Fashion & Merchandising Fads

Frank W. Hoffmann, PhD
William G. Bailey, MA

The Haworth Press
New York • London • Norwood (Australia)

The Haworth Press, Inc., 10 Alice Street, Binghamton, NY 13904-1580

All photographs are used courtesy of the Library of Congress.

Library of Congress Cataloging-in-Publication Data

Hoffmann, Frank W., 1949-
    Fashion & merchandising fads / Frank W. Hoffmann, William G. Bailey.
        p.   cm.
    Includes bibliographical references and index.
    ISBN 1-56024-376-7 (alk. paper).
    1. United States–Civilization–1970- 2. Fads–United States–History–20th century. 3. Fashion–United States–History–20th century. 4. Novelties–History–20th century. I. Bailey, William G., 1947– . II. Title. III. Title: Fashion and merchandising fads.
E169.12.H634   1993
973.92–dc20
                                                                                            92-46036
                                                                                            CIP

CONTENTS

ABOUT THE AUTHORS

Frank W. Hoffmann, PhD, MLS, is an associate professor in the School of Library Science, Sam Houston State University. His teaching responsibilities include library collection development, reference/information services, and a seminar in popular culture. His publications include *The Development of Collections of Sound Recordings in Libraries* (Marcel Dekker), *Popular Culture and Libraries* (Library Professional Publications), *The Literature of Rock* series (Scarecrow), and *The Cash Box* chart compilation series (Scarecrow). He received his doctorate from the University of Pittsburgh and his BA in History and MLS from Indiana University.

William G. Bailey, MA, MLS, has worked in the Information Services division of the Newton Gresham Library, Sam Houston State University, since 1978. He is currently the head of the Reference Department. Due to his daily routine, he is constantly looking for new writing projects to fill information gaps. A fad encyclopedia appeals to his eclectic mind; he is already the editor/compiler of books on such diverse topics as police, longevity, and Americans in Paris. He holds an MA degree in English and American Literature from the University of Houston, and an MLS from the University of Texas at Austin.

Introduction

Life devoid of fads is impossible to imagine. For this to happen we would have to live like the Amish: no electricity, no telephone, no radio or television. We would wear the same modest clothing and genuflect throughout the day. Our food would be plain, our homes clean but drab, and our art restricted to quilt-making. The events of our lives would never waver from established routine and we would care nothing for individual freedom. But fads do enter our lives and are mostly vehicles for amusement.

To say that this volume of 140 fashion and merchandising fads is exhaustive would be amiss. This collection represents a sampling of over 200 years of American fads related mainly to our obsession with clothes, hair, and diet, or in a word–appearance. If you are an avid fad-watcher, the number of fads defined here is far too small. Add to that number the fads already collected in three previous volumes: *Arts & Entertainment*, *Sports & Recreation*, and *Mind & Society*, and the total still falls short. Do you recall these fifty fads that made news in 1990-91?

Fashion

1. *thermochromic dresses:* Black on a hanger, the dress changes colors on the body. Temperature-sensitive chemicals in the ink screen-printed on the fabric make the rainbow effects.

2. *Jesuswear:* Sweatshirts read "UH-University of Heaven" and "God's Last Name Is Not Dammit"; license plate frames announce, "My Boss Is a Jewish Carpenter"; and for kids, a black T-shirt with a yellow dove emblem ("Dove Man") counters the Batman craze.

3. *baseball caps:* With or without the team logo, seen everywhere and worn by all ages, bill either in front or back.

4. *camouflage clothing and the American flag:* U.S. success in the Persian Gulf War triggered patriot garb. Old Glory materialized on blouses, shirts, shorts, and especially bandannas.

5. *torn jeans:* Teenagers no longer have to razorcut denim for that peek-a-boo look. Machine-torn jeans can be bought at the mall. An offshoot are shotgun jeans that are actually tossed in the air like clay pigeons and perforated with holes.

6. *sculptured haircuts:* Lines, zig-zags, initials, peace symbols, a Batman logo, etc., are etched on the head by cutting hair to the scalp to leave the design.

Entertainment

7. *karaoke:* Means "empty orchestra" in Japanese. At a karaoke bar, the participant takes the stage to sing popular songs to recorded music. He or she pretends to be Sinatra, Streisand, or Manilow.

8. *zany fan clubs:* Gumby, Mr. Ed, Bob "Elvis" McVay, Barbara Eden and other unlikely figures of popular culture attract enough fans to form clubs. Arthur Kent, the NBC correspondent who reported from Saudi Arabia during the Persian Gulf Crisis, inspired his own band of ardent followers. Nicknamed the "Scud-stud," the handsome Kent became the immediate object of worship by 1400 fans.

9. *Christo's umbrellas:* The eccentric conceptual artist took six years and spent $26 million to create another of his fad masterpieces. Christo placed 1,340 20-foot blue umbrellas along a 12-mile stretch in Japan, and 1,760 yellow umbrellas over 18 miles of hills in California. The riotous bumbershoots were removed after a few weeks of open-mouthed wonder.

10. *whirlyball:* Two teams of five players ride whirlybugs (vehicles similar to bumper cars), scoring points by using a plastic scoop to throw a ball against a wall-mounted target (popular in 17 cities).

11. *Kitty Kelley:* Queen of the unauthorized biography, Kelly garnered more attention than usual with her life of Nancy Reagan. For her revelations, Kelley became a household name, sold more copies of her libelous chat than Nancy Reagan did of her autobiography, and will host a talk show. In retort, George Carpozi, a former tabloid editor, rushed to print *Poison Pen: The Unauthorized Biography of Kitty Kelley.*

12. *afterlife films:* The great beyond beckoned moviegoers with a host of spirit beings in *Ghost* (the big money-maker), *The Rapture,*

Switch, Ghost Dad, Bill & Ted's Bogus Journey, and others. *Flat-liners,* a film about flirting with postexistence, also did well at the box office.

Cosmetics

13. *colored braces:* Multi-colored bands and wires let shy teen-agers smile broadly to show off their fashionable teeth.
14. *pectoral implants for men:* Wanting total firmness in their sagging chests, men no less than women find support in plastic surgery. Male requests for all types of makeovers are on the rise.

Self-Help

15. *mind machines:* Flashing lights, electrical pulses, soothing sounds and words, motion and ultrasound waves stimulate the brain. Typical apparatus consists of goggles and headphones. Brand names are: SynchroEnergizer, Graham Potentializer, and MC2.
16. *codependency:* The notion that one person becomes so in-volved in another person's life that an obsession develops in the first person to control the behavior of the second. Melody Beattie, who defined codependency, advises 80 million codependent Ameri-cans (her estimate) to "stop controlling others and start caring for yourself."
17. *inner child therapy:* Also called male-mentoring, advocates a return to childhood, i.e., a primitive state, to undo early abuse. Spokesman Robert Bly, a National Book Award winner for poetry in 1968, tells his disciples that all parents abuse their children in one way or another. Bly seeks to heal early abuse by having groups of men go off into the woods to beat drums, dance around a fire, and talk out their hurt–known as "Wild Man" weekends.

Business

18. *outdoor training:* Executives engage in strenuous activities such as mountain climbing, whitewater rafting, and sailing to im-prove their leadership skills and analytical ability. Rope courses are also popular.

19. *corporation bowl games:* American corporations paid millions of dollars for the rights to rename postseason football classics. Instead of the Cotton Bowl, the Mobil Cotton Bowl emerged, as did the Federal Express Orange Bowl, the Mazda Gator Bowl, the Poulan/Weed Eater Independence Bowl, the Domino's Pizza Copper Bowl, and the John Hancock Sun Bowl. Many sports announcers and fans protested, but big business won out.

Merchandising

20. *Certifiably Nuts:* Ten ounces of Georgia peanuts are packed in a straitjacketed, headless doll. At the pull of a string the doll emits a series of crazed, giggling voices. Like the Cabbage Patch Doll adoption papers, Certifiably Nuts comes with a patient history and a certificate committing it to an insane asylum.

21. *microbreweries:* In a very competitive business, 60+ small American beer brewers began production of European-style suds.

22. *Joe Camel:* The ultra-hip dromedary that advertises Camel cigarettes appeals strongly to teenagers. According to an article in the *Journal of the American Medical Association,* illegal sales of Camels to minors rose from $6 million to $476 million because of the "radical ruminant."

23. *camcorders plugged into computers:* For under $15,000, an amateur can buy enough new technology, especially editing devices, to make professional-looking videos. Now the baby's first steps can rival Spielberg.

24. *mountain bikes:* Ten-speeds are out. Their delicate tires pop and riders get tired of hunching over for aerodynamics. This latest breed of bike can take extreme punishment on and off the road.

25. *Krushed Kritter Kompany of Kalifornia:* Markets a stuffed half-cat creation to place on a car windshield. The Kritter appears to have been hit at a high rate of speed. (200,000+ sold so far)

26. *Super-Soaker:* A water gun that shoots a straight line over distance with accuracy. Rambo's answer to the sissy squirt gun.

27. *PowerMaster Malt Liquor:* Contains 5.9% alcohol content versus 4.5% for typical malt liquor and 3.5% for regular beer. Aimed at minorities seeking a macho image.

28. *Stuff-a-Pumpkin leaf bags:* Holds 260 gallons to make the

orange Halloween face come alive; can be seen for blocks. To prevent theft, bricks inside weigh down the bags.

29. *Slap Wrap:* A flexible 9″ cloth-covered ruler slapped against the wrist to form a bracelet. At its peak the novelty sold 500,000 a week.

30. *Saddam Hussein calendar:* Only the first 15 days of January appear, thereafter a blank void. A real collector's item, considering the American blitzkrieg.

31. *real money gift wrap:* Uncut sheets of $1 bills from the Bureau of Engraving and Printing decorate presents in Palm Beach at a chain of clothing stores.

Social

32. *fidelity:* Several well-publicized surveys claimed as many as 90% of married people avow they are faithful and have never had an affair. The Kinsey Institute and other research groups vigorously disagreed.

33. *herbal medicine:* Reminiscent of laetrile (a bitter almond extract purported to cure cancer in the late 1970s), ads tell AIDS sufferers that herbal concoctions can save their lives.

34. *ecotourism:* Whale watching in Alaska, mountain climbing in Nepal, and backpacking in Yosemite attract advocates of pristine wilderness. Unfortunately, the crowds cause more damage to what they want to save.

35. *riverboat gambling:* Illinois, Mississippi, Missouri, and Louisiana either approved or have under consideration the licensing of floating casinos. Free from law, nostalgia and the fast buck reign on the open water.

36. *Super Seven tournaments:* At Trump Castle, contestants play the slots in a race against time to see who can capture the most wins. Each player pays an entry fee of $577 for a $40,077 payoff.

37. *superchurches:* Protestant congregations of 5,000 to 20,000 worshipers who subscribe to a conservative theology, mostly Evangelical, fundamentalist, charismatic, or Pentecostal.

38. *infomercials:* Air early morning or late night on TV and run 30 minutes to push products using high-powered sales techniques. The trend is for a celebrity host to create excitement by repeating, "It's an amazing discovery!" to a spellbound audience.

39. *simplified scripture:* Advertised for today's family, the biblical language has been reduced to primer level. The New Testament is in the stores; the Old Testament will appear in 1996.

40. *city spas:* For the executive-on-the-go, a bath, body scrub, and massage can be had for under $100 in the length of an hour. Regular spas require days to weeks for reinvigoration–far too long away from the art of the deal.

Culinary

41. *canola oil:* Derived from rapeseed, canola is the latest cholesterol-fighter, thereby dethroning safflower oil.

42. *longhorn meat:* Texas A&M researchers have discovered the symbol of Texas is lower in saturated fat than other beef. Ranchers plan to increase their herds.

43. *specialty potatoes:* Yukon Gold, Peruvian Purple, and other designer spuds glitter more on the plate than Idaho browns.

44. *ostrich and garden burgers:* In L.A. the ostrich burger rules the roost. Lower in calories than chicken or turkey, ground ostrich may be appearing in your market soon. On the other hand, the garden burger avoids meat; the patty blends mushrooms, onions, oats, brown rice, low-fat cheese, egg whites, bulgur wheat, walnuts, and seasonings, then is baked not fried. Garden burgers sell well in Hard Rock Cafes, at Sheraton Hotels, and at Disneyland.

45. *specialty vinegars:* Foodtiques now offer champagne, hot pepper, blueberry, and other vinegars to dress up salad. Wine and apple are just too humdrum.

Intellectual

46. *"Who killed JFK?":* Oliver Stone's film about the "cover-up" convinced a lot of people that Oswald wasn't alone. Opinion polls showed a distinct preference for a CIA conspiracy theory with the Mafia theory a close second. All of which prompted the lone-triggerman proponents to accuse Stone of distorting the truth.

47. *self-organized criticality:* The latest physics theory suggests that natural systems organize themselves into a critical state due to having a large number of constituents free to move around. The

"degrees of freedom" are what cause the systems to organize critically. Layperson example: add sand to a sand pile and tiny sand-slides occur. As this happens, the sand pile organizes itself into a conical shape, thus averting chaos. Applied broadly, some physicists believe the theory will explain the evolution of matter in the universe.

48. *cosmic strings:* More theoretical physics: after the Big Bang, cosmic strings (very long, thin strands of pure energy) were left over. So if a spaceship were to fly at nearly the speed of light, the ship could conceivably travel back in time by looping around one of a pair of cosmic strings, that also must pass each other at nearly the speed of light.

49. *SimEarth–The Living Planet:* A computer program that allows the user to play God to create and recreate the Earth spontaneously according to the Gaia hypothesis (Gaia views Earth as capable of monitoring its own needs).

50. *public school reform:* Faced with poor student performance nationwide, some state administrators advocate teacher recertification every five years and doing away with teacher tenure. Besieged teachers point out the real problems: stifling curriculums and overcrowded classrooms.

The media labeled these phenomena of 1990-91 fads. How long these passing fancies stay in vogue is anyone's guess. Thankfully, there is only one pernicious example among them. Just as the Surgeon General was about to declare partial victory in the war against lung cancer, Joe Camel trotted in. It is hard to imagine how a desert-dweller with a peninsular snout could captivate so many adolescents, unless one believes that image is everything. If so, then the advertising agency that created Joe Camel should win an award, albeit a corrupt one. Several mischief-makers that could possibly do damage also appear among the 50 fads listed. In the self-help group, mind machines, codependency, and inner child therapy fall outside the safety net of professional care. Not long ago the Federal Drug Administration would have scrutinized mind machines as it once did fraudulent cancer-cure apparatus. Perhaps we need our watchdogs back. Self-styled gurus, Beattie and Bly, promulgated the two psychotherapies: lacking certification, they are folks helping folks.

This is significant because fads burgeon all the more if they are democratic in nature. Consumers pay greater attention to fellow sufferers cut from their own mold than to remote intellectuals.

Another example of distrust of authority is the allure of herbal medicine. For believers the thinking goes: native people ingest herbs; herbs are natural and magical; herbs work with the body–lab cures work against it. Now that AIDS is full-blown, herbal doctors tout remedies that have little proven efficacy beyond that of mystique. Faddish cures for scourges never quite disappear, but recycle as shamans rediscover them. Herbal treatments for cancer have included chaparral, comfrey, echinacea (purple cornflower), violet leaves, red clover blossoms, burdock root, aloes, cayenne, pepsin, wheatgrass manna, and–whipped up in a drink–Hoxsey Herb Treatment. Merchandisers know that sick people grasping at straws will grasp no less at wheatgrass manna. All it takes to initiate a fad cure is a scourge and marketing acumen. On the flip side of distrust of authority, the FDA conducts serious research on harvesting drugs from plants. The FDA reports that the leaves of a small tree in Samoa might contain a substance to fight AIDS with. Madagascar periwinkle, the May apple, digitalis, and rauwolfia have already been plucked from the wilds to treat other human disorders. Highly regarded, the FDA's Laboratory of Molecular Pharmacology calms consumers skeptical of shamans. So the herbal medicine fad captures both types of consumers: those suspicious of authority and those suspicious of charlatans.

Another intriguing aspect of fads is their ready acceptance as passing fancy. The creator of Certifiably Nuts never intended to replace Planters Peanuts on the grocery shelf. The idea was to sell a few million, then onto another whimsy. Ready acceptance of fads assumes that consumers are always on the outlook for what's new, and they don't know what that is until it is given to them. The image is of a nest full of baby birds straining their necks to devour whatever mother brings home. Along these lines, the slickest packaged deal of the last two years has been the singing-dancing quintet, New Kids on the Block. Maurice Starr, a Boston-based producer, put the Kids together. At first, five white teenagers trying to update the Temptations didn't catch on. Then Starr's master plan took hold. The Kids were to electrify audiences with squeaky cleanness: no profanity or lascivious moves on stage. Aptly named, being new kids on the block in the rebellious world of pop music has paid big dividends. Forbes' latest survey of the highest-paid celebrities places the Kids on top, having grossed an estimated $115 million for 1990-91. To seize that honor, the Kids beat out Bill Cosby, Oprah Winfrey, Madonna, and Michael Jackson. Assembled as they were to bridge the gap between Guns 'N' Roses and Amy Grant, it is unlikely the Kids will repeat their astonishing success or, for that matter, stay together. Conservatism in pop music is usually an anomaly, but in this case worked to perfection.

A social fad like superchurches reveals another aspect of collective behavior. In the grip of mall-mentality, congregating with thousands on Sunday doesn't appear odd. The phenomenon of merchandising religion has endured a decade of growth and scandal. Consumers crowd together to observe a spectacle–the cavernous temple, the charismatic leader, the crescendo of emotion. Freeway billboards and TV spots invite everyone to join in the temple of love. Furthermore, superchurch services are televised, bringing more consumers into the fold. Why do people who apparently once thought religion a private experience flock to great glass houses more profane than sacred? And why do they flock to conservative theology only? The born-again Christian fad of the 1980s holds part of the answer. Unhappy people who wanted a fresh start jumped at the chance to clean the slate. It was so easy to proclaim born-again status, wear a pin, have Christ (the fish symbol) embossed on business cards, and feel absolved of past sins. New alliances flourished overnight, new hope, and regretfully, new segregation. Born-agains cropped up everywhere. They waged holy war to oust pagans from every sector of life. What changed this–killed off the fad–were the misdeeds of the two Jimmys, Bakker and Swaggart. Likewise, misuse of absolution–facing legal charges and trumpeting Christ at the same time–didn't look good. And the vulgar display of wealth as a reflection of God's approval–the rich shall inherit the earth–finally struck people as warped.

The strength of the superchurch phenomenon is size. Providing a larger forum for expression of belief engenders a force to be reckoned with. A small church in which a few people sing off-key cannot compete with a hall full of robust voices. The born-agains of the 1980s have resurfaced and want greater exposure for their conservative theology. Church and state are not always separate as evangelist Pat Robertson demonstrated during the 1988 presidential campaign.

A final twist to fad-watching concerns the esoteric. The theoretical physics fads–self-organized criticality and cosmic strings–are profound concepts that tantalize the public. Being mysterious, yet also somehow intelligible, adds to their allure. These current fads hark back to Einstein. In 1905, his "annus mirabilis," Einstein published four papers that shook the scientific world. By 1920, he was acclaimed as the most famous thinker alive. No matter that the public failed to grasp even the rudiments of his thought on capillarity and Brownian movement, the photoelectric effect, special and general relativity, or unified field theory. Einstein was the cerebral man. What made his theories faddish to the public was that they seemed to explain the workings of the universe, a subject nearly everyone found fascinating. Anyone capable of such brainwork–even in an anti-intellectual climate–deserved accolades. Scientific discoveries of all kinds occur with regularity, though most do not capture the interest of the public. But when a physicist announces a theory that may well hold the key to the universe, people perk up.

We hope you enjoy reading about the fads in this series. Forgive us for having left out any of your favorites. We trust we have shed light on the subject, especially on what constitutes a fad. If you accept today's definition of fad as a passing fancy resulting from our appetite for constant change, then you must agree we are a fad-ridden society. In 1988, a trio of social scientists published a paper on streaking (Aguirre et al., "The Collective Behavior of Fads: The Characteristics, Effects, and Career of Streaking," *American Sociological Review*, 53:569-584). After examining 1,016 incidents of individuals romping nude across campus, they concluded that media coverage and imitation were to blame. In lieu of ever arriving at an exact meaning of fad, these two requisites come close enough.

Before WW II, cancer-cure apparatus such as this elaborate example hood-winked many sick Americans who distrusted conventional medicine. Today, the fad of herbal medicine continues the trend.

The A-2 Flight Jacket

The A-2 Flight Jacket, standard issue in the U.S. Army Air Force beginning in 1931, quickly became the most popular item in the flier's entire wardrobe. Constructed of tough horsehide lined in light brown silk with two patch pockets and knitted cuffs and waistband, it combined utility with an inimitable sense of macho style.

However, by May 1942, General "Hap" Arnold, commanding officer of the Air Force, evidently felt otherwise. During an inventory analysis at the time he held up the jacket and stated, "We don't need leather. Get something better." The Army stopped producing A-2s immediately. But the jacket remained highly visible because airmen were allowed to continue wearing it as long as it lasted, and durability proved to be one of the A-2's greatest assets.

By the end of World War II many of the jackets had become self-contained works of art. Fliers had taken to painting the backs with the same colorful illustrations that adorned the front of their airplanes. Called Nose Art, it featured pinups, slogans, and symbols depicting bombing missions and conquests.

The appeal of the jacket–fueled by posters and World War II films starring the likes of Clark Gable and Spencer Tracy (who wore one in three films, most notably while playing General Jimmy Doolittle in *Thirty Seconds Over Tokyo*)–next spread to the civilian sector. Aero Leather (later, Avirex), one of the companies that originally made them for the government, began producing them for the commercial market in 1942. Over the next 50 years, the A-2 became a staple of men's sportswear, also giving birth to the motorcycle jacket (with a little help from 1950s' rebels like Marlon Brando and Elvis Presley).

The jacket's counterculture chic eventually reverberated back to the military complex which spawned it. In 1987, on its fortieth anniversary as an independent branch of service, the Air Force reinstated the A-2. Blatantly obsolete in an era of enclosed cockpits and a plentiful supply of lighter, cheaper nylon jackets, the Air Force admitted to bringing the jacket back solely to enhance the morale and esprit de corps of its personnel.

BIBLIOGRAPHY

Baxter, Gordon. "Full Leather Jacket," *Flying.* 117:4 (April 1990) 108ff.
Berendt, John. "The A-2 Flight Jacket," *Esquire.* (December 1988) 48. il.
Black, Jeff. "The Bomber Jacket is Taking Lots of Flak," *Daily News Record.* 21:53 (March 18, 1991) 13.
"Cooper Gets Air Force Contract for A-2 Leather Flight Jackets," *Daily News Record.* 18:13 (January 20, 1988) 6. Re. Cooper Sportswear Manufacturing Company.
Scott, Phil. "U.S. Air Force is Hell-Bent for Leather Jackets," *Flying.* 115:1 (January 1988) 98.

The now very familiar face of Jesse Jackson wasn't as well known when the photographer snapped this shot. Sporting a luxuriant Afro, Jackson spoke his mind at the Democratic National Convention in Miami Beach in 1972.

The Afro

The Afro was a direct result of the American socio-political climate in the 1960s. It represented both a break with the integrationist civil rights movement led by organizations such as the NAACP and the Urban League and an aggressive assertion of black pride. A *New York Times* quote of a University of California Afro-American Students Union member in 1967 reflected the forces behind the Afro as well as campus revolts against a Western curriculum bias, enrollment quotas, etc.:

> We decided to remember our African heroes, our American heroes and our culture. We decided to stop hating ourselves, trying to look like you, bleaching our hair, straightening our hair. In high school I used to hold my big lip in.

The Afro came to prominence in 1968, stimulated by the examples set by celebrities such as Sly Stone and James Brown as well as the unqualified support of black power militants like the Black Panthers. The style–due in no small part to its high profile visibility on the wearer–became the most notable image of the black consciousness movement. It also became a linchpin of the Pan-African Renaissance along with articles of clothing like dashikis, bubas, djellabas, kaftans, and agbadas. Colleges were "persuaded"–by force, in some cases–to add African history and culture courses, and blacks attempted to learn Swahili as part of the search for their identity.

In actuality, there was nothing particularly African about the cut. According to Dylan Jones,

> It required frequent combing and, in some cases, trips to the hairdresser to get the shape right. In fact, when it reached Africa, the Afro tended to be worn by rich elites who wanted

to look Western, modern, even American. Tanzania went so far as to ban the Afro, denouncing it as cultural neo-colonialism.

A notable spinoff of the look was the Afro wig. Introduced in 1968, it allowed potentially compromised entertainers as well as average citizens to appear hip and/or politically correct when the occasion demanded it. For example, Diana Ross was able to take time off from her jet set commitments to appear at the London Royal Variety Show in 1968 in an Afro wig, making several "controversial" statements, quoting Stokely Carmichael, among others.

The style's popularity receded with the demise of militant black politics in the early 1970s. By 1973, it had taken on the ghetto stereotype of super bad style and street values.

BIBLIOGRAPHY

Garland, Phyl. "Natural Look," *Ebony.* 21 (June 1966) 142-144ff. il.

Jones, Dylan. "Afro"; "The Afro Wig," In: *Haircuts: Fifty Years of Styles and Cuts.* New York: Thames and Hudson, 1990. pp. 58-59, 61. il.

"Natural Hair, New Symbol of Race Pride," *Ebony.* 23 (December 1967) 139-144. il.

Aiming Toward Punk

Punk fashions took root in Great Britain during the second half of the 1970s as an offset of the music revolution spawned by the Sex Pistols and their mentor, boutique owner-turned-singer Malcolm McLaren. The punk look reflected the anti-establishment stance held by British youth faced with diminished economic prospects (their unemployment rate generally hovered around 50 percent) and a repressive caste system. The strong political overtones of this movement were lost upon American youth who faced brighter economic prospects than their brethren across the Atlantic.

Lacking the core impetus of British punk fashion, the American version–allowing for a small-scale radical fringe–featured a toned-down look, termed by some "Aiming Toward Punk." Given credibility in the mass media by rock stars such as Madonna and Cyndi Lauper, ATP emerged as a dominant fashion trend in the early 1980s.

While individuality and, albeit mild, shock value scored points with the ATP crowd, some of the more general ground rules which could be ascertained included:

- spiked hair for both sexes (minus the exotic coloring used by British punks);
- the ample use of buttons–frequently depicting pop stars such as David Bowie, the Clash, and the Cure–as ornament;
- high-topped tennis shoes, sometimes adorned with paint or graffiti, as opposed to jogging shoes;
- jeans either of the straight-legged, well-worn and tight variety or baggy with lots of pockets and zippers;
- shirts and jackets with the sleeves ripped out;
- black for evening wear;
- exotic sunglasses of various types (e.g., wrap-arounds with narrow eye slits); and

- jewelry salvaged from mom's costume cache, thrift shops, and even Army-Navy outlets.

Parents and other authority figures, evidently forgetful of such past diversions as the zoot suit and the greaser look, exerted a notable degree of effort in attempting to suppress ATP. However, in spite of–or, perhaps because of–such actions, the look maintained its popularity into the 1990s.

BIBLIOGRAPHY

Pugh, Clifford. "Teen Sightings," *The Magazine of the Houston Post.* (July 15, 1984) 17-18. il.

"Punk Look–Fad or Deviance?" *USA Today.* 118:2539 (April 1990) 14. Re. psychological aspects of adolescent behavior.

Alex, the Stroh's Beer-Drinking Dog

Stroh's stock was on the rise in the never-ending beer wars when, in late 1983, it had the hottest ad in television starring a mutt named Alex. The commercial opened with four young men playing poker. Alex's owner ordered the dog to bring four Stroh's. The dog disappeared into the kitchen, and the incredulous guests heard a refrigerator door open and four bottles popping, followed by a lapping sound. "Alex," warned the owner, "you better be drinking your water."

Stroh's had never expected the Alex vignette to end up challenging the long-running campaigns for Miller Lite beer and Pepsi as the most popular ad on TV. The company had tried to be funny in its commercials for eight years without any real success. John Bissell of Stroh's acknowledged, "Humorous advertising is like writing a Broadway show. Some of them turnout to be hits, some of them don't."

With sales up, Stroh's immediately shot a sequel. The young men, out camping, tell Alex to fetch some Stroh's; when Alex's owner hears a car start, he yells, "Alex, you better be taking your own car!" This was, in turn, followed by additional installments. Meanwhile, the company was deluged with fan mail for Alex (whose real name was Pepper), who'd been discovered as a stray wandering the streets of Los Angeles. At the onset of the 1990s, the Alex series was still going strong, a time-honored tradition in its own right.

BIBLIOGRAPHY

"Alex and the Beer Bottles," *Newsweek*. 102 (October 10, 1983) 72.

Dr. Atkins' Diet Revolution

During the 1970s, Dr. Robert C. Atkins' high-fat diet rendered him the nation's leading diet physician. Faced with a weight problem early in his career while serving as a medical consultant for AT&T, Atkins explored the possibilities of a no-carbohydrate diet having the same metabolic effects as total fasting. His eat-a-lot diet proved successful with not only himself, but his clients as well.

In 1964, he became a diet doctor and was soon in demand within show business. A description of his diet appeared in *Harper's Bazaar* in 1966, and in 1970, *Vogue* published a 16-day version under the heading "Vogue's Super Diet." His ideas were collected into a book, *Dr. Atkins' Diet Revolution* (Bantam, 1973), which became a runaway best-seller. By this time his practice was booming, consisting of a swank, 23-room office complex in Manhattan which handled 350 fat patients per week.

The basic premise of the Atkins diet posited that obese individuals had something wrong with the way their bodies handled sugar and other carbohydrates; i.e., they were "carbohydrate intolerant." To control their weight, they needed to cut down or cut out carbohydrates, not calories.

In practice, the diet called for an initial week of zero-carbohydrate menus including an abundance of fats. At this point weight loss would generally range from five to eight pounds. The patient then went on to "Level Two," which allowed for the substitution of foods with carbohydrates (i.e., above five grams daily). This, and succeeding levels (up to "Level Five")–which progressively increased amounts of carbohydrates–were permitted so long as the body remained in a state of ketosis; i.e., a urine test stick did not indicate that the body was no longer releasing ketones, which meant fat wasn't being burned.

Atkins was heavily criticized by the organized medical and nutritional establishment. Frederick J. Stare, professor and chairman of nutrition at the Harvard School of Public Health, argued that it bordered on malpractice to recommend such large proportions of saturated fats and cholesterol when the hazards to the heart were so well known. The chairman of the board of the New York County Medical Society posited that Atkins' book was unethical and self-aggrandizing. Publications attacking the Atkins diet included *The Medical Letter, Medical Opinion, Modern Medicine, American Medical News*, the *Journal of the American Medical Association, McCall's, The New York Times*, the *Washington Post*, and the *Los Angeles Times*. In addition, Senator George McGovern's Select Committee on Nutrition and Human Needs conducted a hearing on April 12, 1973 regarding the safety of the Atkins diet.

Requiring little willpower and going against the grain of conventional wisdom (i.e., high-fat diets are dangerous if only because they can contribute to heart disease), it was understandable that the diet won a substantial following. Ultimately, however, negative publicity–particularly increased attention in the media to the role of fats in causing heart attacks–resulted in its fall from favor.

BIBLIOGRAPHY

"Atkins vs. the AMA," *Harper's Bazaar.* 106 (June 1973) 32-33ff.
Berland, Theodore, and the Editors of *Consumer Guide. Rating the Diets.* Chicago: Rand McNally, 1974.
"A Critique of Low-Carbohydrate Ketogenic Weight Reduction Regimens–A Review of Dr. Atkins' Diet Revolution," *JAMA.* 224 (June 4, 1973) 1415-1419.
"Dr. Atkins' Diet Revolution," *Medical Letter.* 15 (May 11, 1973) 41-42.
"Doctor Meets the Critics," *Newsweek.* 81 (March 19, 1973) 57.
Howard, Pamela, and Sandy Treadwell. "Dr. Atkins Says He's Sorry," *The New York Weekly.* (March 26, 1973).
"Now, the Atkins Diet," *Newsweek.* 81 (January 22, 1973) 79-80.
"Suit Ties Dr. Atkins' Diet to Heart Attack," *American Medical News.* (April 2, 1973) 13.
"When a Best Seller on Dieting Runs Into Medical Critics," *Modern Medicine.* (May 28, 1973) 132-133.

The B-B-B Sweatshirt

Known to classical music enthusiasts as the "three B's," Johann Sebastian Bach, Ludwig von Beethoven, and Johannes Brahms became the subjects of a sweatshirt craze in early 1962. "Be the first highbrow in your neighborhood to own a Beethoven, Brahms or Bach sweatshirt!" trumpeted the ads. The pitch proved so successful that the Eagle Shirtmakers of Quakertown, Pennsylvania had to retool in order to keep pace with orders for some 60,000 units.

The sweatshirts–which featured a silkscreen image and last name of one of the composers on both front and back and retailed for $4–were the brainchild of San Francisco Adman Howard Gossage, who came up with the idea in the midst of a beer commercial project. The garments were available in over 1,000 department store outlets, including upscale chains such as Neiman-Marcus and Bonwit Teller. Celebrity purchasers included Van Cliburn (a Brahms), Janis Paige (a Beethoven), Leonard Bernstein (all three), and Arthur Fiedler, who was photographed by *Life* wearing the Beethoven version at a Boston Pops Orchestra rehearsal in Peoria, Illinois.

BIBLIOGRAPHY

"(Long) Hair Shirts . . . Cool Cats Go Back to Bach," *Life*. 52 (March 30, 1962) 56-57. il.

"BABY ON BOARD" Stickers

The prototype for a deluge of imitations that followed, the stickers were actually canary yellow diamonds each with a suction cup attached at the top. Printed in black capital letters, the plastic diamonds mimicked standard road signs. They also rocked gently back and forth due to the motion of driving. Thus, a motorist desiring self-expression affixed a sticker to the rear window of his or her vehicle and proudly drove down the road, comfortable in the knowledge other motorists would be both watchful and happily entertained.

It all started when Safety First, a Newton, Massachusetts maker of child-safety devices, marketed the first "BABY ON BOARD" sticker to dissuade tailgaters. The company's intention to protect the innocent was certainly praiseworthy and, naturally, no one had any idea where it would lead. On the opposite coast in Los Angeles, Marshall's, a discount department store chain, began giving away "BABY ON BOARD" stickers in 1985 to promote the opening of a new store. The people of that freeway-ensnarled megalopolis practiced tailgating as a fine art and could drive 65 m.p.h. while maintaining minimal clearance between vehicles. Accordingly, the more timid drivers took to displaying the stickers.

Soon, yellow diamonds dangled all over the freeway, although nothing like the field of daffodils later to come. Above all, the stickers generated an emotional response. Californians either loved or hated them. Disgruntled drivers, seeing an empty car seat, shouted, "Where's the baby?" Given the instant notoriety of the stickers, it didn't take long before a novelty company sized up the situation. By early 1986, H&L Enterprises of El Cajon had devised 300 variations on the theme of "BABY ON BOARD" and had shipped them to 20,000 of its accounts. Here's a sample, vintage 1986:

- "WHERE AM I? WHERE'S MY CAR?"
- "IF YOU THINK MONEY CAN'T BUY HAPPINESS, YOU DON'T KNOW WHERE TO SHOP"
- "MAKE ME LATE FOR WORK"
- "GIVE ME THE POWER BUT NOT THE RESPONSIBIL- ITY"
- "EX-WIFE IN TRUNK"
- "EX-HUSBAND IN TRUNK"
- "EX-HUSBAND'S GIRLFRIEND IN TRUNK"

To insure a continuing supply of gag messages, H&L Enterprises offered $25 apiece for acceptable mail-ins from the public.

Fun was fun, but police throughout the nation argued that the stickers obscured the motorist's vision and caused more rubber-necking than usual. Unlike their near-relation, bumper stickers–which have endorsed political candidates, advertised products, publicized recreational areas, supported sports teams, and more–the diamond-shaped stickers lacked staying power. However, bumper stickers have never spawned the same mad rush to buy them as was the case with "BABY ON BOARD" stickers. Even blatantly sexual bumper stickers from the occupational series (e.g., "Librarians Are Novel Lovers," "Welders Know How to Make Things Tight," and "Bronco Riders Stay on Longer") paled in comparison. "BABY ON BOARD" stickers practically forced other drivers to read them; they were just that much more obtrusive.

BIBLIOGRAPHY

"Who Cares Who's on Board?" *Sales & Marketing Management.* 137 (October 1986) 34-35.

Baglets

Baglets–mini handbags smaller than the standard envelope, which could be clutched in the hand, slung across a shoulder, hung from the neck or draped from the waist–dominated the American fashion scene in the fall of 1975. Selling mostly to fashion-conscious women between the ages of 20 and 40, the bags varied in price from $1.50 for a neck basket from Japan or China (available at San Francisco's Obiko Boutique) to elegant models for around $100.

The success of the baglets–also known as bagettes and bicycle bags–surprised even its beneficiaries. Bloomingdale's Fashion Director, Janiana Willner, noted, "Sales have been phenomenal, and price seems to be no object. Honestly, I don't quite understand it because, you know, you can't put too much into it." Others, however, came to appreciate their value. Designer Vera Maxwell admitted that minibags "seemed terribly impractical to me at first." But, she added, "we've finally come down to a great simplicity in clothes. The emphasis is on casual elegance. We all want something understated, not too authoritarian, and these bags work perfectly."

Baglets had other advantages as well. These included the following:

- They were a deterrent for crime, inasmuch as they made a difficult target for purse snatchers.
- They were convenient; by being less bulky than regular-sized handbags, they permitted greater ease of movement as well as allowing for activities which couldn't otherwise be engaged in.
- They were flexible; if a woman decided that one mini had insufficient space, she could belt on two or three.
- They were sexy; New York Designer Albert Capraro noted, "Toward evening when they were slung lower on the hips, they were even sexier."

- Manufacturers liked them because they represented a viable solution for waste; e.g., Maxwell's remnants from her best-selling Ultrasuede dresses were easily converted into Ultrasuede minibags.
- The bags came in countless varieties to suit virtually every taste. Some of the notable models included:

    1. A simple vinyl bagatelle designed by Manhattan's Shirl Miller which–at the retail price of $8–sold over one million that fall.
    2. A flat half circle with a snap-down flap, constructed of suede, leather or printed cotton, by Parisian designer Kenzo, which sold millions in copies by Pappagallo, Miller, and others.
    3. A made-in-Columbia macramé necklace pouch by Kathy McKeany, which retailed for $5.
    4. Bagatelle Creations' snakeskin square with bow-tied front flap and shoulder strap ($45).
    5. Fendi's burgundy suede pouch on matching belt ($85).
    6. A detachable black leather pouch, originally designed by Manhattan's Ruza for the U.S. ski team, which hung from either a canvas belt or a shoulder strap.
    7. Squares of velvets.
    8. Printed velveteen canteens.
    9. Hand-painted leather boxes.
    10. Oblongs of beads.

Capraro alone designed minis for a wide array of clothing, including tunics, jumpsuits, sundresses, pajamas, and long gowns.

Following their debut in the fall 1975 resort-wear collections in Manhattan and Paris, the minibags continued to sell well into the following year. Since that time, they have remained a fixture, albeit on a smaller scale, in the fashion scene.

BIBLIOGRAPHY

"Baglets," *Time.* 106 (November 10, 1975) 93.

The Barbie Doll

Barbie is the most popular doll in U.S. toy history. First marketed in 1958, she helped make her creator, Mattel, Inc., the biggest U.S. toy company by the early 1960s. In addition, her extensive wardrobe rendered Mattel the number one clothing manufacturer in number of outfits made.

Despite countless imitators, the Barbie phenomenon continued to expand right from the outset. Five years after her debut, approximately nine million Barbies had been sold. The doll received 500 letters a week, had a national fan club, and was discussed in syndicated fashion columns (one such writer criticized her for wearing plastic shoes).

Barbie's appeal seemed to rest largely on the fact that she enabled young girls to vicariously live out their fantasies of the adult world. Barbie, 11 1/2 inches tall and shapely in proportion (5 1/4-3-4 3/4 inches), was most decidedly not a childish-looking doll. In addition, the seemingly endless array of clothes available as wardrobe items encouraged the collecting impulse of Barbie owners. And keeping Barbie in fashion was not cheap. Although the doll itself retailed for only three dollars in the mid-1960s (a six-dollar version with variously colored wigs was also available), the clothes ranged in price from one dollar (for a black petticoat, panties, and bra) to five dollars (a red velvet coat and taffeta ball gown). In 1963, her complete wardrobe cost $136; this figure did not include companion dolls such as boyfriend Ken and friends Midge and Allan and cars and other material goods.

Some observers, such as *Ramparts*, saw a sinister side to the phenomenon. In response to a Macy's salesgirl's inquiry, "Why do they sell the dolls cheap ($1.88 apiece during Christmas 1968) but not put the clothes on sale?" the magazine noted,

> . . . the salesgirl is missing the broader picture. What she does not know is that Mattel's research and design group, according

to the report to the stockholders, includes graphic artists, sculptors, writers, and fashion designers. These are people with a lust to influence the young. A good example of their sort of earnestness lies in the slogan coupled with a four-poster Barbie bed manufactured for Mattel: "Toys That Mold Character."

What kind of character is it that the Mattel creative folk are molding? . . . The fiction and feature articles in the fan magazines depict these dolls as having upper-upper-class incomes and lower-middle-class tastes. Barbie is 100 percent Caucasian, and she never associates with a racially impure person. She and her friends live in white houses with blue shutters (symbolizing the white, blue-eyed Anglo-Saxon ideal?) whenever possible, and they strive to have a big garden filled with costly gracious-living gear. There is little or no evidence that they ever read books or listen to music. Clothes and money seem to dominate their conversations and strategies.

In Volume IV, Number 1 of the *Mattel Barbie Magazine*, Barbie says: "Midge! I've got a great idea! Remember the blue dress you wore New Year's Eve?" Midge replies, "Yes, but he's seen that already." In Volume III, Number 6, Barbie tells Midge: "I just treated myself to a marvelous dress for the Society Debs Ball. I hope Ken likes it. He is spending so much money on the tickets." The assumption here seems to be that, while making money is the *summum bonum*, spending it is even more *summum*–especially if you spend it on clothes.

Nevertheless, the Barbie doll continued to prosper. In the aftermath of the conspicuous consumption that typified the 1980s, she remains one of the best-selling dolls–in fact, one of the best-selling toys, period–in the history of the American retail industry.

BIBLIOGRAPHY

Bess, Donovan. "The Menace of the Barbie Dolls," *Ramparts.* 7 (January 25, 1969) 25-28.
Cray, Dan. "Ethnic Barbie Struts Her Stuff on TV," *ADWEEK Western Advertising News.* 40:30 (July 23, 1990) 4.

Cray, Dan. "Mattel's Barbie Ties Charity Drive to Worldwide Summit," *AD-WEEK Eastern Edition.* 31:45 (November 5, 1990) 47.

Fitzgerald, Kate. "Comic Book Barbie; Mattel's Popular Doll Stars in Colorful New Project," *Advertising Age.* 62:2 (January 14, 1991) 40.

Fitzgerald, Kate. "Mattel Fashions Barbie Boutique," *Advertising Age.* 62:27 (July 1, 1991) 3ff. Reports that "The Barbie Shop" will be added to 250 Sears stores, 1000 Wal-Mart outlets and an undisclosed number of Venture stores.

Gibbs, Nancy. "What Do You Want From Santa?: This Year, Parents May Find the Answer Surprisingly Familiar," *Time.* 132:24 (December 12, 1988) 79ff.

Goldsborough, Robert. "Billion-Dollar Barbie the Biggest Hit With Kids," *Advertising Age.* 59:48 (November 9, 1988) 22.

Green, Michelle. "As a Tiny Plastic Star Turns 30, the Real Barbie and Ken Reflect on Life in the Shadow of the Dolls," *People Weekly.* 31:9 (March 6, 1989) 186ff. il.

"It's Not the Doll, It's the Clothes; Barbie Doll," *Business Week.* (December 16, 1961) 48-49ff. il.

Kantrowitz, Barbara. "Hot Date: Barbie and G. I. Joe; Anniversaries Honor an American Love Affair," *Newsweek.* 113:8 (February 20, 1989) 59.

Morgenson, Gretchen. "Barbie Does Budapest," *Forbes.* 147:1 (January 7, 1991) 66ff. il. Profile of Mattel.

"The Most Popular Doll in Town," *Life.* 55 (August 23, 1963) 73-75. il.

"Toys Turn to Social Concerns," *Marketing.* (November 1, 1990) 22.

"Zeitgeist Barbie," *Harper's Magazine.* 281:1683 (August 1990) 20. The doll's résumé as published in the *Barbie 30th Anniversary Magazine.*

Bedecked Beach Hats

Once limited to Caribbean beaches, bedecked beach hats caught on in America in the summer of 1959. The popularity of rough native straws decorated with all manner of objects, flora and fauna, had been growing for several seasons in the small shops in tropical resort towns. Customized to suit individual tastes, these hats cost as little as $2 in Haiti or Jamaica, but rarely survived the airplane trip home intact.

Then domestic hat manufacturers came up with similar reproductions constructed out of more durable materials and retailing in the $5-$17 range. Models in straw included:

- a cloche trimmed by peppers and bow (Therese Ahrens, $7);
- a boater decked out in seashells and a flying fish (Therese Ahrens, $5);
- a porkpie with a bandanna band to which was attached a stop watch and cigarette case, and topped off by a cigarette burning a hole in the brim (Thomas Begg, $8.50);
- a feminine basket shape with a life-sized tropical bird attached to the wide draped band (Therese Ahrens, $17);
- a stovepipe adorned with flowers and built-in sunglasses, the latter of which protected the eyes when the hat was pulled over the face (Therese Ahrens, $11).

After gaining a foothold in the suburbs, the hats began appearing in the cities as an accompaniment to everyday wear. Not particularly practical (enemies included brisk winds and grabby pranksters), the fancily trimmed hats receded from the public eye at the end of the summer. Following years found them relegated largely to the vacation spots from whence the craze had originated.

BIBLIOGRAPHY

"Bedecked Beach Hats Hit the City," *Life*. 46 (June 8, 1959) 65-68.

The Belle Epoque

The Belle Epoque (named after turn-of-the-century coiffures) represented the height of fashion during 1969. Also known as the Char (it looked like the way a charwoman might fix her hair) or "Oscar's hairdo" (after designer Oscar de la Renta, who had all of his models employ it during his spring collections exhibit in November 1969), the style epitomized a sort of graceful neglect in hair care. *Time* noted that for $17.50 at Kenneth's Manhattan salon, a woman could acquire the look via the following treatment:

> The front is pulled loosely up and back into a topknot. Underneath, along with the remainder of the hair, can generally be found several ounces of wool twine or a nylon mesh cushion, the better to swell the structure to second-hand proportions. Hanging down at strategic intervals (at the temples, around the ears, and down the back of the neck), are separate, curling tendrils of hair. The whole thing may look like the work of a bird who flunked building.

The style originated in France where Parisian hairdresser Christophe Carite contrived an early variant in mid-1968. Others credited actress Brigitte Bardot with popularizing it some years earlier in her films. From there, the look was taken up by a string of style-setting clients such as Princess Grace of Monaco and Vicomtesse Jacqueline de Ribes.

Its appeal–aside from its celebrity connections–was attributed to the softness and romanticism it conveyed. One American added that, most important, the Belle Epoque was "not terrifying to a man. To him, it looks as if it's all up there with just one pin, and he's got to think 'If only I can find it, in a matter of seconds it will all be out on the pillow.' "

BIBLIOGRAPHY

"A Sweet Neglect," *Time.* 94 (December 5, 1969) 90. il.

Black Dolls

In December 1968, Lou Smith, CEO for Operation Bootstrap, Inc., noted, "Until now, it's always been a white Christmas. We've been left out. After all, can you imagine black kids trying to identify with blond, blue-eyed dolls?" His company's subsidiary, Shindana, introduced "Baby Nancy" that year, a black baby with Negroid features and "natural" hair that functioned just like the white dolls peddled on Saturday morning cartoon programs. Retailing at five to six dollars, 20,000 were sold at the onset of the 1968 Christmas season; Smith estimated that 80,000 could have been sold if sufficient production facilities had been available.

In addition, the Black Doll Toy Co. of Watts began offering "Soul Babies," as well as a host of other black equivalency toys such as astronauts and jack-in-the-boxes. Robert Welch, co-owner of that company, provided a rationale for his firm's products: "Anything that has white character to it, we want to have black character. Take our spacemen, for example; we're trying to make our children realize that they, too, can be an astronaut."

Parents appeared to be the driving force behind the popularity of such toys. Recognizing the validity of Welch's words, they purchased the black dolls in order to foster a sense of identity and racial pride in their children. In the meantime, mainstream firms were beginning to discover that there was a great untapped market for black-oriented toys.

While major toy companies had been cashing in on the popularity of black dolls for at least two years prior to 1968, their lines consisted of Caucasian-featured dolls with a brown tint added to the mold. Barbie received a black counterpart, as did G. I. Joe. However, in 1968, Remco, one of the largest toy manufacturers, developed its own "ethnically correct" dolls. According to *Ebony*, the Christmas 1968 retail reports underscored the soundness of this move:

. . . the black version of "Tippy Tumbles" is selling one to four compared to the white version, and that is twice the ratio of blacks in the population.

Remco's realistic black dolls also included "Baby-Grow-a-Tooth," "Growing Sally," and "Li'l Winking Winny," who wore a simulated Afro hairdo and had no white counterpart.

Retailers were deriving significant profits from the sales of black dolls as well. In New York, F. A. O. Schwarz noted considerably more interest in them in 1968. The J. L. Hudson Co. in Detroit stocked 32 different black dolls, while Sears and JC Penney Co., in San Francisco, reported that their stock was exhausted just one week into the Christmas season.

Following years saw the expansion of black consciousness into other realms of the toy industry. As a result, black toys have become a permanent fixture in virtually all toy stores across the nation.

BIBLIOGRAPHY

"The Advent of Soul Toys," *Ebony.* 24 (November 1968) 164-170. il. Includes two sidebars, "Afro Shops Offer Black Toys" and "What to Look For In Toys."

"Black Christmas," *Newsweek.* 72 (December 9, 1968) 79-81. il.

"Diahann Carroll Presents the Julia Dolls," *Ebony.* 24 (October 1969) 148-150ff. il.

Blazers for Women

The school blazer, a brass-buttoned, braid-bound, easy-fitting jacket traditionally worn by schoolboys on the playing fields of England, was taken to heart by fashionable American women in 1959. The Paris spring collections played a pivotal role in the breakout of the garment; newcomer Jules Crahay focused on braid-bound suits, and old-timer Coco Chanel emphasized the blazer look that she'd been employing for years. Copies of these styles quickly sold out in the United States. Not to be outdone, American designers developed their own motifs, turning out blazers for all occasions. A sampling of the styles in vogue at the time included:

- an evening jacket that could be worn over a variety of skirts and tops (*Life* exhibited one in blue with brass buttons, piped in red by Junior Sophisticates);
- everyday sportswear (Ellen Brooke had a model available in red wool piped in navy);
- dress for cocktails (Sportwhirl featured one made of sheer organdy bound in cotton braid which could be worn over a plain dark sheath);
- a V-neck version to go with a Chanel suit made of off-white wool with navy binding (copied in the U.S. by Henri Bendel); and
- a cardigan style for evening from the Chanel line.

While blazers were much less in evidence the following year, they have been revived on numerous occasions up to the present day. Their ongoing appeal appears related to the fact that they combine comfort and versatility with classic lines that really never go out of date.

BIBLIOGRAPHY

"The Girls Go to Blazers," *Life*. 46 (May 11, 1959) 111-115. il.

Blue Jeans

During their 140-odd years of existence, blue jeans have evolved from no-nonsense work pants used by miners, lumberjacks, and farmers to fashion statement and cultural icon in our post-World War II global village. It all began in 1850 when a 20-year-old Bavarian immigrant, Levi Strauss, arrived in San Francisco by ship to seek his fortune. He intended to do this by selling heavy brown canvas, which he'd brought with him in rolls, for tents and wagon covers. However, upon discovering that these goods were not in demand but pants were, due to the rigors of mining and other activities, Strauss employed a tailor to make pants. They sold quickly, and he opened a work-clothes and coverall shop in San Francisco. When his canvas ran out, Strauss switched to a tough fabric originally loomed in Nimes, France called serge de Nimes, then denim; sailors from Genoa had long worn pants of similar fabric known as genes, which accounts for the appearance of the associated name, "jeans."

Jeans began expanding beyond their male, blue collar origins during World War II when their production was declared an essential industry, and women started wearing them in war plant assembly lines. In the 1950s, their durability, cheapness, and comfort led to their widespread use on college campuses and by small children. They also became a lightning rod of controversy in high schools when parents and administrators attempted to suppress the sloppy look of rolled-up jeans and shapeless sweaters. The backlash by teens elevated jeans into a symbol of defiance against authority and oppression.

In the 1960s, when one-half of the U.S. population was under 25 years of age and advertising took on a distinctly youth-oriented flavor, blue jeans became fashionable among the mainstream populous. The styles themselves grew increasingly diversified in order to accommodate a multitude of tastes: flared legs, bell bottoms, cuffs, wide-belt loops, tricky pockets, fancy stitching, lighter-weight fabrics, rainbow colors, plaits, and broader cuts.

Youthful trendsetters, rather than abandoning jeans to the middle class, evolved ever more outrageous fashion statements. Holes were covered with patches or embroidery. Torn legs were amputated, resulting in shorts with frayed edges. Rips were covered with a piece of braid. The tattered look was in. Once again, however, big business co-opted the subculture. Machine-embroidered patches were manufactured to be sewn over nonexistent holes by school children. Kits were sold to help produce a worn, faded look with new jeans. Entrepreneurs sprang up to produce various forms of made-to-order blue jean art, from swirling patterns of nailheads and studs to acrylic designs. "Denim has become a living collage," noted Stephen Bruce in 1974, whose New York show, Serendipity 3, presented an exhibition of street-people-and-celebrity jeans at the time, entitled "Rebirth of the Blues."

By the mid-1970s, denim had begun to be used on a seemingly endless array of accessories, including tote bags, automobile upholstery, boots, jewelry, umbrellas, sheets, and book bindings (one edition of a blue denim-covered Bible quickly sold 75,000 copies). Advertising agencies employed jean-clad actors in ads for cosmetics, dog food, liquor, soup, airlines, detergents, cameras, and other commodities.

Cultural observers began searching for new explanations for the staying power of jeans. Yale law professor Charles Reich observed that they "express freedom and wholeness of self." A West German psychoanalyst explained that people want jeans because they have become a uniform binding people together at a time when so much is keeping them apart.

The fascination of foreigners for American life has rendered the denim craze a truly international phenomenon. Reruns of old Hollywood Westerns on TV and made-in-Italy "Spaghetti Westerns" aided considerably in the spread of jeans. Levi Strauss began exporting jeans overseas in the 1960s. The company now has offices in 35 countries and plants in 12 countries, its international division accounting for over one-quarter of its total $750 million in annual sales. Blue Bell, Inc., of Greensboro, North Carolina, the second largest U.S. jean manufacturer, which calls its product Wrangler, markets in 85 countries and produces in 17. In all, jeans are presently manufactured on every continent except Antarctica. Worldwide production surpassed the billion-pair-a-year mark in the mid-1970s.

As more and more people take up the jeans habit daily and more and more long-term users continue wearing them into their middle years, the industry has found its biggest problem to be one of supply. The dye, once brewed from the indigo plant grown in the U.S. cotton belt, but now synthesized by Allied Chemical, cannot be produced fast enough to keep up with demand. The process of making denim–which consists of a twilled cotton (or cotton and polyester) with warp or lengthwise yard dyed indigo (less often, black or green) and white, gray or tinted yarn used for filler in the crosswise direction–is extremely intricate and has led textile companies to hesitate over building new mills. Potential labor shortages, sky-high start-up costs, and fears that demand might one day dry up, compounded by problems in converting such plants to other uses, have all conspired for an essential maintenance of the status quo with respect to American-owned companies; i.e., acceptance of an output which has long lagged behind advance orders. In recent years, foreign companies–particularly those based in the Far East– have helped fill the void, but overall demand has continued to outpace supply. In short, the success of blue jeans seems likely to continue well into the next century.

BIBLIOGRAPHY

Adkins, Jan. The Evolution of Jeans: American History 501," *Mother Earth News*. n124 (July/August 1990) 60ff.

Appelbaum, Cara. "Levi's Takes Control with Stores of Its Own," *Adweek's Marketing News*. 31:38 (September 17, 1990) 8.

Barol, Bill. "Anatomy of a Fad," *Newsweek*. 115:27 (Summer/Fall 1990) 40ff. Re. torn blue jeans. Special Edition: The New Teens.

Block, Jean Libman. "Blue Jean Revolution," *The Saturday Evening Post*. (August/September 1974) 8-12. il.

"Denim Does It," *Women's Wear Daily*. 161 (June 18, 1991) 10ff. Re. Jeans clothing selling well at all price ranges.

Gordon, Mary Ellen. "Fashion Jeans Driving Sales," *Women's Wear Daily*. 161:109 (June 5, 1991) S28. Re. jeans retailer/sportswear report.

Gordon, Mary Ellen. "Handpainted Jeans at $150 a Pop," *Women's Wear Daily*. 161:80 (April 24, 1991) 11.

"Jean Thing," *Newsweek*. 80 (August 21, 1972) 56. il.

"Jordache Joins Legal Fray Over Acid Wash Patent," *Women's Wear Daily*. 160:63 (October 1, 1990) 2.

Lloyd, Brenda. "Western Jeans and Tops Rope Bigger Profits," *Daily News Record*. 21:112 (June 10, 1991) 22.

Mhlambiso, Thembi. "Jeans are Tougher Than Today's Rough Times," *Daily News Record*. 21:88 (May 6, 1991) 11ff. Report that sales are up despite the recession.

Palmieri, Jean E. "Says Patriotism Perfect for Denim," *Daily News Record*. 21:56 (March 21, 1991) 7.

Parola, Robert. "Status Still Sells," *Daily News Record*. 21:90 (May 8, 1991) 1ff. Re. designer jeans market.

"Rags to Riches (Really); Sale of Faded Levi's," *Time*. 102 (July 16, 1973) 52. il.

Bowlers for Women

Bowlers have had a long tradition as a preferred form of head wear for men reaching well back into the nineteenth century. In 1963, however, the hats sold at a furious rate to women–not as gifts for men but rather to wear themselves.

Signs of the craze were everywhere, including the pages of fashion magazines and the mannequins in department-store windows throughout the U.S. But women in public offered the strongest proof, displaying the bowler in myriad forms and styles. Though most popular in straw, they were available in every possible fabric from linen to leopard. In addition, they could be made to look entirely new merely by switching ribbon color or substituting feather for flower.

According to *Time*, the driving force behind women's appropriation of the bowler was the demise of the bouffant hairdo. As a result,

> ... women suffered a serious loss of stature. They were told by reassuring hairdressers that it was more chic to be close-cropped, and advised by the fashion magazines simply to develop a longer neck to offset the loss in head height. But women, who like old tenements are apt to crumble at the very concept of major renovation, found a gradual way of making do. Where once there had been hair, let there be hat.

Bowlers–somewhat more elongated vertically above the brim than has been characteristic of men's models–apparently won the hearts of women because they were neither as impractical (e.g., turbans) nor as small (e.g., caps, berets) as competing forms of headgear.

The popularity of the bowler, however, was short-lived in that reincarnation. Long, straight hair was back in vogue for women by the mid-1960s. The "in" look was natural, and the bowler with its aura of formality definitely didn't fit.

BIBLIOGRAPHY

"Old Hat," *Time*. 81 (April 5, 1963) 77-79. il.

Byronic Locks

Lord Byron cast a long shadow upon the early Romantic era not only within the realm of literature but in the world of fashion as well. Many youths in both America and Europe imitated his long and wavy chestnut hair, then known as "Byronic locks."

These dandies frequently took to slicking their hair into place with the Macassar Oil noted by Byron in his epic poem, *Don Juan*:

> In virtues nothing earthly could surpass her,
> Save thine "incomparable oil," Macassar!

This hair oil was reputed to have been extracted from the nut kernel of trees growing on the Celebes Island. Most of it, however, was locally manufactured from ingredients such as cloves, mace, and oil of cinnamon. The vast popularity of Macassar Oil led housewives to place lace doilies on the backs of chairs and sofas to protect them from the grease used by males to slick and shine their hair. These small oblongs of cloth came to be called "antimacassar," a name they have retained to the present day.

Despite criticism of long hair from many quarters at the time, its continued popularity resulted in its general acceptance by the mid-nineteenth century. Those who could not afford Macassar Oil larded their hair with tallow or bear's grease, which, in turn, led to the widespread visibility of the "cowlick," a single curl over the forehead.

By the 1860s, however, hair length became shorter, following the standard set by London men. An American etiquette manual in 1869, *Good Society*, advised readers that the only men who indulged in long hair were "painters and fiddlers."

BIBLIOGRAPHY

Severn, Bill. *The Long and Short of It: Five Thousand Years of Fun and Fury Over Hair.* New York: McKay, 1971.

Celebrity Perfumes

Celebrity perfumes had become a major force in the four billion dollar fragrance industry by the late 1980s. The first scent to feature a celebrity tie-in was Sophia Loren's, introduced in 1980. The success of Sophia, at a time when perfumes inspired by designers like Oscar de la Renta or Ralph Lauren were the vogue, led to the appearance of more fragrances bearing star names. The most notable examples included the following:

- Forever Krystle, based on the character played by Linda Evans in *Dynasty*, experienced brief success when introduced in 1984.
- Elizabeth Taylor's Passion, which first hit the stores in 1987, quickly ascended to the top ten of popular scents (the only celebrity product to achieve that rank during 1987-1988; see Table 1), grossing $50 million in 1988.
- Herb Alpert's Listen (1988) played on his fame as a musician. The bottle was shaped like the bell of a trumpet, and the ad slogan read: "Once in a great while there comes a fragrance that hits the perfect note. All you have to do is listen."
- Cher's Uninhibited, launched with a big publicity campaign in Fall 1988, sold out almost immediately in many outlets.

As the 1980s drew to a close, at least a dozen other celebrity scents were on the market with more waiting in the wings (e.g., Joan Collins, Priscilla Presley, Mikhail Baryshnikov).

Barbara Kantrowitz explained the factors behind the use of celebrity names by fragrance companies as a marketing tool:

A $175 bottle of perfume can cost as little as $20 to manufacture, not including development or promotion; with this kind of mark-up, a winning brand is liquid gold. Which explains why

TABLE 1. The Ten Best-Selling Scents as of December 1988
(in alphabetical order)

Chanel No. 5
Giorgio
Liz Claiborne
Obsession
Opium
Oscar de la Renta
Elizabeth Taylor's Passion
Shalimar
Vanderbilt
White Linen

competition is so stiff. This year alone, manufacturers introduced more than 40 new scents, bringing the total of men's and women's fragrances on the market to more than 700. . . . Women used to pick a fragrance and stick with it for life; these days, they tend to wear different perfumes on different occasions and switch loyalties often. In such a volatile market, a pleasant smell doesn't guarantee success. "You have to have a hook," says Irene R. Cotter, marketing director of Perfume International. . . . Add a star like Liz, Cher or Sophia and you've got instant publicity even before the first spritz hits a wrist.

Because much depends on the appeal of the star, companies have tried to gauge that potentiality in advance. Prior to formalizing its relationship with Taylor, Parfums International employed market researchers to interview small groups of women in several U.S. cities, focusing on the upscale customer who frequents department stores. The researchers found that Taylor had the greatest appeal, because she was seen as a "survivor" and "the most beautiful woman in the world."

The success of this approach encouraged celebrities outside of the show business mainstream (i.e., actors, musicians, dancers) to consider taking the plunge. As of 1989, the World Wrestling Federation was developing a fragrance for its fans. Michael Stern, the man responsible for Uninhibited, considered athletes to be a good bet, noting "You never know where the personality will emerge who will draw the public attention."

By the 1990s, however, the fragrance market suffered from a glut of products employing celebrity names. As noted by *Sports Illustrated* in mid-1991, the majority of fragrances inspired by sports stars (e.g., Muhammed Ali, Bjorn Borg, Gabriela Sabatini, Iron Mike [Ditka]) fared no better than the typical celebrity product.

BIBLIOGRAPHY

"Celebrity Scents. Celebrities are Nosing Their Way Into the Multimillion Dollar Fragrance Industry. A Report on the Sweet Smell of Success," *Vogue.* 179:9 (September 1989) 352.

Kantrowitz, Barbara. "A Whiff of Glitz at $175 an Ounce," *Newsweek.* (December 12, 1988) 78-79. il.

Lieblich, Julia. "Star Scents," *Fortune.* 119:10 (May 8, 1989) 9.

"Making a List," *Sports Illustrated.* 75:2 (July 8, 1991) 10. il.

Alpert, Herb

"Scents From the Stars," *Time.* 132:23 (December 5, 1988) 77.

Collins, Joan

Mason, Julie Cohen. "A Fading Star," *Management Review.* 80:4 (April 1991) 24ff. Re. Parlux Fragrances Inc.'s "Spactacular" perfume.

Hogan, Hulk

O'Loughlin, Michael. "Eau de Hulk Hogan," *Savvy Woman.* 10:3 (March 1989) 18. Re. Wrestling Federation's plans to put out a perfume.

Hutton, Lauren

"Revlon Sets a Return for Hutton," *Women's Wear Daily.* 158:28 (August 11, 1989) 2.

Miss Piggy

Wood, Dana. "DuCair: Miss Piggy Meets Cardin," *Women's Wear Daily.* 161:62 (March 29, 1991) 12. Re. DuCair Tsumara, manufacturer of children's toiletries is licensed to distribute Pierre Cardin fragrances in the U.S.

Presley, Elvis

"Denny Plans to Launch Elvis Line," *Women's Wear Daily.* 157:98 (May 19, 1989) 14.

Presley, Priscilla

Lippert, Barbara. "An Elvis Souvenir Disguised as Perfume," *Adweek's Marketing Week.* 31:27 (July 2, 1990) 37.

Taylor, Elizabeth

"Calvin's Escape, Liz's Diamonds," *Women's Wear Daily.* 161:102 (May 24, 1991) 1.

Stern, Aimee L. "Divine Extravagance? Liz Taylor Didn't Like the Sound of It," *Adweek's Marketing Week.* 30:5 (January 30, 1989) 52. Column.

White, Vanna

Born, Pete. "Vanna's Turn," *Women's Wear Daily.* 160:105 (November 30, 1990) 13.

Chalk White Cosmetics

Chalk white coloring–as utilized in lipstick and eyeshadow–became the sensation of the cosmetic industry in early 1959. Both products worked best when blended with conventional colors.

Originating in Italy, white lipstick grew steadily in popularity with fashion conscious American women for a couple of years, then, when available in quantities, began outselling all other new spring shades. It provided a pale but dramatic highlight, making the wearer appear as though she had just licked her lips. Added later as a complement to white lipstick, white eyeshadow also gained favor because it produced the effect of larger eyes.

By 1960, chalk white had lost its novelty status and receded back amidst the palette of bright colors produced by cosmetic companies.

BIBLIOGRAPHY

"Make-up in Whiteface," *Life*. 46 (April 6, 1959) 64. il.
Weston, M. "And Now the Pallid Look," *New York Times Magazine*. (July 5, 1959) 10-11ff. il.

The Chase Doll

When her daughters had reached the appropriate age, Martha Chase (b. 1851) constructed dolls for them based upon her own favorite as a child. Her dolls improved upon their prototype in that they were more natural looking and easier for a child to carry about. Helen Young described the Chase creations as being:

> . . . correctly jointed at hips, elbows, knees, and shoulders; the feet were shaped with a flat sole and natural looking toes; the hands were cupped with separated fingers. After much experimenting, Mrs. Chase perfected a head which satisfied her, with a pretty, lifelike face covered with the same kind of spring-knit cloth that was stretched over the underbody. The doll was painted with oil colors so it could be cleaned.

While not especially pretty, Chase dolls were popular due to their durability and sturdiness of construction.

In 1891, after a Boston store buyer had seen some of the dolls and sent in an order, the Chase family established a factory. Made in sizes varying from ten inches to life size, the Chase dolls were immensely popular for almost 20 years. While her best sellers were babies and children, Chase also became the first dollmaker to create dolls adapted from book characters. Six Alice in Wonderland figurines–Alice, Tweedledum, Tweedledee, the Mad Hatter, the Queen, and the Frog–were her first and most popular creations in this line.

When her "stocking dolls" began waning in popularity, Chase turned to making life-sized demonstration dolls for hospital and clinic training, filling a need derived from her longtime knowledge of hospitals (she was the daughter of a physician and married one as well). These dolls came in varied sizes: four infant stages (newborn to one year), a four-year-old child, and a five-foot, four-inch woman. Some included waterproof inner compartments in order to demonstrate various treatments. They also were utilized in training nurses to apply bandages, splints, and slings. The Chase family continued to manufacture these demonstration dolls years after Martha's death in 1925.

BIBLIOGRAPHY

Young, Helen. "Fabric Dolls," In: *The Complete Book of Doll Collecting*. New York: Putnam, 1967. pp. 41-54. il.

The Chemise

Bursting on the scene in the summer of 1957, the chemise dress dominated women's fashions for over a year. Testaments to the impact of the dress could be found everywhere:

- The chemise–and its kissing kin, the flaring trapeze–was selling, according to Eleanor Lambert of the New York Dress Institute, "like nothing since the dirndl skirt of 1932."
- W. D. Aisenberg, vice president of Allied Purchasing Corp., which buys for the 87 Allied department stores, said, "the chemise has definitely saved the dress business–at the very least kept it ahead of the general downward trend of business."
- In New York City, Ohrbach's fashion director Rose Wells indicated that the chemise was accounting for 90 percent of all of the outlet's dress sales.
- In Philadelphia, Blauner's specialty store reported that the chemise accounted for 65 percent of its dress sales.
- In Washington, posh Connecticut Avenue shops credited sales increases of up to 30 percent to the chemise.
- Cynthia Marks, dress merchandise manager for Kirby, Block & Co., noted, "this is not just a big-city look, it's caught on countrywide."
- A Montgomery Ward spokesman concurred, "Two weeks ago we sent a shipment of chemises to Lawton, Oklahoma, and in two days they had sold all but three."
- Betty Shackleton, fashion coordinator for Atlanta's Davison-Paxon Co., stated that the retailer "can't keep chemises in stock."

The chemise had some notable antecedents. In the U.S., Claire McCardell, Larry Aldrich, and Norman Morell all at one time or another put out a tent-like garment. Across the Atlantic, Balenciaga sprang the loose dress on Paris in February 1955, and de Givenchy gave the design added impetus in August of the same year.

The popularity of the dress was more directly attributable to the rise of youth as tastemasters for American society. Tobe Coller Davis, a leading fashion authority of the time, cited the Angry Young Men of literature, theatrical stars such as Audrey Hepburn and Leslie Caron, Parisian designers like the 22-year-old Yves St. Laurent and "small young models [now used] instead of the usual tall willowy mannequins." The youth influence was even more pronounced within the consumer sector. Allied's Aisenberg reported that "the chemise is running 30 to 50 per cent of our misses business and 50 to 70 percent of our junior dresses." Marks agreed, "The juniors started it–not the makers, not the store buyers."

The lower end of the fashion industry–which pushed the trend for all it was worth–also played a major role in the rise of the chemise. Their success, in fact, forced many to change their ideas about the way fashions took root. According to *Newsweek*, fashion insiders:

> have long operated on the theory that after a fashion came from Paris, it would be adopted by U.S. designers and manufacturers, popularized among prosperous (and older) leaders of society and show business, permitted finally to trickle down to the mass market in inexpensive copies. The sack skipped frontline U.S. designers and makers, leaped over most style-setting women, and shot directly into the hands of the girl next door.

Herein lay the core of opposition to the chemise. Jonathan Logan's head designer, Jeanne Carr, felt Fifth Avenue designers were probably annoyed because "the chemise began in small-volume houses" or "because they had been doing it for years and it created no stir." However, the style also drew negatives from journalists, comedians, husbands, certain females, and others. *Parade* magazine fashion editor Virginia Pope conducted a write-in opinion poll in April 1958 and found that men were still opposed to the chemise look, nine to one. Eugene Gilbert, who polled teenagers for *Parade*, found that 86 percent of all boys in this age group disliked the style. Among the female dissenters, actress Constance Bennett declaimed, "I think God made the best-looking figures, and I don't think we ought to make them look like barrels." Critics hung it with such derogatory terms as "the sack," "the bag," "the night-shirt," "the Moslem look," "the shoplifter's delight," and "the limp look."

Still, many had reason to appreciate the chemise. Designers and retailers recognized that the introduction of the style represented "one of the few times since women switched from blue body paint to animal pelts that fashion couldn't be faked on a sewing machine;" i.e., a dress possessing a waistline couldn't be altered to look sack-like. In addition, the accessories market profited immensely from the craze (see Table 1).

TABLE 1. The Accessories Boom Fostered By the Chemise

Stockings–The short length of the dress (up to 18 inches above the floor) helped hosiery manufacturers to move peach and flamingo stockings.

Gloves–Exposing arms below the elbow enabled glove makers to market more elaborate fashions.

Furs–Sales rose due to the fact that furs complemented the dress well.

Hats

Jewelry

Hairdos

The style–albeit via countless variations–thrived into the early 1960s. However, changing social mores (e.g., the birth of a more mainstream brand of feminism, the athleticism ushered in by the Kennedy White House) caused the chemise to be eclipsed by functional and casual–even daring–fashions.

BIBLIOGRAPHY

Chappell, R. "The Chemise–Joke or No Joke . . . Is Filling Sacks of Cash for Business," *Newsweek*. (May 5, 1959) 96-99. il.

"How Long Will the Chemise Last?" *Consumer Reports*. 23 (August 1958) 434-437. il.

Citypants

In Paris, the Autumn 1968 collection of every designer featured pants for women. They bore little resemblance to the traditional slacks employed as casual wear. Called "citypants" or "24-hour pants," these pants–as typified by the trend-setting styles of Yves St. Laurent–were as sober, restrained, and elegant as the mood of men's fashions had tended to be. Generally all black, dark brown, or charcoal gray in color, wide pants were complemented by a long, belted tunic and elongated coat so as to produce a narrow, drawn-out silhouette.

The citypants look caught on almost immediately in the aftermath of the miniskirt craze. *U.S. News & World Report* noted, "The fashion industry is threatening to abolish the skirt and put all women in pants." *Women's Wear Daily* claimed it was happening "in Paris, London, New York, Los Angeles, everywhere." American retailers were ecstatic. A sampling of reactions included:

- Lord & Taylor: "A great collection, a beautiful evocation of [St. Laurent's] style."
- Kimberly Knits: "I loved the pants . . . beautiful."
- Holt Renfrew: "We're not afraid of the pants . . . very revolutionary, very wonderful."

While the U.S. clothing industry struggled to meet retailers' demands, citypants became the rage on college campuses. Although high schools generally held back the tide by requiring skirts, many workplaces gave in to the look. AT&T, Bullock's, Inc., and Garfinkel's were among the companies adapting to the idea of lady employees wearing pants.

Modified versions of citypants remained popular throughout the 1970s, deriving further impetus from the unisex and disco movements. The 1980s, however, characterized by a shift back to more conservative values, heralded a greater emphasis upon dresses in women's fashions.

BIBLIOGRAPHY

"New Boom in Clothing Industry: Women Are Changing to Pants," *U.S. News & World Report.* (September 23, 1968) 78-79. il.

"Pants for the City?" *Life.* 57 (October 23, 1964) 49-50. il.

"Women in Pants," *Vogue.* 144 (July 1964) 45-53. il.

Zinsser, W. "In the Yves of Destruction," *Life.* 65 (October 18, 1968) 12.

The Conk

The conk originated in the 1920s as a result of the efforts of black males to straighten their hair to resemble Caucasian styles. During the Swing Era, the patent leather look popularized by Cab Calloway held sway; however, by the time of the ascendancy of rock 'n' roll, black musicians had begun wearing their conks high. Penny Stallings described them as "pompadours with marcelled sides and a towering cascade of waves and curls."

Blacks were required to work hard in order to achieve the "do." According to Dylan Jones, the process involved the following:

> . . . hours of painstaking straightening, using hot irons and a coagulated gunk, a "relaxing solution." The wet, lank hair was then combed and greased into the conk. Though it could withstand the wildest Lindy-hopping, humid weather played havoc with the conk's construction, turning the hair back to its curly state. For this reason "do-rags" came into being, turban-like stockings which held the conks in place. These "do-rags" have passed into legend: during the mid-eighties several gangs of Bronx b-boys developed a penchant for them (for stylistic reasons only); former hairdresser and funkadelic godfather George Clinton even immortalized the offending article in a song, "Do the Do."

With the notable exception of aging black rock 'n' roll performers, the back-to-the-roots cultural revival of the 1960s and 1970s led to the style's fall from favor. The words of Malcolm X typified the example set by black leaders of the day:

> How ridiculous I was! . . . this was my first really big step toward self-degradation when I endured all of that pain, literally burning my flesh with lye, in order to cook my natural hair

until it was limp, to have it look like a white man's hair. I had joined that multitude of Negro men and women in America who are so brainwashed into believing that the black people are "inferior"–and white people "superior"–that they will even violate their God-created bodies to try to look "pretty" by white standards.

BIBLIOGRAPHY

Jones, Dylan. "The Conk," In: *Haircults: Fifty Years of Styles and Cuts.* New York: Thames and Hudson, 1990. pp. 37-38. il.
Malcolm X. *The Autobiography of Malcolm X.* 1965.
Stallings, Penny. *Rock 'n' Roll Confidential.* 1984.

Convertibles

Ownership of a convertible–or ragtop, as they were commonly called–was long equated with possessing the right stuff. As noted by *Newsweek,* "to a couple of generations of youthful Americans, the sleek, sassy convertible conjured up an image of the hep young playboy and his stunning girlfriend–her hair always flying in the wind–riding down the road to glamour and success." As recently as the 1960s, convertibles comprised around six percent of the car market, or 500,000 units per annum.

Sales began a decline in the late 1960s which dipped as low as 50,000 convertibles in 1974, all of European construction. Factors in the decline included:

1. soaring gas prices in the early 1970s, which discouraged recreational driving;
2. the rising level of carbon monoxide and other air pollutants;
3. the spread of air conditioners in automobiles;
4. a growing public concern over safety (with no more than a canvas or vinyl top, auto manufacturers were forced to compensate with special body construction, creating problems of balance);
5. federal safety regulations (e.g., attaching a shoulder harness required the flexibility of an acrobat);
6. limited top durability, the increased potential for leaks, and other wear-and-tear considerations;
7. compromises in comfort such as wind noises, potential sunburn (in the face of heightened fears over skin cancer), kamikaze insects, and inclement weather (rain, freezes, heat that could scorch seat cushions);
8. poor visibility to the rear with the roof up; and
9. the resolve of the U.S. car makers to phase out the convertible rather than deal with the myriad economic, legal, and engineering problems posed by its continued production.

After the 1980-1982 recession, with convertible sales (still all foreign makes) down to 25,000 per annum, U.S. auto makers began looking at new ways to increase their share. Reasoning that car buyers–particularly baby-boomers with disposable income–were tired of "econoboxes" and wanted something that equated with fun, they began manufacturing ragtops again. Chrysler took the plunge first with the LeBaron-Dodge 400 set in the 1982 model year, and Ford and GM followed shortly thereafter with convertible options for the Mustang, Corvette, and Cadillac Allante.

The nation's sales for convertibles were back up to 130,000 in 1986, reflecting Detroit's growing savvy in detecting the "niche markets" already being mined by foreign car companies. A discernable profile of the typical convertible owner emerged, that of a fashion-conscious, young extrovert willing to pay extra (sometimes over 50 percent more than sedan counterparts) for the open air experience.

With the youth market getting smaller, and the baby-boom generation aging, convertible sales began leveling off in the late 1980s. The growth potential of the genre was also limited by the fact that ragtops continued to display many of the flaws of their predecessors (e.g., marginal cargo capacity, faulty operation of the mechanism for lowering and raising the top). Enough drivers still are finding the convertible an attractive concept, however, to assure their continued popularity well into the 1990s.

BIBLIOGRAPHY

"The Cars of Summer," *Metropolitan Home*. (July 1988) 43-44. il.

Corelli, Rae, and David Todd. "Nostalgia Trips," *Maclean's*. 101:13 (March 21, 1988) 44ff. Covers marketing nostalgia in general; includes a related article on convertibles.

"Gone With the Wind," *Newsweek*. 78 (September 6, 1971) 65. il.

Henry, Ed, and Sherri Miller. "Convertibles: The Sky's the Limit," *Changing Times*. 42:6 (June 1988) 55ff. il.

" 'Miata Mania' Fuels Rag-Top Boom," *Journal of Commerce and Commercial*. 382:27101 (November 9, 1989) 1Aff. Booming Southern California sales attract global auto companies.

Seamonds, Jack A. "Rebirth of Top-Down Driving," *U.S. News & World Report*. (July 13, 1987) 52-53. il.

Strand, Patricia. "Cars Go From Ragtops to Riches," *Advertising Age*. 60:24 (May 29, 1989) 44.

The Corset

Though popularly considered a woman's undergarment, the corset first existed as an outer garment, worn by men as well as women. During the Middle Ages, the male version was a sleeved or sleeveless surcoat. The woman's corset was an outer gown, laced in front and, for cold weather, lined with fur.

By the seventeenth century, the corset had evolved into a type of foundation garment which not only supported, but also shaped the figure by defining or constricting the waist. This type of corset was fashioned in two pieces, called "stays," which laced together in front and in back. The specific contour the lacing created related to the style and "look" of the period which, in turn, reflected the contemporary idea of beauty and the perfect figure. Thus the "heavily-boned V-shape" that dominated the eighteenth century gave way, in the first decade of the nineteenth century, to the "Empire look." This loose, flowing style, derived from the lines of Classical Greek clothing, required less definition of the figure. Therefore, lighter, shorter corsets gained popularity. By mid-century, however, longer, heavier corseting with emphasis on a small waist had become stylish. In *Gone with the Wind*, Margaret Mitchell pictures this type of corseting as "Mammy" helps Scarlett O'Hara prepare for a barbecue at "Twelve Oaks." Scarlett directs Mammy to lace her tighter:

> "Hold onter sumpin' an' suck in your breaf" [Mammy] commanded. Scarlett obeyed, bracing herself and catching firm hold of one of the bedposts. Mammy pulled and jerked vigorously and . . . the tiny circumference of whalebone-girdled waist grew smaller. . . ."

The "hourglass" figure enjoyed popularity in the 1890s, eventually to be replaced by the S-curve of the "Gibson Girl." Both looks required proper corseting to achieve the wasp waist of the hourglass

What more could a man ask for in the way of whittled-down loveliness than this 18-inch waist cinched-in by a clever corset? 1900.

or the low bosom and high pronounced derriere of the S-curve. (Corsets as undergarments for men were offered in the nineteenth century as well, primarily for support, but also to counteract midriff bulge. This type of corset is still available.)

Once into the twentieth century, fashion changed again–this time to the straight, tubular lines associated with the 1920's and the "Flapper." This loose, low-waisted or waistless style required a different kind of foundation garment, one which supported the bust without defining hips or waist. The newly developed, lighter, less-restrictive brassiere served this purpose effectively. As a result of this different type of undergarment and the accompanying change in perception of the ideal figure, the popularity of the woman's corset declined.

In addition to being an item of fashion, the corset for girls and women was also an item of controversy, particularly in the mid-nineteenth century. One side of the debate held that the corset was a necessary item of attire for any respectable girl or woman. Loose (uncorseted) dress was seen as an indication of loose morals. Others asserted that the corset, especially when tightly laced, jeopardized the physical and mental health of the wearer.

–Ann Jerabek
M.L.S.,
Reference Librarian,
Sam Houston State University

BIBLIOGRAPHY

Ewing, Elizabeth. *Underwear: A history.* New York: Theatre Arts Books. 1972.
Mitchell, Margaret. *Gone With the Wind.* New York: Macmillan. 1977. 86th printing.
Steele, Valerie. *Fashion and Eroticism: Ideals of feminine beauty from the Victorian Era to the Jazz Age.* New York: Oxford University Press. 1985.

Cowboy Boots

There was a time when only cowboys wore cowboy boots. Their transition into the mainstream began when country singers adapted them as a vital component of onstage dress. Then, in the mid-1970s, they permeated into the disco scene thanks to the likes of Andy Warhol. By 1978, as a result of trickle-down chic, everyone seemed to be wearing them, including such unlikely luminaries as Catherine Deneuve and Anwar Sadat. At the time, Judi Buie, a transplanted Texan who was selling some 50 pairs weekly in her New York shop, noted, "A year ago, it was only a fad. Now it's fashion."

While Tennessee dominated volume in the then $250 million-a-year business (one factory alone stamped out 40,000 pairs a day), Texas boots were tops in cachet. Most Texan outfits, including the "big three" of Texas bootmakers–(in descending order of size) Tony Lama of El Paso, Justin of Fort Worth, and Nocona of Nocona–as well as countless small-scale custom makers, had their best year ever in 1978. Almost all were far behind on orders, some by as much as three years.

The popularity of cowboy boots continued to rise up through the urban cowboy craze engendered by the film of the same name starring John Travolta. Demand nationwide dropped off sharply in the mid-1980s, however, though boots–as part of the solidly entrenched western wear industry–have remained a staple in the South and West as well as the blue collar population across the United States.

BIBLIOGRAPHY

"All's Well That Ends Well," *Forbes.* 122 (November 27, 1978) 76. il.

"A Boom in Boots," *Newsweek.* 91 (April 17, 1978) 81. il.

"Pushin' Boots for Urban Cowpokes," *Time.* 114 (September 3, 1979) 60. il.

Sodowsky, Roland. "The Origins of the Cowboy Boot," *The Atlantic.* 264:6 (December 1989) 46ff.

Stratton, W. K. "Standing Tall; Handmade Cowboy Boots are Comfortable, Sturdy, Colorful, and Chic," *Americana.* 15:6 (January-February 1988) 57ff. il.

"Western Boots," *Glamour.* 77 (April 1979) 138. il.

Cracker Jack

The Cracker Jack Company has been an American institution for most of the twentieth century. Its practice of packing toys into boxes of caramel-coated popcorn began in 1908, after the confection alone had been marketed for 12 years. Feedback from consumers has convinced the firm that the magic of its success is contained more in the toy than in the popcorn. Cracker Jack also took note of the fact that sales were dismal in those states which used to forbid the inclusion of premiums in packages of edibles.

The premiums have included every imaginable object over the years–boots, dolls, tops, whistles (an early one blew up to four tones), strings of beads, multi-part puzzles, oriental paper fans, miniatures of workshop tools, etc. Runs of each premium have ranged from five million to 15 million since World War II. These items have always been restricted with respect to cost and size (they can't be too large or too small). They also have had to appeal equally to both sexes and across many age groups.

Some grownups can still remember a time when toys in the Cracker Jack boxes were made of wood and/or metal. These were often imported from Japan, Germany, and other places; however, World War II cut off most of these markets and necessitated the heavy use of plastics in their construction. Nevertheless, the quality of these premiums can still lead to letters like the following:

- One man asked for a duplicate of the tiny pair of pliers his son had found in a box. It was the only suitable instrument he'd ever come upon for inserting a wick in his cigarette lighter.
- A miniature sea captain, with a peaked officer's hat, a bar-handled mustache, and a leer prompted concerns that innocent children were being supplied statues of Joseph Stalin.

In actuality, the toy itself has always been less important to the consumer than the element of wonder and surprise that goes with opening up a box of Cracker Jack. According to *Harper's* magazine, "As long as children keep asking 'What is it?' the company will keep packing plastic pig-in-the-poke . . . more than a million times a day, and America will continue to be something like what it used to be."

BIBLIOGRAPHY

"A Million Surprises a Day," *Harper's Magazine.* 217 (1951). il.
"More You Eat: Cracker Jack," *Fortune.* 35 (June 1947) 144.
"Prize Package," *Newsweek.* 53 (January 19, 1959) 66. il.

The Tony Curtis Hairstyle

Throughout his career, Tony Curtis was known as much for his hair as for his acting talents. The Tony Curtis haircut consisted primarily of a curled coif on the forehead, a semi-crew-cut top and a full nape–all accented with a heavy dollop of grease. His hair was first noticed in his second film, *City Across the River* (1949) and his popularity continued growing with each successive release. Although Curtis professed to feel trapped by the work of Hollywood publicity agents, he continued to maintain the Italian cut that had first brought him fame throughout the 1950s, even in historical epics such as *The Vikings* (1958) and Stanley Kubrick's *Spartacus* (1960). Pieces of his locks were sent off to fans by the studio.

Curtis, born into a Jewish Orthodox family in the Bronx, considered his haircut to be phony:

> It all began because I couldn't afford a haircut. Then I thought my very gift was something so mystical and magical that by cutting my hair I thought it would be gone. I could understand what Samson felt. I was afraid if they cut my hair too much they would cut my talent.

Nevertheless, the cut influenced an entire generation of juvenile delinquents, and provided the impetus for Elvis Presley's style.

BIBLIOGRAPHY

Jones, Dylan. "Tony Curtis; The Italian Cut," In: *Haircults: Fifty Years of Styles and Cuts*. New York: Thames and Hudson, 1990. p. 22. il.

"King and Queen of Hearts," *Look*. 18 (February 23, 1954) 50ff. il.

Martin, P. "Perils of Being a Young Movie Star," *Saturday Evening Post*. 224 (February 9, 1952) 22-23ff. il.

Nichols, M. N. "Idle Dreamer to Self-Made Idol," *Coronet*. 43 (January 1958) 10. il.

"Parisian Picnic," *Look*. 19 (November 29, 1955) 90-93. il.

[Portrait], *Look*. 18 (September 7, 1954) 58.

The D.A.

The Duck's Ass–or D.A. for short–was extremely popular with teenage males during the 1950s. The D.A. consisted of overlapping wings of hair combed from the side of the head to the back. Mounds of grease helped keep the hair properly in place, hence the appellation "greasers," which was commonly applied to its exponents.

A South Philadelphia barbershop proprietor named Joe Cirello was credited with originating the style. In an interview published in *The Face* in 1985 he recalled,

> I invented the D.A. in 1940 at 6th and Washington Avenue, on a blind kid. I was just playing around, I had something in mind–I figured this kid can't see what I'm doing, so I kept on practicing. And then the kids started coming in from Southern High (the neighborhood school), they said, "Hey, that looks great, try it on me."

The D.A. spread throughout the youth subculture (and further evolved in the hands of British Edwardians and Teddy Boys), fueled by the example of rock 'n' roll stars and Hollywood exploitation flicks featuring juvenile delinquents of the greaser persuasion. Always associated with working class kids (or middle and upper class teens effecting a form of rebellion against parental mores), the style and its spinoffs–the elephant trunk, the Tony Curtis, the simple quiff, etc.–retained some degree of favor during the initial onslaught of Beatlemania. However, lower class urban teens ultimately turned to the natural, long hair look already in vogue with the majority of late 1960s youth. The D.A., albeit in exaggerated mutations, underwent a limited revival during the punk and neo-rockabilly movements of the late 1970s and early 1980s.

In the meantime, Joe Cirello moved to Hollywood to work as a staff hairdresser at Warner Brothers Studios, cutting the hair of such notables as Frank Sinatra, Eddie Fisher, Bill Haley, Elvis Presley, and James Dean.

BIBLIOGRAPHY

"Ain't Nothin' But a Hairdo; Hair Cut to Look Like Presley's," *Life*. 42 (March 25, 1957) 55-56ff. il.
Jones, Dylan. "Joe Cirello and the D.A.," In: *Haircults: Fifty Years of Styles and Cuts*. New York: Thames and Hudson, 1990. pp. 20-21. il.
Peck, B. "Duck of a Wave," *Mademoiselle*. 43 (August 1956) 80. il.

The "Dammit" (Troll) Doll

In early 1964, everyone from Lady Bird Johnson to hundreds of thousands of college girls found the "Dammit" doll to be lovable. *Newsweek* noted that it was "fast replacing the rabbit's foot as the world's most popular good-luck charm." Advocates included a prominent St. Louis lawyer, who swore his doll had tripled business, and the Coral Gables High School swimming team, which won ten straight meets after adopting one as its mascot.

The doll originated around 1959 when a Danish woodcutter, Thomas Dam, who could not afford to purchase his teenage daughter a birthday gift, carved her his vision of a troll who, according to legend, scampered about the Nordic countryside, bestowing good fortune on humans fortunate enough to catch him. Dam's luck began its upward climb when his daughter dressed the doll and showed it about the village the following day, thereby attracting the attention of a Danish toy merchant.

By 1964, Dam operated doll factories in Denmark, New Zealand, and Hialeah, Florida and had sold more than a million of his creations in the U.S. alone. Mrs. Inge Dykins, who introduced them to the U.S., noted at the time, "The secret of their charm is that they're so ugly you have to laugh. And we Danes have a saying: 'When you laugh, nothing bad can happen to you.'" In fact, "ugly" was an understatement with respect to the doll's appearance. It was jug-eared and potbellied, with eyes as glassy as its grin, with a head that stopped directly above the eyebrows, where it abruptly gave way to a floor-length hank of combed sheep's wool.

In short order, the doll fostered an entire family (ranging in price from $1.25 for baby to $5.95 for poppa), demanded accessories (miniature ironing boards, dishes, motorcycles, etc.), and inspired a slew of imitations (e.g., Wishniks and Drolls). Nevertheless, its popularity waned greatly during 1964 as Americans found new obsessions, most notably Beatlemania.

BIBLIOGRAPHY

"Dammit All," *Newsweek*. 63 (February 3, 1964) 68. il.

The Derby

A hat with a long and rich history, the bowler–or derby–underwent a conspicuous revival in both the United States and Great Britain in 1959. London's *Daily Herald* scornfully commented on the phenomenon:

> This tomfoolery becomes . . . a symbol of decadence. The cure must be short and quick. The bowler hat must be abolished.

The hat fared better in America where it didn't suffer from aristocratic associations. For 20 years, U.S. production had held at 800 or so per year. That spring, however, it surged to 3,000 a week.

In Toledo, which claimed to have more derby wearers than any other U.S. city, 158 citizens formed the Downtown Bowler Club. The older members indicated their liking for the hat to be based upon nostalgia, while younger ones liked the fact that they looked different.

Elsewhere in the states, the derby's popularity owed much to its affinity with the Continental suit. The Continental–which overtook the conservative Ivy League look in fall 1959–exuded a more fitted, dapper look than standard American suits (featuring narrow peaked lapels, a rounded short two-button jacket, slanted pockets, and cuffs on sleeves versus none on trousers); men's clothiers generally recommended derbies as the crowning touch.

BIBLIOGRAPHY

"Big Buzz Over Bowlers," *Life*. 46 (May 18, 1959) 116Aff. il.
"Booming Bowler," *Newsweek*. 53 (January 12, 1959) 72. il.
Palmer, C. B. "New Old Hat; Derby," *New York Times Magazine*. (March 15, 1959) 42ff. il.
"Will Bowlers Come Back?," *Look*. 22 (November 11, 1958) 55. il.

Digital Watches

The digital watch burst upon the marketplace in 1975. Hailed by one manufacturer as "probably the greatest breakthrough in time-keeping technology since the sundial," it displayed time (as well as the month and date on the more expensive models) with glowing numbers rather than hands moving around a marked clock face. Priced between 30 and 3,000 dollars, digitals in 1975 accounted for approximately five percent of all watches sold in the U.S. (i.e., 2.5 million). The watches came in two basic models: the L.E.D. (light-emitting diode) in which the digits lit up at the press of a button or at the flick of the wrist, and the L.C.D. (liquid crystal display), which provided a continuous display but to be seen clearly had to be angled toward the available light.

While the early models were bulky (thereby limiting their appeal to women), digitals appealed to consumers on a variety of fronts:

1. They were considered to be as accurate as any watch then available, losing or gaining only a minute per year.
2. They were constantly dropping in price; it was estimated that they would sell for as little as 20 dollars by early 1976.
3. They were considered a novelty; i.e., the first-on-the-block-to-own-one syndrome.
4. They provide the wearer with a feeling of power; i.e., at the push of a button, he or she could command time.
5. They were practical. Jon Borgzinner, a Manhattan-based writer, noted,

   I like it because when I pick it up at night
   I don't have to figure out from the dial if
   it's ten of six or two minutes before four;
   it simply tells me it's 4:14 or 9:53.

6. They offered exciting new technological possibilities. For instance, Pulsar marketed the "personal information center"

in late 1975–a digital watch combined with a miniaturized calculator.

The digital watch has continued to grow in popularity since its appearance on the market. Its price dropped to where inexpensive models sometimes sold for less than one dollar in the 1980s. Indeed, they were frequently given away as premiums for magazine subscriptions or the purchase of certain products. Their continued ubiquitousness in American life seems assured for years to come.

BIBLIOGRAPHY

"Digital Watches; Bringing Watchmaking Back to the U.S.," *Business Week.* (October 27, 1975) 78-81ff. il.

"Going Digital," *Time.* 106 (December 22, 1975) 48-49. il.

"Good Timing?" *Forbes.* 115 (February 15, 1975) 58-59. il.

"LCD Digital Makes a Comeback," *Business Week.* (April 19, 1976) 40. il.

"Recession Bucker: Digital Quartz Watches," *Time.* 29 (December 1975) 10-12. il.

Smay, V. E. "New Breed of Digital Watches–Far-Out Features, Fewer Problems," *Popular Science.* 209 (December 1976) 48ff. il.

"$20 Digital Watch Arrives a Year Early," *Business Week.* (January 26, 1976) 27-28. il.

"Why Gillette Stopped Its Digital Watches," *Business Week.* (January 31, 1977) 37-38.

The Dodge Rebellion

In 1966, amidst the small car craze fueled by imports and Ford's Mustang, Chrysler Corporation's Dodge Division enjoyed a substantial increase in sales over the previous year (509,000 compared to 481,777 in 1965, both figures covering the January-November period). Much of their success in a declining overall market was attributable to the company's outrageous TV ad campaign featuring Pam Austin, a blonde Hollywood actress who fell off cliffs, bridges, airplanes, and roofs in the best spy capers tradition before making her pitch to "join the Dodge rebellion."

The Austin ads, developed by the Batten, Barton, Durstine & Osborn agency, were termed "the freshest auto sales pitch at least since Volkswagen started thinking small," according to *Business Week*. BBD&O chose the "Rebellion" theme as a means of signifying a break with Dodge's past image. Prior to that time, Dodge had been promoted largely through the *Lawrence Welk Show*–a program extremely popular with women over 50, but a virtual nonentity with youth to whom Detroit was beginning to target heavily. Austin was chosen to star in the ads following a three-month search. Don Schwab, producer of the TV ads, noted:

> We had to develop a whole character, tongue-in-cheek but also slinky. I didn't want to sell just sex, so she had to be wholesome.

The Dodge Rebellion spots quickly became one of the top-ranking TV commercials of the year and were adapted to radio in short order. In 1967, Dodge not only embellished its cliff-hanging TV ads but moved the series into the national print media with captions like "Back the attack," "Revolt against kiddy-car compacts" and "Surrender–you're surrounded with luxury." Evidently, this was not enough for some Americans (who may or may not have owned

Dodges); it was reported that Pam Austin fan clubs were springing up on college campuses at the height of the ad campaign's popularity.

BIBLIOGRAPHY

"Calamity Pam," *Time*. 89 (January 13, 1967) 64. il.

"Dodge Finds Its Fever Contagious for Young; Joan Anita Parker, Dodge Rebellion Girl," *Business Week*. (August 31, 1968) 38-40. il.

"The 'Rebellion' That Caught the Mood of Youth; Dodge Rebellion a Household Word," *Business Week*. (December 10, 1966) 74. il.

Dolls with Human Faces

In early 1965, Americans were snapping up dolls with faces made to order. The New York toy manufacturer responsible for the craze, Jet Party Favors, Inc., claimed in a brochure, "It's a doll with any face you want."

Costing $9.95, the process worked as follows: the customer would mail in a photograph of the person to be modeled, specifying hair and eye color. The photo was reproduced on a strip of photo-sensitive linen, which was put through a pressure-molding process to suggest facial contours such as noses, eyes, and dimples. The hardened, mask-like shell was then touched up by artists, attached to a blank head, and mounted on a standard doll boy, girl, or baby body.

Response was tremendous with more than 16,000 dolls being sold in the first three months. According to Stanley Weber, the firm's marketing director, customers included:

1. parents who considered a stuffed likeness of their child the ultimate in sentiment;
2. grandparents desiring a reminder of grandchildren in remote locations;
3. narcissists wanting dolls depicting themselves as youngsters;
4. necrophiles wanting dolls of deceased relatives; and
5. teenage girls who mailed their images to boyfriends stationed abroad.

Besides satiating the desire for a unique conversation piece or the need to fulfill a strong emotional urge, the process enabled others to indulge in a penchant for the downright bizarre. For example, a Redondo Beach woman ordered a likeness of her departed fox terrier mounted on a doll body.

BIBLIOGRAPHY

"Hello, Dolly?" *Newsweek.* 65 (February 22, 1965) 92. il.

The Drinking Man's Diet

In 1965, overweight Americans were indulging in a new diet craze following guidelines laid down in a softcover booklet entitled *The Drinking Man's Diet*, which retailed for one dollar. The idea sprang from San Franciscan Robert Cameron and his son, Todd, who, upon hearing about the long-popular, high protein regimen known as the Air Force Diet "from an Air Force pilot," concocted the book under the pseudonyms of Gardner Jameson and Elliot Williams.

According to the book, the diet could be summed up in one sentence: "Eat Less Than Sixty Grams of Carbohydrates a Day." What followed in elaborating this premise was referred to by *Time* as "a cocktail of wishful thinking, a jigger of nonsense and a dash of sound advice." For instance, while the book noted accurately enough that distilled liquors and unfortified wines contain negligible amounts of carbohydrates, the argument that alcohol's calories don't count because they somehow disappear in a mysterious metabolic process represented a blatant untruth. In fact, as a number of experts point out, the liver synthesizes the alcohol into a number of by-products including sugar (a carbohydrate), which, if not used for energy, could ultimately turn into fat.

Medical and nutritional experts were vociferous in their criticism of the book. Dr. Philip L. White, The A.M.A.'s top nutrition expert, stated, "The drinking man's diet is utter nonsense, has no scientific basis, and is chock-full of errors." In practice, an individual sticking to the diet might cut down drastically on his or her caloric intake by avoiding bread, potatoes, and other starches as well as the garnishes (butter, sour cream, etc.) usually accompanying them. In short, weight loss could be ascribed to a reduced caloric intake. However, the availability of other diets, supported by experts, offering this same virtue assured the swift demise of the drinking man's diet.

BIBLIOGRAPHY

Alsop, J. "Diet That Finally Did It; Air Force Diet," *McCalls*. 92 (May 1965) 138ff. il.

"The Drinking Man's Danger," *Time*. (March 5, 1965) 72-73. il.

Snider, Arthur J. "Beware the Drinker's Diet," *Science Digest*. (August 1965) 13-15. il.

Wernick, R. "I Wrote the Drinking Man's Diet," *Saturday Evening Post*. 238 (May 22, 1965) 84ff. il.

"What About That Painless Air Force Diet?" *Readers' Digest*. 87 (July 1965) 89-92. Abridgement of Alsop article.

Drive-in Banking

Drive-in banking began inauspiciously in 1936 with the City National Bank of South Bend, Indiana announcing its intention to provide "bank curb service" in order to better utilize its useless alleyway. By mid-1948–and the complete resumption of normal business activities in the wake of World War II–the phenomenon had spread to 250-odd banks in 18 states.

The Exchange National Autobank, perhaps the largest and most complete drive-in, illustrated the rapid growth of the practice. Opening in late 1946, the Autobank made money at a growing clip, almost doubling its deposits during its first two years of operation despite a nationwide decline in bank receipts. From 50 cars daily at the onset, car-borne customers rose to more than 600 by late 1948, accounting for close to half of the bank's deposit business.

The advantages of this service were a testament to its success. These included:

1. Greater safety for the customer. Businessmen, for example, could lock themselves into their cars with the day's receipts, drive right up, and make a deposit.
2. Greater safety for the bank. As of late 1948, no major holdups with drive-in windows (which were often comprised of sheet steel and bulletproof-glass booths) had been recorded; as a result, insurance companies had not raised rates for such operations.
3. No parking problem–generally a headache for banks located in urban centers.
4. Convenience for the customer. Housewives who didn't want to dress up could do their banking, clad in a house dress, from within their cars. Children–generally considered a nuisance in the main lobbies of banks–could even be brought along.
5. Speedier handling, primarily because the physical barriers

present in drive-in banking cut down on the amount of gossiping between patron and teller.

6. No stand-in-line waiting. Any waiting necessary could be done comfortably from within the car.

7. Valuable promotion for banks. Exchange National estimated that half of its new customers came aboard due to its autobanking facilities.

8. Economy. A bank experiencing heavy use could install a drive-in outlet for less expense than it could enlarge its lobby.

In addition to these advantages, banks such as Exchange National handled not only deposits but loan payments, foreign exchange, bond purchases, check certification, etc. In cases requiring the assistance of a bank officer, the teller could send paperwork and/or documents to him via pneumatic tube, thereby assuring that they would receive quick attention.

In 1941, *The Manchester (N.H.) Union* joked about the onslaught of drive-in banking in an editorial:

> If, while the customer is depositing his $9.76, an assistant teller cleans his windshield, while another fills his radiator, and a third checks his air and hands him a road map, the problem of what to do with all those [depression-closed] vacant bank buildings may yet be solved.

Indeed, drive-in banking acquired institutional status during the post-World War II era, offering–in addition to the aforementioned advantages–expanded banking hours which reached their optimum level with the spread of 24-hour automated teller services. Largely as a result of the American romance with the automobile, many related drive-in services evolved during this period, including restaurants, libraries, and movie theaters.

However, the refinement of one of the by-products of drive-in service, electronic banking, may contain the seeds of its ultimate demise. But, for now, drive-ins remain a potent force within the industry, particularly in small-town America.

BIBLIOGRAPHY

"Deposit and Drive Away; Curb-Teller Installations," *American City.* 67 (December 1952) 104-105. il.

"The Flourishing Drive-Ins," *Newsweek.* 32 (August 16, 1948) 63-64. il.

"Snorkel; Curbstone Banking," *Time.* 53 (February 14, 1949) 89. il.

Electronic Clothes

Diana Dew was the rage of the fashion scene in 1967 because she accomplished something that nobody had thought of doing before; i.e., to make clothing that switched on and off. By using thin, luminated, pliable plastic phosphorescent lamps sewn into the clothes in segments and connected to a rechargeable battery pack worn on the hip (which kept the wearer flashing on and off for five hours and could be recharged on house current), she was able to produce minidresses with throbbing hearts and pulsating belly stars, as well as pants with flashing vertical side seams and horizontal bands that marched up and down the legs in luminous sequence.

Dew migrated to New York City in the mid-1960s with hopes of becoming a fashion designer. When no one there expressed an interest in her ideas, she relocated to Cambridge, Massachusetts and opened her own boutique, Isis, on Harvard Square. It was not a success because "I couldn't turn the stuff fast enough," she noted. "And, anyway, the people who liked my things couldn't afford them."

In late summer 1966, she became a designer for Puritan's Paraphernalia division. By the end of the year she was such a hit that they established a special division called Experipuritaneous (Experimental Puritan Outrageousness) and made her president of it. Her electronic fashions hit the market in February. Because of their relatively high prices ($125-$225) and the long hours required to construct them, they were offered in very limited quantities. Nevertheless, they caused a stampede–not so much for the clothes (many potential buyers were afraid they might be electrocuted when wearing them), but for Dew. She appeared on Johnny Carson's *Tonight Show*, and the fashion writers at *Harper's Bazaar*, *Vogue* and *Mademoiselle* welcomed her innovations with open arms. Suddenly, nothing was more identifiably "in" than a Diana Dew electronic dress.

"My clothes are designed to turn people on," she said at the time. "Get rid of their inhibitions. Like taking LSD–with none of the hang-ups." Much of her inspiration came from two vastly different contemporary sources: hippies–with their playful costumes, bright colors, psychedelic effects, acid trips, freedom, pleasure, and new levels of communication; and astronauts–with their world of spacesuits, electronics, new materials, and new dimensions.

After a year with Puritan, Dew went out on her own. Some of her new projects included music (she formed a band with three other girls called Creamcheese which wore electronic clothes) and interior design. With the decline in appeal of Pop Art in the early 1970s, however, her idiosyncratic psychedelic-electronic creations dropped out of the cultural mainstream.

BIBLIOGRAPHY

Dew, Diana. "Aglow: Electronic Clothes; Interview," *New Yorker.* 42 (January 28, 1967) 26-28.

Hymon, Tom. "Turn On Your Dress, Diana!" *Saturday Evening Post.* 241 (January 13, 1968) 26-29. il.

"Turn On, Turn Off," *Time.* 89 (January 20, 1967) 80. il.

Fallout Shelters

One notable offshoot of the Cold War hysteria gripping Americans after World War II was the fallout shelter. Encouraged by public figures as wide-ranging as Ann Landers and President John F. Kennedy (who deemed it "every citizen's duty to protect his family in case of attack"), many families fell prey to the marketing strategies of companies that sold fallout shelters and survival supplies. Above all, shelters were seen to represent the sole means of maintaining the semblance of normalcy should there be a World War III as well as a vastly preferable alternative to living in a public shelter alongside absolute strangers.

A host of publications appeared in the 1950s and 1960s geared to assisting citizens in the establishment and maintenance of bomb shelters. The office of Civil and Defense Mobilization compiled a shelter supply checklist in 1969 which included the following items:

- paper plates, cups, and napkins (a two-week supply);
- a battery-operated radio with the CONELRAD frequency marked;
- flashlights and electric lanterns;
- a ten-gallon, lidded garbage pail serving as a toilet;
- reading material; and
- educational games for children (if present).

In 1961, *Time* devoted a cover story, "The Sheltered Life," to the phenomenon which included warnings against bogus supplies such as radiation salve, anti-radiation pills, and "fallout suits." Chuck West, in his *The Fall-Out Shelter Handbook*, offered basic survival skills such as reading constellations to get one's bearings and making bread and medicinal teas. The OCDM's *The Family Fallout Shelter* provided elaborate plans for five types of shelters, ranging

Afraid of nuclear warfare that would render ground-level living impossible for a number of months—if not longer, Americans in the 1950s shopped for fallout shelters.

from the inexpensive Basement Concrete Block to the deluxe six-person Underground Concrete Shelter with baffle walls, centrifugal blower, termite shield, and twelve-gauge corrugated metal door to keep out intruders.

For those unable–or uninclined–to build their own, numerous commercial models were advertised via catalogs. The Armco Steel Corporation of San Francisco offered a prefab modular shelter, while Lone Star Steel of Dallas made one which featured a trompe l'oeil picture window on the wall, depicting a two-dimensional landscape. Pool tables, wine cellars, and other luxury items were available with top-of-the-line shelters.

The 1961 Texas State Fair, in which the fallout shelter exhibition drew larger crowds than the venerable prize-cattle exhibit, offered further proof of the public's fascination with these structures. Shelters remained a fixture on the American social landscape up through the 1960s, albeit with less intensity than that characterizing the earlier part of the decade.

By the 1970s, however, shelters had lost their allure to most Americans, a victim of growing public sophistication regarding the hazards of a nuclear holocaust. The old "duck and cover" sloganeering had long since fallen into disrepute; avoidance of conflict was viewed as the only sure means of survival. In addition, the lessening of Cold War tensions, fueled by Détente, the Salt Treaty and Nixon's China trip, helped seal their fate. Even the revival of Commie-bashing during the Reagan years proved incapable of resurrecting shelters as part of a serious survival strategy; this despite the fact that the U.S. government has yet to come up with any viable public alternative.

BIBLIOGRAPHY

Brant, I. "Who Shall Be Saved By Shelters?" *New Republic*. 146 (March 5, 1962) 7.

"Civil Defense is Possible," *Fortune*. 58 (December 1958) 98-101ff.

"H-Bomb Shelters Provide 3:1 Survival Rate," *American City*. 72 (September 1957) 177ff.

Levin, Eric. "It's Strictly a Hole in the Ground, But John Hay's Doomsday Domicile is on the Market for $3.3 Million," *People Weekly*. 30:1 (July 4, 1988) 59ff. il.

"Life and Love in Your Own Shelter," *Nation.* 189 (July 18, 1959) 22.

Rockefeller, Nelson A. "Importance of Shelters in Nuclear Age; Address, March 4, 1960," *Vital Speeches.* 26 (April 15, 1960) 411-413.

Rothman, S. "Shelter Debate," *America.* 107 (July 28, 1962) 543-545.

"Shelter Boom," *Newsweek.* 58 (September 18, 1961) 31. il.

"Sheltered Life," *Time.* 78 (October 20, 1961) 21-25; 79 (March 9, 1962) 26. il.

"Sheltered Life; No Market for Shelters," *Newsweek.* 64 (July 27, 1964) 75. il.

"Shelters Again; Incentive Program," *New Republic.* 146 (May 25, 1963) 6.

"Spare Room Fallout Shelter," *Life.* 48 (January 25, 1960) 46. il.

Stern, Jane, and Michael Stern. "Mr. and Mrs. Average," In: *Sixties People.* New York: Knopf, 1990. pp. 200-231. il.

"Their Sheltered Honeymoon," *Life.* 47 (August 10, 1959) 51-52. il.

"What the Citizen is Not Being Told," *Nation.* 193 (October 14, 1961) 237.

"Where are They Now? Fallout-Shelters," *Newsweek.* 74 (August 25, 1969) 10.

"Your Cellar Could Mean Your Life," *Science Newsletter.* 77 (May 14, 1960) 314-315. il.

The Feather Wave Cut
and the Revival of Hairpins

In a rare case of government policy dictating fads to the general public, Washington deep-sixed the ladies' long shoulder hairdo (à la Veronica Lake) by severely curtailing the manufacture of bobby pins. WPB order L-104, developed to conserve approximately 6,000 tons of steel, left American women with three options: (1) letting hair grow and putting it up old-fashioned-like, (2) adopting a mannish cut, or (3) indulging in a new feather wave cut. The majority of females seemed to prefer the latter.

In the wake of the ruling, the first move of the hairdressing industry was to shunt the allotment of steel for bobby pins (only one-eighth of the amount used during 1941 was permitted for the following year, thereby rendering it impossible to employ high-carbon steel, the only means of supplying sufficient spring tension to make the pins stay put) to hairpins. Nothing in L-104 affected enameling, an important process in the manufacture of hairpins.

The hairpin had been hanging on in the marketplace for a generation since women had begun cutting their hair and using bobby pins. Hairpin sales were also boosted by the fact that sanitary laws in about thirty states disallowed beauty shops from using them a second time. The feather wave cuts, which required hairpins for setting but none after the customer left the shop, did not especially please hairpin makers. They fondly recalled the consistent turnover in the product when used with long hair styles; millions tumbled annually to sidewalks as well as bathroom and bedroom floors and were swept away into oblivion. Nevertheless, the patriotic war effort effectively put a lid on complaints and the new short bobs reigned supreme through the mid-1940s.

BIBLIOGRAPHY

Sayler, O. M. "War Styles the Coiffure," *New York Times Magazine.* (September 27, 1942) 24. il.
"WPB Coiffure," *Business Week.* (May 23, 1942) 30.

The Five-Gallon Hat

The ascendancy of Lyndon Johnson to the White House proved to be a boon to Western hat manufacturers. Not only did the President wear a stylish "five-gallon" hat, but his practice of giving them to favored guests caused quite a stir within Washington, DC society. As noted by an official of the Byer-Rolnick Hat Corporation, the Garland, Texas firm which made Johnson's hats,

> There are many people in Washington wearing LBJ hats the President gave them. There are also a great many others who bought the same style hat, creating the impression that LBJ gave them one, too.

Stores in the Capitol such as the tony haberdashery firm of Lewis & Thomas Saltz, Inc.–which immediately fired off an order to Texas for six dozen "exact duplicates" of the hat–found the five-gallon hard to keep in stock as even normally hatless men (mostly loyal Democrats) went under cover.

The President was known to keep approximately 30 different-sized hats on hand for purposes of giving away. Costing him 20 dollars apiece, his five-gallons differed from the "store boughten" ones (which retailed for 25 dollars) in one notable respect. The bona fide LBJs had a small gold-colored map of Texas on the inside silk lining with the words "Johnson City" and, in the President's own handwriting, "LBJ Ranch." A white star inside a lariat loop highlighted the location within the state.

Whereas only "drugstore cowboys" wore Western hats prior to the LBJ White House, according to Byer-Rolnick vice president Kenneth L. Topletz, the style began winning many new converts in 1964. Byer-Rolnick–which had been turning out 250,000 Westerns in about 50 styles at prices from $12.50 to $250 (the latter being mink-trimmed specials for the Dallas-based Neiman-Marcus chain)–was only one of many companies profiting from the boom.

The Western hat mania crested around the time of LBJ's re-election to the White House in late 1964. However, as his popularity began to wane in the wake of domestic upheaval (e.g., Civil Rights riots) and growing public disenchantment with the Vietnam War, the five-gallon–and its relatives–likewise fell from grace.

BIBLIOGRAPHY

"The '5 Gallon,' " *Newsweek.* 63 (February 10, 1964) 68. il.

Nash, L. M. "Hat That Crowned the West: Cowboy's Stetson," *Coronet.* 50 (August 1961) 54-56. il.

Flashfashions

Flashdance–which chronicled the life of a Pittsburgh girl (starring Jennifer Beals) who was a welder by day, go-go dancer by night and full-time ballet hopeful–inspired a full-scale merchandizing bonanza during the summer of 1983. The film grossed nearly 50 million dollars in the first couple of months following its release in April 1983, and its title song, "Flashdance–What a Feeling" (performed by Irene Cara on the Casablanca label), was the number one single for six weeks.

The film also spawned a genre of exercise and dance videos as well as a fashion look termed "raggedy chic" by *Newsweek*; i.e., shorts or a mini and an artfully torn, off-the-shoulder T-shirt or sweatshirt. Boutiques like Metropolis in Los Angeles and Commander Salamander in Washington specialized in Flashfashions, the latter even offering "custom ripping, either on or off the body," with the purchase of a $7.99 T-shirt. Other customers did their own alterations at home–slashing necklines, hacking off sleeves, and unraveling hems.

Wearers offered a variety of testimonials to the appeal of Flashfashions, once the sole province of jocks, dancers, and a few avant-garde Japanese designers.

- Flashdancers said their saggy shirts–often layered over tank tops or undershirts–kept them cool during fancy footwork.
- A 21-year-old secretary in Atlanta, Paula Eckman, exclaimed, "I love clothes that look like they're gonna fall off because the guys think they're gonna see something."
- New York art director Dayna Winston indicated an appreciation for the look's practicality, stating, "It's easy, it goes with everything, and I can wear it for any occasion except a wedding."

The look was gradually subsumed by a broader, watered-down form of punk fashions popularized by pop singers like Madonna and Cyndi Lauper in the mid-1980s. The new style featured rainbow hair dyes, spiked hair, and rag-tag layered clothing.

BIBLIOGRAPHY

Langway, L. "Flashdance, Flashfashions," *Newsweek.* 102 (July 4, 1983) 55. il.
"What a Feeling! Chic Dressers are Turning Maniac for That Sexy, Torn-Up Flashdance Look," *People Weekly.* 20 (August 8, 1983) 70-71. il.

Footsees

On occasion, some toys will achieve greater success the second time they enter the marketing merry-go-round. The Footsee was a case in point.

After a similar product enjoyed fleeting popularity in 1964, the Footsee returned in summer 1968 to become the rage of the playground set. About four million were purchased in the U.S. at a retail price of $1.29 during its first three months in the stores.

Robert Asch, president of Twinpak Ltd. of Montreal, manufacturer of the toy, got the idea from watching Arab children in Jerusalem playing with similar contraptions. It consisted of a plastic ankle ring to which was attached a 30-inch string with a bell-shaped weight at the other end. The object was to twirl the string with one foot and hop with the other. Some youngsters were able to master twirling several Footsees at once.

By 1969, however, the toy was history. Further attempts at reviving it proved to be comparative failures.

BIBLIOGRAPHY

"Fads; Return of the Oldies," *Time.* 92 (October 11, 1968) 87. il.

G. I. Joe

By Christmas 1966, retailers had shelves spilling over with military toys that were not selling. Harvey Cole, a wholesale distributor in the Seattle area, attributed this situation to the fact that "People are sickened by anything painted in olive drab."

G. I. Joe, an 11 1/2-inch-high doll launched in 1963 by Hassenfeld Bros. of Pawtucket, Rhode Island, proved the exception to the rule. His face–a composite of 20 Congressional Medal of Honor winners–was a fixture in some ten million homes by that time.

G. I. Joe's success seemed to rest with several factors. His 21 movable parts enabled him to salute, grasp the fork of a tiny mess kit with ease, crouch in a foxhole or squeeze into a Jeep. One tyke, Chicago's Jon Anderson, observed that "He's like a real person." Fathers who worried that doll-playing was sissified, found Joe "real gutsy." Mothers appreciated the outlets the doll provided for vicarious fantasizing; e.g., deep sea diving, driving a tank through the desert.

Perhaps most significant of all, the host of accessories available for G. I. Joe appealed to the collecting impulse in boys, while making a dent in the pocketbook of mom and dad. Although the basic doll cost only four dollars at the time, the complete arsenal of equipment–including ski and scuba gear, assorted weapons and clothing–ran about $200. New additions for the Christmas rush included a Mercury capsule with solid silver spacesuit ($10), a sea-sled that operated under water ($14) and a six-man international task force of "action soldiers of the world" (i.e., French, German, Japanese, British, Australian, and a fur-capped Russian).

Despite the competition of similar dolls–Stone Burke, paratrooper, James Bond, Illya Kuryakin, Captain Action, etc.–G. I. Joe remained the best-selling single new toy around. Following a lull in the late 1960s and early 1970s in which Joe's military instincts were submerged (his company used him to capitalize instead on the

93

moonshot craze) so as to retain public favor, he emerged again in all his warlike splendor (in a 3 1/2" size) during the belligerent Reagan years. Lionized in comic book titles and on Saturday morning cartoons, G. I. Joe almost single-handedly held his own against the onslaught of electronic gadgets and video games in the 1980s. Attempting to capitalize on the Gulf War merchandizing bonanza, Impel produced a trading card set devoted to the character in mid-1991.

The original G. I. Joe (11 1/2" size) has become very desirable to doll and toy collectors. Prices in the collector market will vary according to condition, originality, and rarity, particularly in the Southeast where G. I. Joe is especially sought after. If Joe's popularity with children diminishes, he can be assured of immortality with nostalgic adults who may be seeking to recapture their childhood, to collect military history, or perhaps simply to make an investment for the future.

BIBLIOGRAPHY

"Front & Center," *Time*. 88 (December 23, 1966) 62. il.

Fuller, J. G. "Trade Wind; Influence of Military Toys on Children," *Saturday Review*. 48 (December 25, 1965) 7.

"G. I. Joe Talks; Hassenfeld Bros. Products," *Newsweek*. 69 (March 13, 1967) 99.

Garfield

According to comic strip artist Mort Walker, 1982 "[was] the year of Jim Davis." America's love affair with Davis's cartoon creation, Garfield, began amidst a nationwide feline fetish which first became apparent in 1973, when George Gately's *Heathcliff* was introduced to newspaper readers. Some two years later, a whimsical paperback, *Cat*, by cartoonist Bernard Kliban, became a runaway best-seller. Another 250-odd cat books followed, including *The Official I Hate Cats Book* and *101 Uses for a Dead Cat*. The animal was also featured on screen (*The Cat People*, *Cat's Eye*) and stage (the Broadway smash musical, *Cats*).

While the general cat craze may have assisted Davis's climb to success, his trademark sense of humor played a major role. His light touch—not the topical humor of a *Doonesbury* or the philosophical reflections of a *Peanuts*, but, in his words, "the kind of laugh that leaves you feeling a little better"—came through in classic Garfield lines like "I'm not overweight—I'm undertall" and "Show me a good mouser and I'll show you a cat with bad breath."

Davis created Garfield in 1976, after spending seven years as an assistant for Tom Ryan, creator of the comic strip *Tumbleweeds*, and after five years of rejection slips for his strip, *Gnorm the Gnat*. Davis reflected on the circumstances behind Garfield's creation: "I took a long, hard look at the comics. I saw there were a lot of dogs doing very well—Snoopy, Marmaduke . . . I didn't know of any cats." The cat was modeled and named after Davis's grandfather, Garfield, known for being stubborn, opinionated, and cantankerous. While Davis portrayed himself as Jon Arbuckle, Garfield's owner, the average guy who was the butt of all the jokes, others have seen some of the cat in its creator. Desiree Gayette, the lyricist and singer for a TV special soundtrack, *Here Comes Garfield*, observed, "Garfield is Jim's alter ego. He is that person all of us would like to be, if we were totally honest–a person who gets what he wants when he wants it."

During the two years before Davis accepted a deal with United Features Syndicate leading to Garfield's newspaper debut, the physical make-up of the feline underwent considerable modification. Davis noted that he grew stripes and "his eyes got larger to get more expression; so did his mouth. His body got a little smaller just so I could get him around easier. His limbs got longer to make him more animated and his ears got a little shorter because I didn't need them." His personality remained intact, though; i.e., this thing against cute ("Cute rots the intellect") and dogs ("They're rusting our nation's fire hydrants").

Shortly after his contract with UFS in January 1978, Garfield became a phenomenon. By 1982, the strip had an estimated 55 million readers in 1,200 newspapers (making it the fastest growing comic in history). In addition, 16 books–beginning with *Garfield At Large* in 1980–had sold seven million copies (with an unprecedented half dozen simultaneously on the *New York Times* best-seller list). A TV special, *Here Comes Garfield* (CBS) was supported by 100,000 soundtrack albums and 495,000 Ballentine paperbacks listing at $4.95 apiece. Some 1,500 Garfield products–including a 50-dollar lasagna dish, 69-cent bookmarks, $200 stuffed cats and Garfield clothes and sheets–had earned close to 20 million dollars as well. Davis maintained a close connection with all of these projects via Paws, Inc., a company begun in 1981.

Garfield kept a high profile throughout the 1980s, and seemed likely to remain popular for some time to come. By the latter part of the decade, he and his creator were hired as spokespersons for the Red Roof Inns chain. Arlene Scanlan of United Media Enterprises, the company licensing Garfield products, underscored this point:

> Mothers between the ages of 18 and 34 are cat lovers, so we targeted our marketing to that audience. From there it seemed to evolve to kids, 8 through 13. Then we found that Garfield is a phenomenon on college campuses. Now we are seeing that men love Garfield–men who don't love cats . . . Snoopy is a way of life. Garfield will be.

BIBLIOGRAPHY

"Garfield Gets in the Picture," *Saturday Evening Post.* 256 (November 1984) 45-51. il.

Miller, H. G. "Jim Davis: He's Got the World by the Tail," *Saturday Evening Post.* 256 (November 1984) 52-53ff.

Vespa, Mary. "Garfield Goes Hollywood–With Jim Davis on his Cattails–For Feline Fame and Fortune," *People Weekly.* 18 (November 1, 1982) 88-91. il., cover story.

The Gatsby Look

The Gatsby look began in the summer of 1972 with Parisian designer Kenzo Takada's revival of the classic V-neck, red-and-blue-bordered tennis sweater. When it became an immediate success, Kenzo expanded on the tennis theme in earnest in his Spring 1973 collections. The style received a further boost with the release in 1973 of a film based on F. Scott Fitzgerald's novella, *The Great Gatsby.*

The keynote was a calculatedly casual, languid elegance punctuated by the message (as quoted from Los Angeles designer Marilyn Lewis) "I'm not working. I'm disporting myself with physical pleasure because I have the leisure." The basic elements of the look included, in addition to the ubiquitous tennis sweater (which was often complemented by a matching long cardigan),

- a three-piece suit in white or pale flannel or muted plaids;
- wide-legged baggy pants, cuffed or pleated or both;
- pin stripe shirts with big butterfly bow ties;
- two-tone spectator shoes;
- little white pleated shirts ending just above the knee and small cloche hats pulled down to the eyebrow as daytime wear for women;
- soft and flowing chiffons and crepe de Chines, bias cut to drape close to the body, for female evening wear;
- natural fabrics–e.g., wool, linens, pure cotton–which exhibit a tendency to become rumpled; and
- red, maroon, navy blue, dark or pale green, basic black, and white (predominating in several hues–stark, off-white and creamy–a flaunting of practicality) as the preferred colors.

American retailers and manufacturers enthusiastically embraced the style. Boston's Jordan Marsh reported that the tennis look sold well as resort wear. Lord & Taylor pushed the collection designed by Walter Albini, dubbed the godfather of the Italian Gatsby look. New York's Alexander's promoted the Gatsby theme in every department. Even Levi Strauss produced wide-legged, cuffed pants and V-neck sweaters.

The very impracticality of the look–which led to its relatively rapid fall from favor–was summed up by designer Halston: "Women have finally settled down to pants, and that's the way it will be for a long time. Do you expect a woman today to go back to garters?" The aura, sans the details, of the jazz age–as reflected in the clothes–was embraced merely as a nostalgia trend rather than as a sensible accompaniment to the 1970s lifestyle.

BIBLIOGRAPHY

"Great Scott? The Great Gatsby Look," *Newsweek.* 81 (March 26, 1973) 61. il.
"The New Old Sports," *Time.* 101 (March 26, 1973), 98-101. il.

Gibson Girl

Artist Charles Dana Gibson's conceptualization of the ideal American woman first appeared in *Life*, a weekly humor magazine, in 1890. Gibson hardly could have imagined that his willowy, athletic, shirt-waisted creation, clad in a "flowing skirt," and sporting a "pompadour crow's nest topped by a hard straw hat," would transform him into the most influential and highly-paid illustrator of his era.

Indeed, she "stepped out of *Life* into life," for during most of the next quarter century, women at home and abroad turned to Gibson's drawings for guidance on how to "dress, stand, sit, walk, shake hands, enter vehicles, or eat." Besides adorning the pages of books, magazines, and newspapers, the Gibson Girl's stately image graced china, silverware, calendars, matchboxes, wallpaper, pillow covers, handkerchiefs, scarves, and commemorative plaques. Hobbyists eagerly purchased pyrography kits in order to burn her silhouette onto almost every imaginable wooden or leather household item. Gibson Girl dolls delighted countless little ladies. Popular songwriters and playwrights rendered homage to her beauty. Vaudeville troupes praised her charms. Silent, motionless actors portrayed scenes from her life in *tableaux vivants*, the "living pictures" popular at church bazaars and charity events of the period. Polkas, waltzes, and two-steps bore her name. Manufacturers, advertisers, editors, and clothiers scrambled to win her favor. She even received fan mail–so much that Charles Gibson's young sister had to cease her attempts to answer it. In short, the Gibson Girl's vogue "cut across class, age, and regional lines."

A "torrent of print" was devoted to the question of the identity of Gibson's original model. In actuality, the first Gibson Girl was an ideal composite rather than an individual portrait. On occasion, however, Gibson drew his wife, Irene Langhorne, who was considered one of the world's most stunning women. At times, young socialites posed for the eminent illustrator. This practice forced him to wear a disguise in public, since wherever he walked, "whole streets full of women would start striking Gibson attitudes and blocking traffic." Consequently, he tended to restrict himself to professional models for most of his serious work. Still, he based the Gibson Man, the Gibson Girl's tall, clean-shaven companion, upon the likeness of his good friend, Richard Harding Davis.

Love, courtship, and marriage comprised Gibson's major themes. His glittering setting was New York's High Society, which he gently satirized. In an age when the news media focused upon the doings of wealthy heiresses, Gibson depicted the "trials and tribulations" of love between "incredibly handsome, well-bred young people." Members of all social classes aspired someday to find their own Gibson Girls or Gibson Men in "flesh and blood." The Gibson Girl embodied the achievable American dream that Charles Dana Gibson himself had realized in his own life.

Gibson set out to draw a girl "so alluring that other young men would want to climb into the picture and sit beside her." Fortunately, recent technological advances in photoengraving permitted his fine craftsmanship to be reproduced accurately for mass distribution. Accordingly, his superb technique and mastery of the vignette caused a "considerable portion of a great nation" to try to "live up to a series of pen drawings."

In the United States, lithographers traditionally had created "most of the dominant models of female beauty." Gibson disliked the heavy, voluptuous woman who had reigned as the American ideal since the 1870s. Instead, he was attracted to the classical types favored by his idol, the Paris-born black-and-white artist George Du Maurier. Once more, Charles Dana Gibson was in step with his times. Starting around the mid-1800s, the popularity of the bicycle combined with the movement for healthy reforms in women's dress paved the way for a more athletic ideal. By 1895, a "new woman" had appeared in America. She was visible in education, sports, reform, and the work force. Like the Gibson Girl, she played tennis, golfed, bicycled, bathed in the ocean, and drove automobiles. Gibson's "potent blessing" further encouraged U.S. women to engage in any sport, so long as they were "graceful about it."

The Gibson Girl was "braver, stronger, healthier, more skillful,

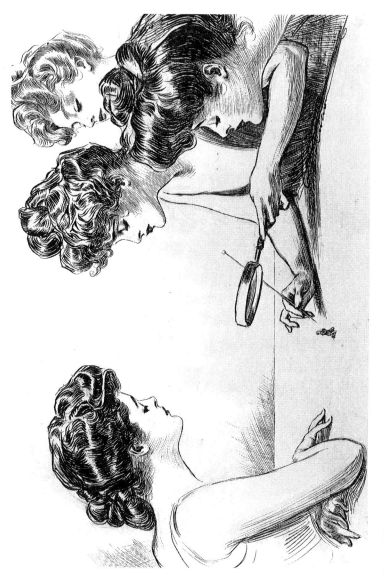

These Gibson girls are about to dissect the "weaker sex." At the turn of the century feminism was just starting to percolate, so that many young women delighted in Charles Gibson's provocative drawings.

more human," than her voluptuous predecessor. Feminists of the time often viewed her as a "prototype of the 'new woman.'" Still, Charles Dana Gibson did not sympathize with "organized feminism." He felt that politics tended to masculinize females. In one sense, "the independence of the Gibson Girl did not go much beyond playing sports, wearing comfortable clothing, and looking self-reliant." She served as a "fantasy figure" who made it possible for poverty-stricken, oppressed women to cope with the economic depression and social strife of the 1890s through romantic escapism. Yet, on the other hand, the Gibson Girl was meant to be popular, not radical. Even as she was, she represented the far-reaching changes women in the United States had undergone throughout the course of the nineteenth century.

In 1912, the Gibson Girl triumphantly symbolized the ideal American woman. A year later, the flapper began to depose her. "Petite girls, thin girls, hoydenish girls, who would have had a terrible time trying to look Gibsonian, won their day in the sun in the compensatory swing of the cycle of fashion." The flapper's appearance "marked the fruition of a sensual revolution among American women that had begun in the 1890s and that the Gibson Girl image could only partly accommodate." The Gibson Girl's type of emancipation was out of style. Nevertheless, to this day, Charles Dana Gibson's lady on a pedestal continues to evoke the haunting romance of a vanished age.

Frank Marotti
Librarian
Gresham Library
Sam Houston State

BIBLIOGRAPHY

Banner, Lois W. *American Beauty*. New York: Alfred A. Knopf, 1983.
"Charles Dana Gibson," *Hobbies*. 55 (December 1950), 33.
Chiara, Joan. "Gibson Girl Doll." *Hobbies*. 83 (June 1978), 83.
Downey, Fairfax. *Portrait of an Era as Drawn by C. D. Gibson: A Biography by Fairfax Downey*. New York: Charles Scribner's Sons, 1936.
"Frankly Romantic," *Time*, January 1, 1945, 52.
Gibson, Charles Dana. *The Gibson Girl and Her America: The Best Drawings of Charles Dana Gibson*. New York: Dover Publications, 1969.

"Life calls on the Charles Dana Gibsons," *Life.* October 12, 1942, 132-134.

Meglin, Nick. "Charles Dana Gibson and the Age of Exclusivity," *American Artist.* 39 (March 1975), 62-63.

Pitz, Henry C. "Charles Dana Gibson: Creator of a Mode," *American Artist.* December 20, 1956, 50-55.

Rawls, Walton. "Wake Up, America!" *American History Illustrated.* 9 (September 1988), 32-45.

Rogers, Agnes. "The Undimmed Appeal of the Gibson Girl," *American Heritage.* 23 (December 1957) 80-98.

Glitter Tops

In 1972, the primary fashion statement consisted of setting off casual clothes with touches of camp or swank. This trend usually found its embodiment in the wearing of snazzy, jazzy individualistic tops as counterpoint to proletarian denims.

These sweaters, T-shirts, tank tops, and long-sleeved shirts exhibited a wide array of designs:

- festooned with rhinestones, sequins, silver threads, gold sparkle dust, and paint;
- abstract designs in an Art Deco vein;
- representational images (e.g., Marilyn Monroe pin-ups via silk screening, Bette Midler's face in sequins, flowers, and animals in sparkle dust);
- words and numbers for funny messages ("Keep on Truckin'), advertising slogans ("Palm Springs: P.S. I love you"), tribute to a favorite athlete by wearing his/her numeral, etc.

Though generally priced for the jean wearer's budget (i.e., $11-$20), premium lines were also available, such as Right Bank Clothing's "America" top (which featured a confetti-like array of multicolored rhinestones surrounding the lettering (priced at $72). Some affluent customers–e.g., Barbra Streisand, Sally Struthers, Diana Ross–teamed the tops with satin pants, tweeds, and other expensive items.

Clothing manufacturers attributed the craze to the inflationary economy, which made a bit of glamour at moderate prices attractive. Ronnie Gross, president of a group of sportswear firms that included Quips, Questions and Quotations, gave credence to the idea by noting,

What does the working girl do when she can't afford to spend money for regular clothes? She can either buy a lot of cheap, imitation designer clothes that don't fool anybody. Or she can go kicky, buy a flashy shirt, and say it is something for a giggle.

By fall the trend had spread from the junior-sportswear division to all sectors of the clothing industry. The tops were being paired with dress slacks and sporty blazers. The nation's leading chains scrambled to keep up. The upscale Saks Fifth Avenue, for instance, set up a new boutique devoted to spangled goods entitled "The Treasure Chest."

While the craze did slack off somewhat during the winter of 1973-1974, glitter tops have remained a fashion fixture, albeit on the fringes of the mainstream, into the 1990s. Most clothing stores continue to stock them as a sideline.

BIBLIOGRAPHY

"Flash and Trash; Second-Hand Denim Encrusted With Sequins and Rhinestones," *Newsweek*. 82 (November 12, 1973) 106. il.
"Glitter-Giggle Tops," *Time*. 102 (October 22, 1973) 86-87. il.

Greasy Kid Stuff

For a brief span in the early 1960s, Kid Stuff Products, Inc., of Chicago competed successfully with the giants of the hairdressing industry, including the very company whose product it had started out satirizing. During the first half of December 1962, more than 50,000 four-ounce bottles of Greasy Kid Stuff (GKS) retailing for 98 cents apiece were sold in Chicago alone. The initial order of 130,000 bottles sold out almost immediately, and by the end of that year Kid Stuff Products had outlets from Texas to New York as well as Canada and was adding more daily.

The enterprise was sparked by a television ad for Bristol-Myers' Vitalis in which a star athlete, combing his hair before a locker room mirror, asked a young player, "Are you still using that greasy kid stuff?" (He then advised switching to Vitalis.) Larry Frohman, then a 22-year-old senior in advertising at Babson Institute, and William Cole, a 20-year-old pre-med student at Emory University, responded by pooling 50 dollars apiece and developing a hairdressing alleged to contain lanolin and GKS. Obtaining Food and Drug Administration certification in July 1962 and filing for a trademark, they began production shortly thereafter.

The concept captured the public's imagination. WFUN, a Miami Beach radio station, gave it a free plug, as did Johnny Carson on the *Tonight Show*. Frohman and Cole obtained the backing of two lawyers named Ring (Jack and Leonard), who helped form Kid Stuff Products and lined up investors.

Bristol-Myers officials gave their approval to the enterprise, noting that GKS seemed to do Vitalis more good than harm. They even had Frohman in to talk about a future with Bristol-Myers. Frohman would've done well to seize any offer while it stood; by mid-1963 the novelty value of GKS had ceased earning dividends and the product dropped from sight like a brick.

BIBLIOGRAPHY

"Hitching Your Wagon to Another Guy's Star," *Business Week.* (December 29, 1962) 38. il.

Hacky Sack

In mid-1978, Hacky Sack seemed poised to rival Frisbee and the Hula-Hoop as an outdoor recreational activity. Hacky Sack–which employed a soft, golf-ball-sized leather bag–was invented by John Stalberger while in his 20s as a means of strengthening his knees after a football injury. In the eight months following its introduction into the market in September 1977, some 77,000 bags–at five dollars each–were sold.

The object of Hacky Sack was to keep the bag in the air, using the knees and the feet, without letting the bag touch the ground or the player's upper body. Each "kick" counted as one point. In competition, points were given for the number of kicks and for form, including grace and agility. It could be played alone or in doubles, where two players took turns keeping the bag in the air; in team play, three or four worked together as a group.

Hacky Sack's appeal lay in part with the humor implicit in attempting to master the difficult moves required to keep the bag in the air. In addition, as one 13-year-old in Portland, Oregon noted, "It builds up your coordination, balance, and muscles."

As the activity caught on, Stalberger established a National Hacky Sack Association to govern its growth and referee rules disputes. By 1978, it was being taught in grade schools all over Oregon, Washington, and Southern California, and at least three Oregon colleges were fielding Hacky Sack teams. Most notable of all, the bag was seen on college campuses throughout the nation.

Hacky Sack's popularity has continued unabated up to the present day, albeit minus the hype surrounding its sell-them-while-they're-hot early days. Its chief appeal now rests in its employment as a brief, leisure-time respite from the pressures of everyday life.

BIBLIOGRAPHY

"A Whole New Ball Game," *Newsweek.* 91 (May 22, 1978) 69. il.

Handbags for Men

In late 1969, increasing numbers of men began carrying handbags in public. The practice owed something to male dress at the time; with trousers slim and pocketless and Edwardian jackets cut to hold little more than the wearer, another method was needed for toting around one's everyday necessities. The examples set by hippies and trendy individualists such as designer Rudi Gernreich and author Truman Capote helped pave the way for acceptance of the handbag by more self-conscious men.

Capote considered the trend long overdue, noting, "I don't see how people get along without some sort of little satchel." As to what items he included in his bag, he added,

> I keep my money in it. And a book, in case I have to wait for someone. And the papers I'm working on. Four or five pairs of glasses. And a toothbrush and toothpaste, because you never know where you might spend the night.

While the accessory originated in 1967 when Gucci marketed a line in Italy, U.S. sales were concentrated in stores on both the coasts. In California, I Magnin's, Saks Fifth Avenue, and other top-end outlets offered a variety of styles, ranging from a heavy vinyl satchel ($17.50) to Vuitton's convertible shoulder-strap model retailing for $125. More economical versions began cropping up in abundance at discount stores the following year. An industrial designer named Darrell Howe, who liked the fashion enough to design a shoulder bag for his Los Angeles staff, admitted that there were still certain parts of the American heartland "where you would be eaten alive" for wearing one.

Psychiatrists had a field day analyzing the trend. Jerome Jacobe saw it as a healthy development, explaining, "It could indicate the disintegration of the more superficial aspects of role differentiation." Leonard Olinger, however, regarded it as "an overreaction that tends to deny the real differences between the sexes, just as in the past we have been forced to be terribly different when there isn't that much difference. The truth lies somewhere in between."

Evidently enough men had doubts about the use of handbags to keep their use from reaching truly universal proportions. Nevertheless, a healthy percentage of men have continued to carry them around in places where alternatives such as the gym bag, luggage case, and backpack would seem out of place.

BIBLIOGRAPHY

"Their New Bag," *Time*. 94 (September 26, 1969) 58. il.

Hood Ornaments As Jewelry

In early 1987, hood ornaments had moved from cars to teenage jewelry; i.e., necklaces, bracelets, keychains. The hood ornaments were generally taken from expensive cars such as Mercedes-Benzes and Cadillacs, although Volkswagens and various sports cars were also targeted. "About $7 for a Mercedes, about $5 for a Cadillac," said one teenager to a *Houston Post* reporter. "You can get $25 for a big one if you find the right person–if he wants it bad enough." The practice appeared in many cases to be related to membership in particular cliques.

Some felt the phenomenon was tied to a music video by the rap duo, The Beastie Boys, in which one of them wears a Volkswagen hood ornament around his neck. However, Harold Schmidt, a long-time Mercedes dealer, recalled that stealing these and other automobile accessories was also popular during the 1960s.

School officials as a whole cracked down on the practice of wearing them by means of "unofficial" dress codes and similar strategies. Ginger Hester, spokeswoman for the Spring (Texas) Independent School District, stated, "Our principals are making it clear to all our students in all our buildings they are just not to wear them at school."

Some youths got involved through legitimate means by purchasing smaller, legal facsimiles of the ornaments that were available at jewelry stores. School authorities appeared to be unanimous in allowing students to wear these copies.

BIBLIOGRAPHY

Hensel, Bill, Jr. "Hood Ornaments Now Hot Jewelry," *Houston Post*. (April 3, 1987) 10a. il.

Hoop Skirts

The hoop skirt reached its apex of popularity when introduced in 1854 in modified form by the Empress Eugenie, wife of Louis Napoleon, the Emperor of France. Contemporaries have noted that the Empress was extremely hard to please in matters of fashion; she criticized, altered, and rejected incessantly the creations of her well-meaning dressmakers and tailors until the costumes had been re-composed to her satisfaction. The original concept of the hoop skirt featured a whalebone construction in the shape of a beehive. The largest circumference was around the hips, from which the dress fell in perpendicular lines; another popular variant consisted of hoops arranged like those on a barrel.

Eugenie's invention, however, was made of graduated steel wires covered with a woven cotton netting held together by perpendicular straps of broad tape. Her prominence as an arbiter of fashion led to the spread of its popularity throughout Europe and North America. More unassuming followers of fashion lined the edges of their gowns with horsehair and their flounces with stiff muslin. Petticoats were also constructed with casings around them at intervals, into which canes were run.

The hoop skirt was the object of widespread derision dating back to its earliest use. Critics noted its ugliness, high cost, and inconvenience–even danger–to both the wearer and innocent bystanders. The dress was said to be noisy and "engrossing of place and room" in omnibuses, rail cars, and church pews. It was collapsible and very easily broken. Accounts can also be found of women whose voluminous skirts caught fire.

While Eugenie's style was not without a semblance of grace, more exaggerated forms in the 1860s featuring an increasingly wider circumference were universally worn by women of all classes. Correspondingly, the chorus of jeers and jibes evident in contemporary accounts grew ever more strident in condemning the hoop skirt. A popular song from that era observed,

Hoop skirts freed the woman of starched, padded, or stiffened petticoats that weighed her down and created an endless laundering problem. Circles of spring steel made the lighter cage under the fabric work. 1860s.

Now crinoline is all the rage with ladies of whatever age,
A petticoat made like a cage–oh, what a ridiculous fashion!
'Tis formed of hoops and bars of steel, or tubes of air which
lighter feel,
And worn by girls to be genteel, or if they've figures to con-
ceal.
It makes the dresses stretch far out a dozen yards or so about,
And please both the thin and stout–oh, what a ridiculous fash-
ion!

The historian, Justin McCarthy, in his *Portraits of the Sixties* (New York, 1903), offered the following account:

There is one peculiarity belonging to the early sixties which I cannot leave out of notice, although assuredly it has little claim to association with art or science, with literature or politics. The early sixties saw in this and most other civilized countries the reign of crinoline. It is well for the early sixties that they had so many splendid claims to historical recollection, but it may be said of them that if they had bequeathed no other memory to a curious and contemplative posterity, the reign of crinoline would still have secured for them an abiding-place in the records of human eccentricities. I may say, without fear of contradiction, that no one who was not living at the time can form any adequate idea of the grotesque effect produced on the outer aspects of social life by this article of feminine costume . . . The fashion of crinoline defied caricature for the actual reality was more full of unpicturesque and burlesque effects than any satirical pencil could realize on a flat outspread sheet of paper. The fashion of crinoline, too, defied all contemporary ridicule. A whole new school of satirical humour was devoted in vain to the ridicule of crinoline. The boys in the streets sang comic songs to make fun of it, but no street bellowings of contempt could incite the wearers of this most inconvenient and hideous article of dress to condemn themselves to clinging draperies.

Ultimately, the critics held sway and the reign of the hoop skirt began to recede in 1865. Despite efforts on the part of some garment makers and retailers to keep the style in favor, it disappeared forever at the time the rule of Louis Napoleon was coming to an end.

BIBLIOGRAPHY

"If Crinoline Came Back," *Atlantic.* 129 (June 1922) 854-856.
McClellan, Elisabeth. *History of American Costume, 1607-1870.* New York: Tudor, 1937.

Hot Pants

During the wintery months of early 1971, department stores and boutiques could not stock their shelves fast enough with hot pants for women. Also known as short shorts (so-named after their less skimpy predecessor of the 1950s), cool pants, short cuts, and les shorts, they were quickly accepted everywhere–in restaurants, offices, churches, and even black-tie dinners. Generally augmented by boots and tights used as body stockings, they eschewed the sturdy materials used in the sportswear type of shorts–i.e., denim and broadcloth–in favor of mink and monkey fur, silk and satin, calfskin, chiffon, and cut velvet.

Fashion experts generally attributed the craze to a general reaction against the prim and dowdy-looking midiskirt. Manhattan Boutique proprietor Jimmi York noted, "The way women are buying and men are reacting, it would seem legs have been out of sight for ten years, not ten months." Women also appreciated the fact that they could indulge in activities such as dancing and walking up stairs without having, in the words of one wearer, "to remember to keep your knees together."

Despite their widespread popularity–as evidenced by wearers, ranging from celebrities like Jackie Onassis to career girls to teenagers, braving icy weather and by the commitment of designers like Halston, Adolfo, Sant' Angelo, and Betsy Johnson–hot pants ceased to be fashionable, oddly enough, with the arrival of the peak summer months. In all probability, this decline was hastened by the limitations of the average female physique. As designer Rudi Gernreich admitted, "[hot pants are] great, but for great bodies."

BIBLIOGRAPHY

Edmiston, S. "Hotpants: the Heat's Off!" *Seventeen*. 30 (July 1971) 157.
"Hot Pants: A Short But Happy Career," *Life*. 71 (December 31, 1971) 14-15. il.
"Hot Pants: Legs Are Back," *Time*. 97 (February 1, 1971) 48-50. il.
"Hot Pants: Shorts," *Life*. 70 (January 29, 1971) 36-39. il.

Ironing Hair

Ironing hair began as a fringe movement among Boston school-girls, who were revolting against the tyranny of bouffant hair teasing and sleeping on rollers. The practice gradually spread West to be emulated by high school and college girls across the continent, fueled by the example of female folk singers (e.g., Joan Baez, Mary Travers of Peter, Paul, and Mary) and the lank-haired models of television and fashion magazine advertising. "Everybody in school is ironing their hair," exclaimed Sharon Black, 15, a sophomore at Andrew Warde High in Fairfield, Connecticut in January 1965. "Even the people with straight hair are ironing it to make it straighter."

Ironing appealed to economy-minded girls who would rather use a home appliance than spend up to 25 dollars for a beauty shop anti-permanent. Home hair straighteners, although relatively inexpensive at $2.25 a jar, took 45 minutes to apply and, according to one teenager, "[smelled] to high heaven."

The ironing method was simple in nature. The girl would bend herself to the ironing board while her friend ironed an inch of hair at a time. The process took from ten minutes to a half hour and lasted until the next hairwashing.

The practice did have its drawbacks. A 19-year-old junior at Bennington College noted, "If you do it too often and have too hot an iron, you break the hair." Dr. Robert Berger, a dermatologist at New York University, warned that constant ironing "[might] cause so much breakage that the hair [would] look thin in places." Psychological problems were also documented; 14-year-old Gay Stilley of Glen Oaks, New York claimed to have found it hard to sleep without the feel of curlers in her hair. In addition, friendships may well have been taxed. A University of Wisconsin freshman accidentally burned an iron-shaped wedge in her roommate's hair.

Ironing persisted throughout the 1960s during the vogue for

straight hair (despite short runs for the pixie cut and Afros). In the 1970s, the wave returned to fashion and ironing receded into the background.

BIBLIOGRAPHY

"All Ironed Out," *Newsweek.* (January 11, 1965) 53. il.
"Ironing Hair Fad," *Look.* (April 20, 1965) 104-107. il.

Jax Slacks

Jax slacks were the rage with women during the mid-1960s. "I wear Jax, Jax, Jax all day," exclaimed Mrs. Loel Guiness at the time. Other celebrity wearers included Audrey Hepburn, Marlene Dietrich, the Kennedy sisters, Natalie Wood, and Candice Bergen.

The slacks–which clung "like oil to water"–required both money (they retailed for as much as $60) and a slim physique. Elizabeth Taylor was considered too "buxom" for the style, but she purchased $3,000 worth anyway in March 1964. One notable reason for the slacks' tight fit was the location of the zipper up the back where it didn't bulge as do side zippers.

The originator of the craze, Jack Hanson, was 24 and an ex-short-stop for the Los Angeles Angels when he set up shop designing peasant skirts, blouses, and slacks in Balboa, California on a $500 loan. Unable to afford mass media ads, he had his salesgirls model pants in the store windows. The promotion caught on, leading to a second store in Beverly Hills. The smash success of the latter outlet brought fame and fortune. The Jax chain had spread eastward as far as Manhattan (encompassing seven stores) by early 1964, with new openings planned for Southampton and Paris. With an estimated $4,000,000 income, a house in Beverly Hills, and a cream-colored Rolls-Royce, Hanson settled down with his favorite salesgirl, Sally (size 8).

"We were the first," Hanson noted, "to realize that a girl's fanny is cute." Maybe so. Judging from the onslaught of imitators over the years, however, not the last.

BIBLIOGRAPHY

"Bottoms Up," *Time*. 83 (April 3, 1964) 60. il.

Hanson, J. "He Shows You the Girl; President of Jax Stores; Interview," edited by M. Byers, *Life*. 59 (October 8, 1965) 55-56ff. il.

Jenkins, Dan. "Life With the Jax Pack," *Sports Illustrated*. 27 (July 6, 1967) 56-62. il.

Jumpsuits

Jumpsuits–basically streamlined spinoffs of the overalls worn by plumbers, carpenters, and garage mechanics–were the hottest garment on the U.S. fashion scene in 1975. Cinnamon Wear, a New York fashion house, filled 10,000 orders for its lower-priced lines ($45-$50) between spring and fall of that year, while Saks Fifth Avenue stores nationwide sold thousands in the early fall. Brenda Bird, a buyer for Alexander's, the New York department store chain, exclaimed, "We can't keep them in stock. Price is no object." Kal Ruttentstein, a Saks vice president, added, "It's the only fashion silhouette this fall." *Women's Wear Daily* reported that retailers and manufacturers "are already viewing it as the sleeper of '75." Even then first lady Betty Ford was reported to have purchased one.

The jumpsuit vogue began in Paris in the fall of 1974 and was brought to the United States by models who had attended those fashion shows. The first Parisian designer to produce a high-fashion jumpsuit for the U.S. was Yves Saint Laurent, whose collection included a black acrylic with drawstring waist ($375), a turtleneck number ($355), and one in classic poplin ($205). Other top designers followed with jumpsuits in jersey, Liberty prints, slinky evening models, and versions with Kabuki sleeves and toggles. Kenzo introduced a wide-wale corduroy in slate gray accented by banded trouser bottoms which went well with construction boots.

Best-sellers tended to be more inexpensively priced numbers such as Victor Joris' self-belted gabardine suit with pleated pants–at $110, some 600 stores had ordered 38,000 midway through fall 1975–and the Esso suit, a loose overall in cotton emblazoned with Exxon's familiar name. Accessories also sold well, including plumbers' satchels from Denmark ($25) and Saint Laurent's serapes ($100).

Like other upwardly mobile work clothes (e.g., jeans, sweatshirts), jumpsuits became fashionable because of their functionality. Comfortable at all times, they precluded the need to coordinate tops with pants and were easy to put on and take off. One New York shopper was recorded by *Time* as saying,

> After packing separates in a suitcase most of the summer weekends, I found that I spent the whole day in my jumpsuit. Then I ended up just adding a scarf at night. A jumpsuit is such easy dressing. It does as much as a well-tailored pair of pants to make you look dramatic.

These factors have proven sufficient to keep the jumpsuit a strong performer up to the present day. It is available in virtually all American clothing outlets as well as through countless mail order catalogs.

BIBLIOGRAPHY

"Overall Chic," *Time*. 106 (October 13, 1975) 88. il.

Kewpie Dolls

The name Kewpie was a diminutive of Cupid. Kewpies–possessing the essence of infant charm with rounded tummies, golden topknots and a pair of tiny blue wings–first appeared as drawings to illustrate Rose O'Neill's poems in a series originating in the *Ladies' Home Journal* in 1909. This series was followed by paper doll Kewpies in the same magazine and, later by demand, bisque Kewpies manufactured by the J.D. Kestner Company of Germany and distributed in North America by the George Borgfeldt Company.

By 1913, some five million Kewpies had been sold. In addition to bisque, a small number of the Kestner output consisted of celluloid. With the advent of World War I and the termination of trade with Germany, American manufacturers replaced the bisque models with dolls made of celluloid, cloth, composition, rubber, and metal. Eventually, in the post-World War II period, a small number of bisque Kewpies were imported again from Germany; however, by then the market for Kewpies was dominated by American companies.

The early Kewpies were as popular with adults as with children. They were frequently used as decoration, whether in conventional clothes or with a huge bow of ribbon tied around the tummy. One popular custom consisted of dressing a pair of miniature Kewpies as bride and bridegroom, and placing them atop a wedding cake.

The great popularity of Kewpies led to their being made in a wide variety of models. The dolls were usually made in sizes ranging from one to twelve inches; however, there were a few life-size models, and some as small as half-inch ivory charms. Action Kewpies were also widely available.

Kewpies continue to be manufactured to the present day. But their primary appeal in recent years has been as knickknacks made of porcelain or glass.

In the 1920s cute-as-pie Kewpie dolls made out of bisque or celluloid inspired human imitators. It is unlikely this flesh-and-blood Kewpie ever stayed home alone on Saturday night.

BIBLIOGRAPHY

Young, Helen. "German and American Bisque Dolls," In: *The Complete Book of Doll Collecting*. New York: Putnam, 1967. pp. 104-117. il.

Knickers

Knickers–or knickerbockers as they are called in Great Britain (because the former term refers to ladies' underpants in that country)–first appeared in the mid-nineteenth century. According to John Berendt, they were inspired by the somewhat baggy knee breeches seen in George Cruikshank's illustrations for Washington Irving's *A History of New York*; the name, in fact, was derived from "Diedrich Knickerbocker," the pseudonymous author of the book. Knee breeches themselves went back as far as the sixteenth century and had been the dominant form of men's pants for over 200 years prior to the French Revolution. Their identification with the deposed aristocracy led to the rise of the more egalitarian trouser; the garment was henceforth relegated to formal dress, court attire, and sport.

Knickers went on to become extremely fashionable in England in the early decades of the twentieth century. Although never as popular with American men, they became a mainstay with boys in this country. The reasons for their appeal included:

1. Comfort.
2. Functionality. Long after they went out of style, climbers, skiers, woodsmen, and other sportsmen continued to wear them in order to avoid snagging the lower part of the trouser cuff. With respect to golf, they were even alleged to prevent cheating; when wearing knickers a man couldn't drop a ball down his trouser leg so as to obtain a better lie on the fairway.
3. Health. George Bernard Shaw, an active member of the Healthy and Artistic Dress Union, wore them because he was convinced overlapping trousers and socks were bad for circulation.
4. Aesthetics. Oscar Wilde took a liking to their looks, denouncing trousers as "boring tubes."

Knickers declined around 1930 due to one notable factor: many people–whether because they had skinny legs, fat legs, bowed legs, etc.–simply didn't look good in them. After almost a half century of only marginal use, knickers have undergone a modest revival. By the late 1980s pro golfers such as Payne Stewart and Patty Sheehan were seen wearing them. In addition, mail order catalogs (e.g., L. L. Bean, J. Peterman) were offering them, and Ralph Lauren added them to the Polo line.

BIBLIOGRAPHY

Berendt, John. "Knickers," *Esquire.* 111 (April 1989) 46. il.

Koosh Balls

Oddz On Products Inc.'s Koosh Ball was an especially hot toy during the 1988 Christmas season. Described by some as a cross between a bowl of Jell-O and a porcupine, the Koosh Ball was made up of thousands of rubber filaments (sporting a seemingly endless variety of color schemes) radiating from a central core. Melissa Armour of Imaginarium, a San Francisco retailer selling hundreds weekly at that time, noted, "[Kids] pick up a ball out of curiosity and just can't put them down." The toy's appeal appeared to reach across the age spectrum; an Oddz On spokesman intimated that 40 percent of all Koosh Balls ended up in adult hands.

Koosh Balls were invented by Scott Stillinger, a former computer engineer, and his brother-in-law, Mark Button, who had previously marketed Barbie dolls for Mattel. Their Oddz On factory in Campbell, California, shipped "millions" to outlets across the nation, including such upscale establishments as Macy's, Neiman-Marcus and the gift shop at the Smithsonian Institution. The toy, which retailed for five to twelve dollars, was given added credence by the appearance of a user's guide, *The Official Koosh Book*, which listed 33 games it had engendered (e.g., Bop the Brother).

The ball remained a fixture in stores up through the early months of 1992. It appeared more and more likely that Koosh Balls would not become the "Pet Rock of the '80s," but rather a timeless classic along the lines of the Frisbee.

BIBLIOGRAPHY

"A Cross Between Jell-O and a Porcupine," *Newsweek*. 112 (December 26, 1988) 72. il.

The Veronica Lake Hairstyle

According to reports of the time, the 49th minute of the film *I Wanted Wings* (1941) was almost instantly recognized as a historic moment in the annals of the cinema. When the then unknown young actress Veronica Lake entered center stage and shook her mane of long blonde hair at a transfixed public, she set into motion a trichological sensation unmatched since Jean Harlow had launched the platinum-blonde rage in 1930.

Alternately termed the "strip-tease style," the "sheep-dog style," and the "bad-girl style," Lake's hairdo was admired by men, imitated by girls, cursed by their mothers, and viewed with alarm by moralists. By late 1941, *Life* noted that Lake had found herself "the owner and custodian of personal property comparable in value, fame and world influence to Deanna Durbin's voice, Fred Astaire's feet or Marlene Dietrich's legs." The style retained favor throughout much of the 1940s, despite various inconveniences such as:

- rude comments from males;
- the natural tendency to get caught in objects like buttons, jewelry and appliances;
- the gaucheness of having the hair fall into one's food; and
- the danger of having it catch fire near an oven or while smoking.

By the middle of the decade, however, the Veronica Lake look was on the way out as a result of both the actress's mediocre talent, which led to diminished roles, and the resurrection of the short bob due to the shortage of metal hairpins during the war effort. Lake contributed to her own decline by having her locks shorn in a show of patriotic duty.

BIBLIOGRAPHY

"I, Veronica Lake," edited by N. Busch. *Life*. 14 (May 17, 1943) 76-78ff. il.
"Puts Up Her Hair as a Safety Measure," *Life*. 14 (March 8, 1943) 39-40. il.
"Veronica Lake's Hair is a Cinema Property of World Influence," *Life*. 11 (November 24, 1941) 58-61. il.

Leg-of-Mutton Sleeves

Between 1825 and 1835, leg-of-mutton sleeves represented the most striking article of the female wardrobe. According to fashion historian Elizabeth McClellan, "It is not known who invented these sleeves or gave them the name which so well describes their shape, but like most popular fashions they increased in size until they became absolutely grotesque."

A pair of these sleeves necessitated virtually as much material as did the skirt of the gown, despite the fact that the latter was larger in size than it had been for many years. The sleeves were so voluminous that the wearer found it necessary to pass through an ordinary doorframe sideways. A contemporary of the style noted that when situated behind a pair of leg-of-mutton sleeves, one could always discern a curious creaking sound resulting from their rubbing together at the back.

During the 1830s, exaggerated leg-of-mutton sleeves were even worn by boys. Portraits from that era indicate that not only the sleeves, but the trousers also followed this shape; the most pronounced examples belonged to prepubescent youths.

BIBLIOGRAPHY

McClellan, Elizabeth. *History of American Costume, 1607-1870*. New York: Tudor, 1937. il.

The Licensing
of Familiar Media Characters

By early 1983, the licensing of familiar movie or cartoon character names had become a $20.6 billion per year industry (up from $6.6 billion in retail sales for 1978). Seth Siegel, vice president of Hamilton Projects Inc., licensing consultants in New York, attributed part of the trend to the sluggish economy, noting, "When times are bad, a manufacturer who wants a good market share doesn't have the time or money to create a fast market awareness." Accordingly, toy manufacturers turned increasingly to the licensing of characters with built-in media exposure, which increased the appeal of these products to video-oriented children.

Some of the more successful characters have included the following:

- the *Star Wars* menagerie which, up through the release of the sequel film, *The Empire Strikes Back*, had earned Twentieth Century Fox as much as $75 million in licensing revenues (based on retail sales of $1.5 billion), in addition to up-front money.
- E.T., whose likeness adorned some 200 items. While Kamar International, like many other toymakers, initially considered the alien to be "an ugly little creature," its brown vinyl E.T. dolls helped triple overall company sales in 1982.
- the Smurfs, who brought Wallace Berrie Co.–the North American licensee for these characters–at least $650 million in retail sales in 1982.
- Pac-Man, whose trademark was on nearly 300 items by early 1983 (up from 100-odd products in May 1982), all without a film to back up its popularity.

Business Week noted that these success stories were no accident. The big winners were the artists who were highly cognizant of the marketing possibilities. The usual financial arrangements included a hefty up-front payment to the film/video game company as well as seven to ten percent of the wholesale price of each unit shipped. Mark Pepvers, vice president of Twentieth Century Fox Licensing Corp., stated that George Lucas envisioned Star Wars "with the toy byproducts in mind. He was making much more than a movie."

Despite such successes, the licensing of familiar characters remained a financial gamble. Movies, television programs, and arcade games may prompt consumer interest, but some characters did not find favor no matter how exhaustive the hype. The movie *Annie* seemed like a can't miss hit and led toymakers to scramble for licenses; however, the film bombed at the box office and the licensed characters experienced flat sales.

BIBLIOGRAPHY

"E.T. and Friends are Flying High," *Business Week.* (January 10, 1983) 77.

Long Hair on Men

Long hair worn by men has historically come into vogue in cycles; the most recent explosion took place in 1964 with the arrival of Beatlemania on American shores. Soon male moptops seemed to be growing everywhere. As the length kept getting longer, the original Beatle hairstyles would come to seem short by way of contrast (the group's album covers, in fact, offer a chronological journey through the evolution of men's hair fashions during the 1960s). The trend received added impetus when the hippie movement sprang up out of the ashes of the West Coast beat culture. Girls also joined in, first with matching Beatle bobs, then with straight, shoulder-length hair.

Barbers predicted long hair would doom their trade. Shops were being forced to close at the rate of 100 per month according to one estimate. Bill Severn notes, however, that some barbers found opportunity in the face of this crisis.

> But others who modernized their methods and surroundings found business and income booming. Instead of the traditional quick trim, they offered consultation in the styling and care of the new coiffure and turned their establishments into masculine beauty shops. Young men with money to spend, and older men who began to let their hair lengthen in the wishful pursuit of youth, discovered what women always had known, that long hair required attention.

Services offered by such salons included individual styling, hair problem and hair personality analysis, wave straightening, thinning, restoring, conditioning, coloring, massage, sunlamp tanning, facials, and mudpacks. Accessories sold for home use included masculine perfumes, lotions, astringents, skin creams, tubes of liquid makeup in sun bronze and wind buff, and face powders to improve sallow complexions.

Long hair reflected a change in attitudes as well as in fashions. Shielded from the basic deprivations their parents had experienced during the depression and ensuing war, baby boomers desired more than steady employment, life in suburbia, and the accompanying status symbols such as expensive cars and jewelry. Rather than just beatniks, surfers, motorcycle gangs, and other social outcasts, this new ethic had infiltrated the mainstream. As a result, long hair–perhaps more than any other cultural icon–became a symbol of deviant status. It encompassed free love, drugs, rock 'n' roll, and rebellion against conventional social mores of Nixon's Moral Majority in general. The keepers of society's status quo were worried. Long hair was banned in schools, at work, public meeting places, and in nearly every home with children.

The New Yorker cited a typical case in early 1968 where 53 long-haired boys were suspended by the principal of a Norwalk, Connecticut high school. Such treatment–which struck many Americans as patently unfair if not downright silly–ultimately gave rise to a backlash against those meting out the punishment. *The New Yorker* noted, "The chief function of a suspension hearing seems to be not that of an educational conference for the good of the child but that of a mechanism designed to support an arbitrary decision by the school authorities." *America* asked,

> Why all the fuss, especially in view of the absence of comparable attention to really serious problems of adolescents such as steady dating, heavy drinking and reckless driving? We are not making a case for long hair. The whole matter hardly seems that important. But if it keeps adolescents happy, why not indulge their latest fancy?

Hair also polarized people in political campaigns, in advertising, and in the arts. Poll-takers, psychologists, sociologists, columnists, and commentators made it a central theme. The basic split on this issue did not merely pit youth against authority figures. Severn summarized the situation as follows:

> To many of the older generation, the question was not length of hair but proper respect for authority, maintaining standards, decorum, discipline, and classroom control. As a

Norwalk, Connecticut, school system director put it in 1968, "The setting of values and guidelines for the community's youth is part of the educational process . . . a basic responsibility of the public schools."

On the other side were parents and educators who considered anti-hair edicts an attempt by government to dictate personal lives, to usurp family decisions, invade individual privacy, enforce conformity, and crush youthful questioning or dissent. By trying to tell students how to wear their hair, some charged, schools created problems of discipline and caused rebellion. Others saw more serious dangers, government violation of civil liberties and of basic constitutional rights, and the threat that a school which tried to make all students wear hair alike was only a step away from telling them to think alike.

The controversy had become stifled somewhat by the late 1960s as the vogue spread beyond its initial constituency. A *Time* editorial observed in 1967,

> . . . long hair has outgrown its parameters, traditionally described by the rebelliousness of youth and the self-consciousness of show business. It has become grey, middle-aged, ubiquitous and eminently respectable, a coast-to-coast phenomenon that has infiltrated even the U.S. Army, that last bastion of the butch.

Sociologists, psychologists and other observers of the human condition offered many theories as to why long hair was in. One camp held that it represented a concerted male effort, led by youth, to blur the lines distinguishing the two sexes. The hippie variant was dismissed by some as mere juvenile protest; i.e., "he wears his hair extravagantly long because short hair was once the Establishment's style, and he opposes the Establishment." Another theory set forth that the human peacock was merely showing his true feathers. Psychologist Robert D. Meade of Western Washington State College argued, "Perhaps man is coming into his biological destiny, suppressed in our Puritan milieu. It is the male in all nature, you know, who spreads his gorgeous tail feathers and erects his ruff for the inconspicuous little brown mate." Those attempting to explain the conversion of more mature, establishment types posited that the 50-year-old may not look any younger or more like an actor if he lets his hair grow out, but he thinks he does.

Long hair gradually went out of fashion during the 1970s. During the reign of disco fashions in the latter part of that decade, male haircuts became significantly shorter as more rebellious or fashion-conscious youth reverted back to shorter styles as exemplified by the punk and new wave movements of the late 1970s. (One can observe in photos from that period the supreme irony of the more rural-based and conservative elements of society deeming long hair stylish and adopting the very look they had criticized previously.) While the more individualistic approach typifying male fashions over the past couple of decades has allowed for a small enclave of holdouts, long hair in males no longer dominates the horizon.

BIBLIOGRAPHY

"Big Sprout-Out of Male Mop-Tops; Revolt Against the Close-Trimmed Male Haircut," *Life*. 59 (July 30, 1965) 56-59ff. il.

"The Long-Hair Controversy," *America*. (November 12, 1966) 578.

"Longer Hair Is Not Necessarily Hippie," *Time*. (October 27, 1967) 46. il.

"Notes and Comment; Male Hair Length and Puritan Conscience," *New Yorker*. 43 (June 10, 1967) 29.

"Rights," *The New Yorker*. (February 17, 1968) 24-25.

Severn, Bill. *The Long and Short of It*. New York: David McKay, 1971. il.

"Splitting Hairs Over Moptops; or, How Lunatic is the Fringe?," *Senior Scholastic*. 87 (October 14, 1965) 20. il.

"Unkindest Cut for Student Moptops," *Life*. 59 (September 24, 1965) 4.

Macrobiotic Food

By the mid-1960s, a motley assortment of students, writers, musicians, artists, and philosophers were advocating the benefits of MB or "macrobiotic" food (taken from the Greek word "makrobiotos," meaning "the art of prolonging life"). The components of the diet–grain soup with wheat noodles and lily roots, mealy bread buttered with a gooey paste, steamed wheat, a bit of seaweed, pale tea, and the grand entree, a bumpy glob of brown rice so sticky that it was reputedly impaled on a chopstick and eaten like a candy apple–were believed to clear up asthma, stop headaches and cure back problems, reduce weight, increase energy and powers of concentration, and even trigger hallucinations.

The MB regimen was allegedly based on Zen principles, a balance of the opposing but complementary forces of yin and yang. Illnesses supposedly arose from living in extremes and following a diet either too rich in yin foods (e.g., ice cream, fruit) or yang foods (e.g., meats, eggplant); because grains fit within the extremes, they became the staple of the diet. Allan Warsowe, a 1964 Harvard honors graduate affiliated with Cambridge's East-West Institute, noted, "[The MB diet is] a little like drugs, only better, because you're not depending on stimulants. Your mind escapes from your body. You're free to work."

The Institute, presided over by Michio Kusli, who claimed to have been introduced to MB by Oriental philosopher Georges Oshawa, pioneered the diet. It spread along the Eastern corridor, becoming particularly popular in New York's Greenwich Village community. One Cooper Union student claimed, "It helps you leave the Great American Deception which is a self-deluding stimulus that makes you content in a kind of fat, disgusting way."

The diet also had its detractors. Dr. Frederick Stone of the School of Public Health argued,

Macrobiotic effects have nothing to do with the magical properties of brown rice. They are simply symptoms of mild starvation accentuated by psychological suggestion.

Nevertheless, MB retained its following throughout the 1960s, gradually feeding into the back-to-nature, whole earth diets of the early 1970s.

BIBLIOGRAPHY

"Yin, Yang, and MB," *Newsweek.* 65 (April 5, 1965) 90-92. il.

Madras Plaid Clothing

India madras plaids have been a part of the American fashion scene since the late 1930s. Their appeal–first in the form of shirts and, by the 1960s, in practically everything else in the male wardrobe–was a result of (1) their bright palette of color, (2) the coolness of the handwoven cotton, and (3) brilliant advertising. Most influential of all in turning Americans on to madras were the efforts of two individuals–Ellerton Jette, president of Hathaway shirts, and David Ogilvy, a big-time adman.

Jette, during one of his frequent trips to London's custom tailors, noticed the use of plaid madras in shirts. His company had been employing madras–a loosely woven, ultrafine cotton muslin–in shirts for years, but only in plain white. Its popularity in Great Britain was the result of civil servants bringing the material back to England following tours of duty in India. The plaids were an expression of India's longstanding fondness for Scottish tartans. Cognizant of the commercial possibilities, Hathaway added plaid madras shirts to its line in the waning years of the Great Depression.

Almost immediately, the boom subsided as customers started returning the shirts, complaining that the colors were fading in the sun and bleeding in the wash. Stores panicked and unloaded their stock at bargain basement prices. The problem was a result of the vegetable dyes utilized for coloring which faded naturally. Ogilvy, hired by Jette to resuscitate the madras shirts, instituted an ad campaign that trumpeted the fabric's tendency to fade, as if fading were a virtue. The Ogilvy ads did for madras shirts what Tom Sawyer had accomplished for whitewashing fences, with proclamations like:

- "Magical things happen to this shirt when you wash it."
- "Hathaway guarantees that your shirt will fade in the wash. . . ."
- "This [fading] gives the shirts a look of good breeding and maturity, which no mass-produced fabric can ever aspire to."

• Faded shirts were "dustily well-bred" and "marvelously muted."

In addition to giving madras shirts a classy aura, Ogilvy in 1960 recounted in his ads how Yale University had grown in part due to the sale of madras cotton. Endowed with such a lofty pedigree, madras became the Ivy League fabric of record, surging ahead of chino, Harris Tweed, and other cherished threads. The institutional status of madras was now assured and, indeed, it has remained a fixture in male dress up to the present day.

BIBLIOGRAPHY

Berendt, John. "The Madras Shirt," *Esquire*. 111 (June 1989) 46. il.

The Mail-Order Catalog Business

The mail-order business proved to be the retailing revolution of the 1980s. According to the Direct Marketing Association, Inc., the number of catalogs mailed per year grew from 5.8 billion in 1980 to 12.4 billion in 1988. Computerized mailing lists played a major role in this growth, causing the shopper who bought an item from one or two catalogs to get inundated with dozens more. By the end of the decade, mail carriers were claiming that they sometimes had to make more than one trip a day to deliver some people's mail due to the glut of catalogs.

The mail-order industry as big business dates back to the turn of the century when department store chains such as Sears sought customers in rural America. Specialty companies–e.g., book and record clubs–also thrived over the years by offering convenience, price incentives, and even artistic advice.

The catalog market owed its phenomenal growth in the 1980s to several more recent developments:

1. The substantial increase in numbers of working women in the last 20 years, which expanded household incomes.
2. The limited time available to many families for shopping.
3. The rise of couch-potato consumerism fostered by the pioneers in the mail-order field.

The bonanza reaped by retailers such as L. L. Bean, Lands' End, and homewares colossus Williams-Sonoma attracted a flood of imitators. In addition, established catalog houses found it necessary to excel in one or more of the following areas:

1. The provision of unique and/or high quality merchandise.
2. Efficiency in targeting the right customers; e.g., being more specific about the mailing lists employed.

3. The quality treatment of customers; some examples of above-and-beyond service have included (a) the provision of swatches of material and wardrobe coordination (Jos. A. Bank), (b) allowance for fax ordering, and (c) the institution of a special consumer hotline on which experienced outdoorsmen answer questions on anything from kayaking to ice climbing (Patagonia).
4. The production of "magalogs"–catalogs that offer literary features along with shopping information; e.g., Lands' End has included employee profiles, travel features, and product pieces such as one on how cashmere is made.
5. Involvement with goodwill causes; e.g., Telltales, a Maine-based children's book catalog, helps combat illiteracy by sending newborns their first book, and Patagonia donated ten percent of its pretax profits to environmental causes.
6. Adoption of new technologies; by the late 1980s Brownstone Studio was experimenting with "video catalogs," and a number of online information services were offering a shop-by-computer feature.

The field faced a number of stiff challenges besides a glut of players at the outset of the 1990s. Although mail-order companies historically didn't have to charge sales tax because most orders came from out of state, approximately half passed new laws in the late 1980s to reserve that policy. Mailing costs–both for catalogs and merchandise–were steadily on the rise; catalog mailing costs alone jumped 25 percent in 1988. Nevertheless, with sales continuing to grow at twice the rate of store retailers, survivors appeared likely to reap windfall profits.

TABLE 1. A Sampling of Mail-Order Companies

A & S
Archie McPhee and Co.
B. N. Genius
Ballard Designs
Blackhawk Video
Bloomingdale's
Brown & Jenkins Trading Co.

Brownstone Studio
CML Group, Inc.
The Compact Disc Centre
The Company Store
Eddie Bauer, Inc.
Faith Mountain Co.
Gifted Children
Hanna Anderson
Holy Cow, Inc.
Inmac Corp.
J & R Music
JCPenney
J. Crew
Jos. A. Bank
L. L. Bean
Lands' End
Last Chance Records
Lillian Vernon
The Love Tapes
Mary's
Mellow Mail
Movies Unlimited
Nieman Marcus
The Paragon
Patagonia
Quill Corporation
Sears
Smith & Hawken
Spiegel
Swiss Colony
Telltales
Tweeds
Undressed To Kill
Video Yesteryear
Williams-Sonoma

BIBLIOGRAPHY

Gumpert, D. E. "Mail-Order Success Only Looks Easy . . . ," *Working Woman*. 14 (July 1989) 37-38ff. il.
Lubove, S. "Bargain-Hunting," *Forbes*. 145 (June 11, 1990) 196-198. il. Re. computers through the mail.
Miller, Annetta and Lourdes Rosado. "'Up to the Chin in Catalogs," *Newsweek*. (November 20, 1989) 57-58. il.
Pomice, E. "Catalog Firms Bite the Hand That Squeezes," *U.S. News & World Report*. 107 (July 31, 1989) 44. il. Re. move to impose state sales tax.

Marilyke Dresses

The Marilyke look was a fixture in many U.S. clothing stores during the mid-1950s. It enabled potential customers to select dresses worthy of bearing a tag proclaiming them fit for a Roman Catholic girl.

Each tag, which cost retailers three cents "to cover the cost of shipping and mailing," was illustrated with a picture of the Virgin Mary, the trade name "Marilyke," and the motto, "Whatever our Blessed Mother approves." Also included were a list of specifications for Marilyke dresses, including:

- full coverage for the bodice, chest, shoulders, back, and arms;
- no cutouts lower than two inches below the neckline;
- no transparent or flesh-colored materials to give the impression of nudity;
- sleeves halfway between shoulder and elbow; and
- nothing that will "unduly reveal the figure of the wearer."

The labels also bore the legend "Copyright by Rev. B. Kunkel," who'd started a "crusade" for maidenly modesty out of his home base of Bartelso, Illinois (population 304) in 1944. Kunkel founded an organization named the Party Crusaders of Mary Immaculate, and in 1953 began the Marilyke tagging system. The movement expanded rapidly, with about 75,000 dresses having been tagged by June 1955. By then, a factory in Bartelso was manufacturing Marilyke clothes as well.

Other priests took up the Marilyke program, most notably the Rev. Charles Varga, pastor of St. John the Apostle Church in Linden, New Jersey. All retailers in his parish accepted the tagging agenda; one shopkeeper noted, "What are we going to do–commit business suicide? This is a 65 percent Catholic community." Some retailers submitted to the process more enthusiastically. One buyer in a large Manhattan department store declared that "some of [the Marilyke dresses] are so cute we've put them in the Junior Department."

BIBLIOGRAPHY

"Catholic Crusade for Modesty," *Literary Digest*. 82 (August 30, 1924) 25-26. il.
"The Marilyke Look," *Time*. 65 (June 27, 1955) 64.

Master Mind

America–like a large portion of the world–was captivated by Master Mind in the mid-1970s. Between 1973, when the game first appeared on the market, and late 1975, approximately five million sets were purchased in 60 different countries. Almost 100,000 were sold in the U.S. alone from spring to fall of 1975 at prices from $2.50 to $20. Those playing the game frequently professed to be thoroughly addicted.

The game was invented by Mordechai Meirovich, a postal employee in Israel, who first exhibited it at the 1971 Nurnberg Toy Fair. Representatives from Invicta Plastics, a Leicester, Great Britain games manufacturer recognized its potential and arranged to produce, package, and retail four different models. After achieving popularity of epidemic proportions there it spread to the status where its success was largely duplicated.

The basic rules of Master Mind were succinctly laid out in *Time*:

> . . . one player, known as the "codemaker," picks four pegs from a choice of six colors and places them in any order he chooses under a shield on one side of a board. The object of his opponent, the "codebreaker," is to place four pegs in holes on his side of the board, attempting to duplicate the color and order of the hidden pegs in a maximum of ten tries. After the codebreaker has set up his four pegs, the codemaker gives clues by placing in four small holes either black markers (for correct color, correct position), white markers (correct color, wrong position) or no markers (wrong color). The code breaker next arranges another row of pegs and is given more clues, repeating the process until he has deduced the hidden "code." Then the players switch positions; the winner is the one who figures out the code in the least number of tries.

The popularity of the game rests at least in part on its appeal to the relative skill of the player. Joe Ballester, assistant games buyer for the Brentano's bookstore chain, noted, "Chance plays an important element in the first three tries. After that it's logic." This dimension has even led to its utilization within the classroom. Manufacturers of educational materials such as Cuisenaire in New Rochelle, New York, and J. L. Hammett in Braintree, Massachusetts, for instance, promoted the game as a means of teaching logic in schools. Georgia State University student Gene Lewallen cited the fact that "it's easy to understand the rules, and it's not long and drawn out like chess (average time to crack the code: 15 minutes)." Television producer Lis Nygaard added, "You can break the ice with people. You get to know a lot about them: how they think, even what colors they like."

These strengths were sufficient to keep the game extremely popular in the U.S. throughout the balance of the 1970s. Interest in it appears to have dropped off significantly at that point, probably due to the appearance of other games of intelligence, most notably Trivial Pursuit.

BIBLIOGRAPHY

"And Now, Master Mind," *Time.* 106 (December 1, 1975) 73. il.

Matchbox Vehicles

Matchbox vehicles–modeled after real-life cars and trucks–have been a staple toy for young children for two generations. The manufacturer, Lesney Products & Co., Ltd., started in 1947, when Leslie C. Smith and John W. Odell set up a die-casting shop in a bombed-out London pub. They began producing die-cast toys as a sideline, really making an impression in 1953 with a finely detailed one-inch model of Queen Elizabeth's coronation coach which sold about one million units.

Having found its market, the company embarked upon an extraordinary expansion program. By 1966, Lesney had seven plants which produced 130 million toy vehicles–in approximately 120 different models–annually. These cars and trucks comprised 90 percent of what was then a 30-million-dollar-a-year business with sales of around 500,000 units per week in the U.S. alone.

The keys to the success of the Matchbox vehicles were (1) loving attention to detail, (2) sturdy construction (able to withstand the most rambunctious child as well as the tread of unsuspecting grownups), and (3) efficient production techniques that permitted low retail prices (55 cents and up in the U.S. in the mid-1960s). *Business Week* noted that the company's mode of operation was not very different from its full-scale relations in Detroit:

> To start, [a] designer . . . made precise drawings of the real thing. [A] model maker . . . hand-tailored a prototype, and from this draftsmen projected how the actual model would be produced–what parts would go where, and how they would be assembled.
>
> Meanwhile, a wooden pattern was made, about five times bigger than the planned model. From this, resin molds were made, and sealed back down to final size on a pantograph die-making machine, which turned out dies in chrome-vana-

dium steel. It's during the pantograph process that the details are added; toolmakers use jeweler's lenses to add authentic bits of trim.

All of Lesney's die-casting machinery, plastic injection machines, and other specialized tools were designed by its engineers . . . fully automatic die-casting was essential because of the huge volume, and the equipment had to be made in the shop because the necessary combination of speed and precision was simply not available on the open market . . . Lesney also developed its own paint spraying equipment. In one machine, the tiny auto bodies are spun rapidly on spindles in front of a spray gun, then pass into an oven. . . .

In the final assembly, there is a great deal of hand work, though moving belts and automatic controls help to keep the flow even to make sure that no assembler runs out of parts, and so holds up the show; each job is coded to control belts running from the huge stockroom, where parts for 30-million cars are kept. . . . Moving belts also take the completed cars to the packing room, where the work is again done by hand except for a machine that opens and closes the boxes.

With Lesney's policy of constantly seeking out new markets and predisposition for modeling "big, colorful, and noisy" vehicles (which have tended to outlast faddish types), the company continued to thrive into the 1970s and beyond. Despite the inroads made by a host of new competitors within the toy industry, particularly from the electronic media, there appears to be something elemental in the appeal of the Matchbox line to youth, perhaps, in part, the subconscious wish to act out one's fantasies as an adult complete with all the trappings of that world.

BIBLIOGRAPHY

"Little Big Wheel in the Auto Industry," *Business Week.* (March 26, 1966) 178-180. il.

Men's Pajamas

The $35,000,000 men's pajamas industry experienced a bad year in 1949; sales fell to 18,000,000 pairs, or 65 percent below 1948 figures. Some felt the drop was attributable to the fact that ex-GI's, who weren't issued sleeping clothes in the service, had gotten out of the habit of wearing them. Others saw it as part of the overall decline in the soft-goods business.

Manufacturers set out to reverse the trend by bringing out a vast number of eye-catching new styles. A major strategy consisted of bringing pajamas out of the bedroom and into the livingroom.

The new models seemed to offer something for everyone. There was a lounge-coat type designed for television viewers, and a knitted jersey pair for puttering around the house or for indoor sports like table tennis. A pantless outfit was earmarked for men preferring to wear just the tops of pajamas to bed as well as a topless pair for those who were used to retiring in only the bottoms. Husband-and-wife combinations ended up becoming especially popular, a notable example being BVD's "Cellmates," featuring a black-and-white-striped, prison-type look with a heart over the left breast where normally the pocket would be located.

Manufacturers also employed new fabrics. The "caveman" type would find comfort in a leopard skin-like material. There was a sheer outfit with short sleeves and legs for use in hot weather. In addition, nylon and rayon became increasingly employed.

The industry's efforts proved overwhelmingly successful. Sales for the first half of 1950 were up an estimated 50 percent over the same period in 1949, with June sales (fueled by Father's Day gifts) up 100 percent over the previous year. The popularity of pajamas continued throughout the decades, abetted no doubt by the sanitized domestic images of the American family provided by television; i.e., *I Love Lucy, My Little Margie,* and *The Joan Davis Show,* among others, exhibited both men and women late at night wearing pajamas.

The garment slipped from favor somewhat in the 1960s, perhaps because it was viewed by the younger generation as a badge of uptight conformity. Nevertheless, pajamas have remained an institution for sleep up to the present day, for women, albeit to a lesser extent, as well as men.

BIBLIOGRAPHY

"Disaster; Movement to Keep Pajamas Alive," *New Yorker.* 25 (July 30, 1949) 18-19.
"Men's Cotton Pajamas," *Consumers Research Bulletin.* 27 (January 1951) 24-25. il.
"Pajamas Back in Favor," *Newsweek.* 35 (June 19, 1950) 74. il.
"Undercover Survey; Pajama Wearing," *Collier's.* 126 (July 22, 1950) 74.

Microwave Ovens

Microwave ovens were the fastest-selling appliance during the 1970s. This proved to be a welcome development to an industry hard hit by the energy crises (shortages of supplies, rising costs, etc.) and recessionary tendencies of that decade. In 1975, for instance, the year microwave ovens achieved a larger volume of sales than did gas stoves ($370 million and $356 million, respectively), they recorded a 28 percent increase–on top of a 64 percent jump the previous year–while sales of gas ranges dropped 17 percent and electric range sales plunged 31 percent.

In the early years of its commercial existence, however, few would have predicted such a success story for the product. In the late 1960s and early 1970s, consumers worried about excessive radiation leakage. But in 1971, the Food & Drug Administration's Bureau of Radiological Health set tough new standards on allowable leakage and followed them up with strict inspection and enforcement procedures.

Declining consumer concern over safety represented only one of many factors behind the rise of microwave oven sales. Others included:

1. the availability of new features vastly improving performance such as (a) units with variable power settings (replacing units that could run only on full power), (b) special browning devices, and (c) new temperature controls;
2. their reputed energy efficiency (resulting in energy saving of anywhere from 20 to 75 percent depending upon the source); and
3. the fact that microwave oven sales were not yet tied to new housing construction (at that time a depressed industry).

In the latter years of the decade, the microwave oven boom appeared to be losing its momentum (e.g., through June 1978 factory shipments of the appliance ran only 14 percent ahead of the first six months of the previous year, a dramatic decline from the increases of 45 percent or more chalked up in the same time frame between 1974-1977). Weakening demand was attributed to price persistence, a proliferation of brands and models that confused consumers and retailers alike, continued fears of hazardous microwave radiation (recently fanned by Paul Brodeur's book, *The Zapping of America*), and complicated controls that made the ovens look too much like computers. With respect to the latter point, Anna Cummin of Cappy's Appliance Co. in Woburn, Massachusetts, noted in 1978, "[Consumers] think you have to be a genius to run a microwave oven."

While sales flattened out, however, food processor and food-packaging producers continued to see microwave ovens as their single most important growth market. Pillsbury Co. was one of the pioneers in these sectors, introducing a whole line of foods for the device, beginning with one-minute pancakes and three-minute popcorn. The pioneering of paper and plastic containers (following earlier misadventures with aluminum, which occasionally caused sparks to jump between containers and oven walls, sometimes damaging the power systems of the ovens) was particularly helpful in stimulating the growth of products geared to microwave ovens.

The growth of the microwave food market, in turn, helped revive flattened sales of the appliance. Enticed by the convenience of preparation promised by the use of microwave ovens, sales revived and continued at a high rate well into the 1980s. Many homes had two or more of them in use, and they were highly visible in the workplace as well. Added proof of their high profile in American society came with the increasing tendency of builders to place them in new homes as a standard kitchen appliance alongside the range. At present, microwave ovens appear likely to remain an American institution for years to come.

BIBLIOGRAPHY

Edgerton, J. "Joy of Zapping," *Money.* 7 (December 1978) 68-70ff. il.
"Microwave Oven Sales Lose Some Speed," *Business Week.* (July 31, 1978) 99-100. Graph. Includes sidebar, "Will New Foods Help the Market for Ovens?"

Pauly, D. and W. Schmidt. "Really Cooking," *Newsweek.* 86 (September 15, 1975) 64-65. il.

"Sales are Sizzling for Microwave Ovens," *Business Week.* (February 9, 1976) 32-34. Graphs.

"Should You Buy a Microwave Oven?" *Good Housekeeping.* 187 (December 1978) 280ff. il.

Steinmann, M. "Waves of the Future?" *New York Times Magazine.* (November 7, 1976) 78-80ff. il. Re. radiation hazards.

The Midi

As the tumultuous 1960s–with their fanciful, often outrageous, fashions–came to a conclusion, John Burr Fairchild, head of Fairchild Publications, which included amongst its properties the influential trade tabloid, *Women's Wear Daily*, decreed 1970 the year of the midi. His publication immediately began pushing the midi, beginning with careful attention to semantics. Although the term would eventually come to mean anything from below the knee to the ankle, it still meant mid-calf at the beginning of 1970. Accordingly, Fairchild coined the word "Longuette" and, in an attempt to keep abreast of European fashion developments, propounded the theme: "The whole look of American women will now change, and die-hard miniskirt adherents are going to be out in the fashion cold."

American designers and retailers felt little recourse but to go along, and midis were hastily placed on the marketplace in January to the virtual exclusion of mini-fashions. While midi coats and sport-skirts, particularly in junior styles, sold well in the majority of outlets, daytime dresses in the longer lengths failed to move. Combined with the 1970 recession, the fashion industry entered a tailspin: fabric mills slowed down, some clothing manufacturers went out of business and retailers garnered red ink.

Even worse, the industry suffered through a severe public relations debacle. Men openly denounced the midi as a threat to the golden days of mini ogling, while women insisted that it would make them look old, ugly, dumpy, or sawed-off–or all of these. When major U.S. clothes designers presented their fall-winter collections in New York in May, various women's groups protested in the streets. "Keep the Mini on the Market," pleaded the supporters of GAMS (Girls/Guys Against More Skirt) while FADD (Fight Against Dictating Designers) threatened to exercise "purse power" by boycotting all department stores that stocked only midis for fall.

Retailers, however, remained largely behind the midi bandwagon banking on the prospect that if hemlines went down far enough, women would have to buy complete new wardrobes: midi dresses, skirts, coats, belts and bags, higher-heeled shoes, and boots. As noted by Katherine Murphy, a fashion coordinator for Manhattan's Bloomingdale's: "Look, this isn't fun and games. We have a multi-million-dollar business to run, and we're not laughing all the way to the bank. Our whole economy is based on planned obsolescence."

Despite the high profile backlash against the midi, substantial segments of the female population appeared relieved to have an alternative to mini-styles. In addition to the fringe crowd–those wanting to be first with anything new, no matter what, as well as individuals who would do things just to be different–there were obviously women who wished to hide unattractive legs or simply the ravages of time. Many also had considered the mini to be both uncomfortable and impractical for dealing with a host of everyday occurrences (e.g., sitting in chairs). Still others had been alienated by the sheer exhibitionism of the style. As a result, the sales of midis picked up during the fall of 1970. Nevertheless, it was the mini-midi controversy which garnered the larger share of the headlines and this standoff helped engender the hot pants craze early the following year as a substitute for the vanquished mini.

BIBLIOGRAPHY

Lobsenz, N. "Mini-Midi-Maxi Madness," *Good Housekeeping.* 171 (August 1970) 61ff. il.

"Midi Muscles In," *Life.* 69 (August 21, 1970) 22-29. il.

"Onward and Downward with Hemlines: The Midi Look," *Life.* 68 (March 13, 1970) 38-45. il.

"Out on a Limb with the Midi," *Time.* (September 14, 1970) 76-81. il.

Owett, T. "Midi Without Fear," *Ladies Home Journal.* 87 (August 1970) 74-75. il.

"Skirt Skirmishes," *Newsweek.* (May 18, 1970) 90. il.

"Stuck With the Midi and Pushing Hard," *Business Week.* (October 10, 1970) 106-108. il.

The Model T

The Ford Model T was far more than the first notable success story for the fledgling automotive industry. According to Richard Nichols,

> Almost alone, the Model T wrought a social revolution across North America. It brought small communities previously isolated by a two-day horseback journey within easy reach of each other and of large towns. It mechanized the activity of city dweller and farmer alike. It was practical, reliable, adaptable and, above all, affordable. More than any other item, invention or product associated with the internal combustion engine, it . . . dragged the Western civilizations into the 20th century.

The Ford Motor Company, founded in 1903, following on the heels of the Detroit Automobile Company (1899) and the Henry Ford Company, represented Henry Ford's third attempt at proving his theory that the achievement of financial success lay through making and selling large numbers of cars at low prices with small profit margins. Early models (the A, B, C, and N) sold well enough to provide Ford with the capital and resolve to produce a light-weight, 20-horsepower, four-cylinder vehicle capable of carrying five passengers in comfort, which would be within the means of all Americans. The culmination of this vision, the Model T, began production in Detroit on October 1, 1908. Priced at $850 in its Touring form (it was also available as a Town Car, Runabout, Coupe, or a Landaulet), it sold a hitherto unheard of 17,000 units in its first year of production. Four years later, the production rate had increased ten-fold to 170,000 (more than the volume sale of the Galaxie, Falcon and Fairlane models some 50 years later).

The continually increasing rate of sales, the substitution of lower quality materials (e.g., leather door trims replaced by pressed steel, the brass portion of headlamps and radiators gave way to an all-steel configuration), and assembly line refinements resulting in greater production efficiency enabled Ford to continually lower the price tag of the Model T. By 1923 the car cost $260–brand new and available in "any color you like as long as it's black"–and sold more than 2,000,000 units.

While the Model T was not especially innovative from a mechanical standpoint (one new feature was the monobloc engine casting with bolt-on cylinder head), its success was in no small part due to its remarkable efficiency and durability in performance. As noted by Nichols,

> The roads of the time were little more than dirt tracks, and [the Model T] was well suited to them. Its lightweight frame, made from steel channel, flexed in response to rough surfaces and complemented the work of the rather rudimentary suspension of the time–its transverse leaf springs had no form of shock absorber at all. But its unsprung weight was low. The 30-inch wooden spoked wheels weighed very little, and they also afforded a high (10-inch) ground clearance, which was important at the time.

A victim of changing fashions and the opulence of the Roaring Twenties, the Model T ceased production in 1928, after more than 15,000,000 had been sold. The adoption of the left-hand drive configuration as the norm in the United States represented yet another legacy of the car; while unusual in this respect at the time of its first appearance, the vast number of Model T's sold reversed the equation in a short number of years.

BIBLIOGRAPHY

"Henry's Wonderful Tin Lizzie," *Newsweek.* 62 (August 12, 1963) 67. il.

Lefferts, B. "Revolution of the Tin Lizzie," *New York Times Magazine.* (July 28, 1963) 18-19. il.

Nevins, T. A. "Untold Story of the Model T," *Popular Science.* 183 (July 1963) 68-72ff. il.

Nichols, Richard. "Model T," In: *Classic American Cars.* New York: Exeter, 1986. pp. 6-11.

Ortner, E. H. "Any Dope Could Drive a Model T," *Popular Science.* 183 (July 1963) 73-74ff. il.

Musical Toys by Mattel

In 1945, when Mattel, Inc., was merely a small workshop in a garage, most American-made musical toys were of the mass-produced variety that tended to break after minimal handling. Comparable European products performed a lot better but cost as much as twenty-five dollars.

At this point in time a movie studio music arranger showed Mattel's owners–35-year-old Elliot Handler and his wife, Ruth–a crude wooden music box he had designed. The device, which had stiff wires of graduated lengths, held together in a zinc base and twanged by knobs on a rubber belt, differed drastically from European boxes, which produced their melodies through a row of "tuned" metal strips flicked by cogs on a revolving drum.

The Handlers, who up to then had concentrated on general toys and novelties, immediately grasped the box's possibilities and bought the rights. It was simpler and less expensive than European boxes, yet relatively durable. Best of all, the device's small size–only one-half-inch in width–meant it could fit into all kinds of toys.

By 1951, all Mattel toys were musical, and most of the musical toys made in the United States bore that company's name. Ranging in price from 98¢, to $2.19, Mattel grossed around $4,500,000 that year. Products utilizing the music box included plastic guitars, a miniature covered wagon that played "Oh Susannah," organ grinders with dancing monkeys, nursery-rhyme books, and a jack-in-the-box that played "Pop Goes the Weasel." In addition to licensing other musical-toy makers in Latin America, Mattel found itself receiving orders from Europe, including Switzerland, original home of the handcrafted music box.

During the 1950s, Mattel wisely embarked upon a policy of product diversification, most notably the Barbie doll. By the time musical toys had become more technologically sophisticated, Mattel was securely perched at the top of the toy industry.

BIBLIOGRAPHY

"All's Swell at Mattel," *Time*. 80 (October 26, 1962) 90. il.
"Mattel Inc.," *Forbes*. 117 (March 1, 1976) 27-28. il.
"Music by Mattel," *Newsweek*. (December 10, 1951) 77-78. il.

The Mustang

While strongly influenced by the two-seater classics of the 1950s–the Corvette and Ford's own Thunderbird–the Mustang quickly acquired its own niche as the greatest single automotive success story of the 1960s. Introduced in April 1964, it sold 680,000 units in the first nine months of production, setting an all-time record for first-year sales of a new model. The Mustang maintained comparable sales figures through 1966, the last year in which it had the "muscle car" (or "pony car," in recognition of its impact on the industry) field to itself. According to Richard Nichols,

> The real secret of the Mustang's appeal was hidden in the option boxes on the dealer order blanks. Buyers were able to order a basic compact of a full-house race car via the possible mix of three- or four-speed stick-shifts, handling package, disk brakes, power steering, air conditioning, tachometer, bench or bucket seats, you name it. Naturally there was also a selection of special badgework, stripes and body moldings available on option.

In addition, the basic model bore a sticker price of $2500–a bargain even before one considered its sporty good looks and performance capabilities.

In 1967, the Mustang's totals dipped below one-half million units as competitors rushed out their own versions, most notably General Motors' Camaro/Firebird models and the Mercury Cougar. In an attempt to revive its image, Ford supplied the Mustang with big-block engines–a 335 horsepower, 390-cubic inch version as well as a 390 hp 427–in 1968. This was followed by its first major facelift in 1969, the Mach 1. This version set the tone for the 1970s, being longer, lower and wider, and including dummy hood scoops, vents,

Proclaimed the year of the Mustang, 1966 witnessed the rise of the domestic sports car and of its most vocal proponent, Lee Iacocca, executive vice president of Ford Motor Company. The Mustang excited buyers because they could chose from a myriad of options to personalize the car.

and a rear deck spoiler. While sales had fallen below 200,000 in 1970, the Mustang continued to pace the muscle car division. In the face of growing legislation aimed at promoting fuel efficiency, greater safety and cleaner air, the Mustang power plant gradually diminished in size and output. By the mid-1970s, it was reduced to competing with a host of inexpensive subcompacts and mini-cars from abroad as well as Detroit entries like the Dodge Colt, Chevy Chevette, and Ford Maverick.

BIBLIOGRAPHY

"Appeal to Youth; Ford's Concentrating on Youth Market," *Time*. 83 (January 3, 1964) 74-75. il.

Nichols, Richard. "Mustang," In: *Classic American Cars*. New York: Exeter, 1986. pp. 110-115. il.

O'Shea, P. "Ford's Wildest Mustang," *Hot Rod*. 17 (June 1964) 26-29. il.

The Nerd Look

In 1984, evidence everywhere indicated that nerds were "in." David Link, publicity manager at Twentieth Century Fox–the studio responsible for the hot film, *Revenge of the Nerds*–delineated the signs of the encroaching craze:

> You see lots of guys with their shirts buttoned all the way up, and even cool guys are wearing white T-shirts under their regular shirts. You see a lot of high-water pants like Michael Jackson wears. And people are walking around with computers attached to their belts . . .

The forces behind the rise of the nerd included, first and foremost, the computerization of society. Hackers–the type of computer whiz kids glorified in *War Games*–have become the new campus heroes. In addition, there appear to be a lot of closet nerds; i.e., people who go home and dress like nerds because they feel more comfortable that way. Link also noted,

> . . . with the advancement and concentration on high technology now, fashion has gotten into what traditionally has been nerd territory. I mean, the whole look out here in L. A. is more efficient dressing, and nerds are into efficiency.

Perhaps, most telling of all, media stars have been exhibiting the look. Among musicians, Elvis Costello and the band Devo epitomized the nerd with their owlish, horn-rimmed glasses and gawky poses as early as 1976, followed by Thomas Dolby (seen wearing bermuda shorts and knee socks in his MTV videos) and Michael Jackson. Designers Perry Ellis and Ralph Lauren displayed the white socks and black loafers which Andy Warhol had made his trademark back in the 1960s. Pee Wee Herman, considered by many to be the quintessential nerd, achieved cult status and sired a whole school of socially regressed stand-up comedians, including Howie Mandel and Richard Lewis.

In the wake of such developments, Link authored a loose-leaf *Nerd Planner* aimed at the nerd inside each of us. Ingredients included:

- a plastic pen pack with an extra pocket for a calculator;
- a screwdriver to fix computers;
- an official nerd comb with a back clip to adhere on a pocket and thereby keep from losing;
- two kinds of rubber bands—one for regular use and the other to keep a trouser leg from getting caught in bicycle spokes;
- a plastic container that laces onto your shoes in which you may stash your video game tokens or key to the computer club; and
- an official Nerd Association card with spaces to fill in your I.Q., highest video game scores, SAT scores, and Mom's telephone number.

Twentieth Century Fox also published a nerd handbook and released a sequel to *Revenge of the Nerds*. Other studios also mined the nerd craze with titles like *16 Candles*, *Weird Science*, and *Can't Buy Me Love*.

By fall 1984, even mainstream fashion had jumped on the bandwagon. Designers paired clashing plaids, mixed patterns and textures, and generally played havoc with prior taboos. And what the industry overlooked, style mongers carried off with a little imagination; e.g., wearing striped ties with patterned shirts.

The nerd look lost some of its appeal in the late 1980s; however, it appeared likely that committed practitioners would never again be regarded as quite the social pariahs they once were.

BIBLIOGRAPHY

Black, M. "Nerd News," *Mademoiselle*. 90 (August 1984) 90. il.

Cohen, B. "Who (and What) is a Nerd?" *Personal Computing*. 8 (April 1984) 203-207. il. Re. computer programmers.

Landers, Margaret. "Now It's Nerds, Naturally!" *Houston Post*. (August 19, 1984) 4G il. Supplied by Knight-Ridder Newspapers.

The New York World's Fair of 1939

The 1939 New York World's Fair was a product of its age. It symbolized an America which had survived the Great Depression and–in slowly regaining that trademark optimism for which the country was known around the world–looked boldly to the future. Above all, it represented the ultimate party in a decade known for its excesses; glitzy Hollywood musicals, lavish parties for well-heeled debutantes, jazz performed by expanded big-band combos of orchestral proportions, and wild promotional stunts such as flagpole sitting and marathon dancing. As noted in *This Fabulous Century, 1930-1940*, the fair

> was the biggest, giddiest, costliest, and most ambitious international exposition ever put on. Even before it opened, on April 30, 1939, amid a blaze of fireworks and a blast of windy publicity, it had cost more than $150 million. Its 1,216-acre grounds in Flushing Meadows, Queens, had been made to order by filling in the entire Queen city dump and planting it with 10,000 trees and one million tulips from Holland. Upon this tract had been built 300 massive, futuristic buildings to house the Fair's 1,500 exhibitors. They included 33 states, 58 foreign countries and 1,300 business firms, ranging from the Ford Motor Company to Dr. Scholl's Footease, which maintained an emergency clinic to treat fairgoers whose arches had sagged along the exposition's 65 miles of paved streets and footpaths.

The president of the fair, Grover Aloysius Whalen, christened it "The World of Tomorrow" and dedicated it to both the blessings of democracy and the wonders of technology. With respect to the latter, the fair certainly delivered, functioning as a showcase for such futuristic products as television, nylon stockings, and robots.

A night view of the New York World's Fair in 1939 surpassed even Oz. Dorothy and Toto never saw such a proliferation of sleek design and technological wonders as this.

But it was more than that. During its two-year run, the 45 million visitors to the fair saw glimpses of the past, present, and future presented via a bewildering assortment of technological marvels, promotional gimmicks (e.g., Planters Nut & Chocolate Company's film, *Mr. Peanut and His Family Tree*, feasting on soup and pickles at Heinz, getting a shave at Remington Rand), sideshows (e.g., Billy Rose's Aquacade), and downright corn (e.g., Borden's Elsie in a box stall disguised as a four-poster bed). Sidney M. Shalett wrote in *Harper's* magazine in 1940, "It was the paradox of all paradoxes. It was good, it was bad; it was the acme of all crazy vulgarity, it was the pinnacle of all inspiration."

BIBLIOGRAPHY

Bainbridge, J., and C. McKelway. "That was the New York World's Fair; Mr. McAneny and the Little Girl from Jackson Heights," *New Yorker.* 17 (April 19, 1941) 44ff.

"The Big Fair," In: *This Fabulous Century, 1930-1940*, edited by Ezra Bowen. Volume IV. New York: Time-Life Books, 1969. pp. 266-283.

Eustis, M. "Big Show in Flushing Meadows," *Theatre Arts Monthly.* 23 (August 1939) 566-577. il.

"Fair's Farewell," *Business Week.* (November 2, 1940) 18ff.

Harding, G. "World's Fair," *Harper's Magazine.* 179 (July 1939) 193-200.

"New York Fair Studies Its Mistakes," *Business Week.* (October 28, 1939) 17-18.

Shalett, S. M. "Epitaph for the World's Fair," *Harper's Magazine.* 182 (December 1940) 22-31.

"Tomorrow and 1940," *Time.* 34 (October 23, 1939) 77-78. il.

900 Numbers

The presence of 900 number services was so prevalent in American society by the late 1980s that few remembered its modest origins earlier in the decade. When AT&T first marketed 900 numbers in 1980, they were consigned to the periphery of the phone industry. Dominated by sex, entertainment, sports, and gab spots during the early years (and advertised largely on late night television), the business notably expanded in volume and diversification in 1987, when Telesphere Communication, Inc., a small Chicago long-distance carrier, instituted a national 900 service that for the first time permitted interaction by callers, whether through a line operator or via a computerized voice-playback system. In short order, the major long-distance players–AT&T, MC Communications and U.S. Sprint Communications–followed with interactive 900 Services.

At the onset of the 1990s, callers could select from an astonishing array of services, including:

- horoscopes;
- sports scores and injuries offered through *Sports Illustrated*;
- baseball card valuations and market trends addressed by one entrepreneur via 900-420-CARD;
- celebrity gossip from the likes of Madonna, Janet Jackson, Paula Abdul, and leading rap stars;
- dial-a-stock quotations and commentaries from stockbrokers and business publications (e.g., *Wall Street Journal*);
- dial-a-porn–long the staple of the market–featuring confessions and racy messages from sexy phone voices. The ad section in the June 27, 1991 issue of *Rolling Stone* included the following:

"Women's Most Intimate True Confessions 1-900-USA-GIRL 24 Hours! 7 Days! $3.00"

"1-900-646-4646 GIRLS! GUYS! DATES! TALKING PER-
SONALS! DATES AND FRIENDS IT'S FUN-SAFE-EASY
Connection USA $2/min."

"Women's Secrets! You won't believe what you will hear!
1-900-820-2828 7 Days, 24 Hours. $3.00"

"U.S.A. Dreamgirls LIVE ADULT 1 ON 1 1-900-988-6900
ALSO TRY: 1-900-988-7900 $10 per call nationwide 24 hrs."

"LIVE TALK! 1-900-847-7529 $2.00 per min. MAKE THE
CALL OF THE WILD 1-900-VIP-PLAY"

- the marketing of fringe rock bands through national information services such as Music Access.

Almost from the beginning, large numbers of citizens complained to politicians and governmental regulators about the sleaziness and ubiquitousness of these services. Parents, in particular, were outspoken about the problems inherent in misleading ad charges as well as controlling the temptations of unsupervised youth. The phone companies, intimidated by proposed FTC investigations and ever mindful of negative PR fallout, attempted to be responsive to more acceptable modes of usage, most notably within the business sector. By 1990, many legitimate businesses were seeking to cash in on the apparent national mania for instant, conveniently accessible information (i.e., gratification). In October 1990, Crossroads Communications launched a 900 line for high school students that featured recruitment presentations by over 300 colleges. *The New York Times* offered crossword hints at 50 cents a minute, and *Consumer Reports* would provide the value of a specific year and model used car for $1.50 a minute. In June 1990, MTC Information Systems Corp. began selling TRW Business Credit Reports on companies for 28 dollars, billed as a 900 call (the reports were delivered by mail, facsimile, or overnight express). Other firms, such as Lotus, offered problem-solving by technicians on the phone. Callers to Traf/Fax Inc. in Marina del Rey, California, could get maps of Los Angeles traffic jams every ten minutes. Many smaller firms found 900 numbers to offer a cost-effective means of offering valuable support services. Dee Dee Walsh, the marketing communications manager of one such operation, Button Ware (a software company in Bellevue, Washington), noted, "We thought every one of our customers would hate us because we were charging them for information we offered for free. But since the company could afford to hire more operators and service improved, no one complained."

With countless low profile entrepreneurs and professionals getting into the act of owning 900 lines, both long-distance and local phone companies began marketing the concept to the private sector. By late 1990, the market was awash in discounts and fee waivers. Any interested individual could dial (at $9.95 per call) *InfoText* magazine's 900 INFOTEXT for a free subscription and help in setting up a line. With agencies such as the National Association for Information Services available to aid the prospective 900 line owner in projecting budgetary revenues and costs, in addition to sifting through ever tightening rules regarding content, advertising, service to minors, etc., the industry seemed likely to evolve in totally unforeseen directions during the 1990s. What appeared safe to project, however, was that 900 numbers would continue to occupy a key place in the socio-economic landscape of the U.S. for years to come.

BIBLIOGRAPHY

Armstrong, Larry, and Peter Coy. "900 Numbers Are Being Born Again," *Business Week*. (September 17, 1990) 144-146. il.

Coy, Peter, and Michele Galen. "Let's Not Let Phone Pollution Hang Up Free Speech," *Business Week*. (August 19, 1991) 32.

Dunkin, Amy. "1,001 Things You Can Do With Your Own 900 Line," *Business Week*. (November 5, 1990) 162-163. il.

Gamerman, Amy. "Phone Rock: Punching in Toxic Armpit," *Wall Street Journal*. (March 6, 1991) A8.

Nathans, Leah J. "Reach Out and Touch the Market's Latest Fad," *Business Week*. (May 22, 1989) 144-145. il.

Neff, Craig. "Games on the Line," *Sports Illustrated*. 72 (March 12, 1990) 10. il.

Purvis, Andrew. "Reach Out and Cure Someone; A New 900 Number Offers Medical Advice by Phone, But Can It Replace a Family Physician's Personal Touch?" *Time*. (July 22, 1991) 54. il.

1950s Teen Fashions

Strongly influenced by the "beat" movement as well as the rise of youthful anti-establishment celebrities (e.g., Marlon Brando, James Dean), teenagers had evolved their own fashion subculture by the mid-1950s. For boys, the desired look generally included leather jackets, sweat shirts or T-shirts, blue jeans, and motorcycle boots; for girls, T-shirts and jeans, or V-neck blouseless sweaters and tight skirts, or party dresses weighed down with ornate jewelry.

School authorities appeared almost unanimous in their belief that the wearing of such clothes contributed to juvenile delinquency. R. B. Norman, principal of an Amarillo (Texas) high school at the time, noted, "You can't put a kid into a monkey suit like one of those blue-jeans outfits and expect him to make any record for himself." Dr. Joseph Manch, associate superintendent in the Buffalo, New York public school system, addressed the correlation even more directly: "The way in which boys and girls dress is frequently reflected in their behavior."

At the 1957 convention of the National Association of Secondary School Principals, Manch described the first year of "The Buffalo Plan," a voluntary drive for a school dress code aimed at improving behavior and courtesy. In it, the Inter-High School Student Council recommended appropriate clothes for the district, including ties, sweaters or jackets, and clean, polished shoes for boys; suits, jumpers, and conservative dresses–all fitting "appropriately and modestly"–for girls. These recommendations were posted in all homerooms.

While such efforts at "reform" proved to be of dubious value, they effectively delineated the boundaries of the then much written about (and discussed) generation gap, with the adults generally taking on the role of hysterical guardians of conformity and the status quo and youth the part of pilgrims in search of truth and self-actualization. In retrospect, future youth fashions would render 1950s styles seemingly tame by way of comparison.

BIBLIOGRAPHY

"Debutante Slouch is Back," *Look*. 20 (February 21, 1956) 107-109. il.
"Teen 'Monkey Suits,' " *Newsweek*. (March 11, 1957) 102.
"Undressed Look," *Time*. 68 (August 13, 1956) 64ff. il.

Nostalgia

Nostalgia has fond connotations for most people; however, the word actually has negative overtones. Webster's defines it as "the state of being homesick; a wistful or excessively sentimental, sometime abnormal yearning for return to . . . some past period." Columnist George F. Will has been even harder on the term, dismissing it as "narcissism . . . modern man's worship of himself through veneration of things associated with his development."

Nevertheless, nostalgia always seems to be sweeping the country; there has always been a nostalgia boom. From year to year, the prime variant consists of who is feeling nostalgic about what. Michael Barrier noted, "Nostalgia is like sex: Every generation thinks it is discovering it for the first time." With respect to nostalgia in the late 1980s, he added,

> Most people, as they approach middle age, sense that their lives have settled into patterns that may not change significantly for many years to come. They look back longingly at a time when youth seemed endless and opportunities boundless. We are now at a peak in the nostalgia cycle because so many people are reaching an age when nostalgia comes most naturally.

The nostalgia experienced by baby boomers covered a vast array of fields, most of which became big business. These included:

1. baseball card collecting;
2. classic era (1938-1948) jukeboxes;
3. Elvis Presley memorabilia;
4. rock 'n' roll recordings reissued on virtually every audio format from the now obsolete 78s to compact discs;
5. comic book collecting;

6. sightseeing at cultural shrines such as Woodstock, Presley's Graceland mansion, etc.; and

7. eating at diner-style restaurants and 1950s-style drive-ins.

Barrier qualified just what constitutes nostalgia, arguing that it wasn't the same as mere enthusiasm for what is old. For example, an interest in Egyptian statuary would not be considered "nostalgia." In short, true nostalgia has always been based upon the living memory of artifacts and events from the past whether originating in private, personal memories or in the shared experiences of a generation.

Despite the ever-present spectra of crass commercialism, the nostalgia boom has had its positive features. It has functioned to bring the cherished past alive in the present, thereby making lives seem whole. In addition, it has served to refresh and comfort those in need of a break from the tedium of everyday life.

BIBLIOGRAPHY

Barrier, Michael. "Memories For Sale," *Nation's Business.* (December 1989) 18-26. Includes sidebar, "A Business That Outgrew Nostalgia," about a comic book distributor.

Jaynes, G. "Old and in the Way," *Life.* 12 (August 1989) 14. il.

Kellogg, M. A. "Please Spare Me the Nostalgia Craze," *Glamour.* 86 (September 1988) 208. 11.

"Nostalgia," *The New Yorker.* 64 (May 16, 1988) 30-31. Re. *Nostalgia News*, published by Jack Smith.

"Nostalgia: Not What It Used to Be," *Fortune.* 117 (February 15, 1988) 8. il.

Advertising

Kanner, B. "Themes Like Old Times," *New York.* 22 (January 30, 1989) 12ff.

Oopsie-Daisy

"Every year, there's a doll, and this is the year of Oopsie-Daisy," noted Howard W. Moore, executive vice-president of retailer Toys 'R' Us, Inc., in December 1989. Despite its rather unremarkable looks and behavior ("She crawls, falls down, and cries, only to pick herself up again"), the doll, which retailed for $44.95, helped propel its parent company, Tyco Toys, Inc., close to the top of the toy industry.

Once a lackluster producer of boys' playthings such as toy trains and racing cars, the company earned the nickname of "Little Hasbro" in recognition of its emulation of Hasbro Inc.'s pioneering efforts in implementing a diversified approach to toymaking so that success would not be dependent on a single product. As a result of this strategy, Tyco could boast of a record unrivaled in the industry by the end of the 1980s: five years of consecutive earnings and sales increases. In 1989 alone, analysts projected a 28.2 percent rise in profits, to 15 million dollars, on a 44 percent sales gain to $380 million. The company's healthy financial status enabled it to keep the supply of Oopsie-Daisies down (below retail demands) with the aim of managing the frenzy beyond one or two faddish years.

Tyco's commitment to diversification began after sales of racing cars and trains tumbled in 1983. Chief executive officer Richard E. Grey introduced Super Blocks, a cheaper, compatible version of Lego, and Super Dough, a competitor to dominant Play-Doh, shortly thereafter. The company really took off in early 1989 after it obtained rights to Oopsie-Daisy from its distributor in Canada, where the doll had been a huge success during the 1988 Christmas season. Then, in September 1989, Grey paid 44 million dollars for View-Master Ideal Group, Inc., which gave Tyco control of such perennial big sellers as Betsy Wetsy, Tiny Tears, and View-Master 3-D viewers. Given Tyco's commitment to cautious planning, it appeared likely at the onset of the 1990s that Oopsie-Daisy would be a fixture with American youth for years to come.

BIBLIOGRAPHY

Roman, Monica. "Oopsie-Daisy, Guess Who's Tops in Toyland Now?" *Business Week*. n3138 (December 18, 1989) 102.

The Op-Yop

The contemporary look characterizing Op-Yop when it was first marketed in 1968 belied its derivation from the ages-old button-on-a-string toys. Manufactured by Kramer Designs of Royal Oak, Michigan, it consisted of twin twirling disks colored in psychedelic hues. When the string was pulled taut, the disks whirled apart, then clopped together in mid-spin, sounding like, according to *Time* magazine, "a shark with loose plates chewing on an oyster."

Like countless other nonsensical objects of a similar strip, its essential appeal proved impossible to fathom. Nevertheless, approximately two million Op-Yops were sold that year before the product sank like a stone in 1969.

BIBLIOGRAPHY

"Fads; Return of the Oldies," *Time*. 92 (October 11, 1968) 87. il.

Paper Dolls

Paper dolls, as we know them today, were first sold in Germany, France, and England in 1790. Early on, sheets of them were bound together in sets, resembling our paper doll books. Because they had to be tinted by hand, the price was high.

Advertising proved to be a particularly fertile area for paper dolls. American firms employing them during the Victorian era included Bull Durham, Singer Sewing Machine Company, Spalding Sporting Goods, and William A. Rogers, Ltd. (silversmiths).

Refinements in color printing in 1880 brought about a drastic reduction in the cost of manufacturing paper dolls. As a result, newspapers and magazines began printing more and more of them. The *Chicago Record-Herald* started including them in 1901; soon many periodicals were utilizing them as a means of heightening reader interest, thereby ushering in the heyday for paper dolls.

The first magazine paper dolls were two series drawn by Sheila Young, Lettie Lane, and Betty Bonnet, which ran in the *Ladies' Home Journal* from 1908 through July 1915 (then followed by "Betty Bonnet's Dearest Dolls"). The *Ladies' Home Journal* also introduced the paper doll format of Rose O'Neill's Kewpies in 1909. A competing magazine, *McCall's*, also printed several notable series of paper dolls: Dolly Dimple, Billy Bumps, and others designed by Grace Drayton, whose plump children also appeared in ads for Campbell's Soups.

The continued association of paper dolls and advertising reflected the socio-economic mores of a bygone age. In the early decades of the twentieth century, most advertising was done in women's magazines or in newspapers; therefore, the bonuses–such as paper dolls–were of a kind to appeal to females of all ages.

The rise of new media in the post-World War I years–first radio, and then television–provided new advertising outlets catering to a broader demographic audience. Accordingly, paper dolls receded in importance, as they became relegated primarily to paper doll books.

Most of these volumes consisted of several dolls–generally celebrities of one sort or another (e.g., Queen Elizabeth, Shirley Temple, Blondie)–accompanied by dozens of interchangeable outfits. Coloring books, available for years at dime stores, also belong to this genre, and continue to be available up to the present day.

BIBLIOGRAPHY

Young, Helen. "Paper Dolls," In: *The Complete Book of Doll Collecting.* New York: Putnam, 1967. pp. 27-40. il.

Patches Worn on Women's Faces

The women's fashion of wearing patches was passed on from Great Britain during the final days of the reign of Charles I (d. 1625) to the English Colonies in Virginia, Maryland, and the Carolinas. One historian, Elizabeth McClellan, notes a reference to them in 1650:

> Our ladies have lately entertained a vain custom of spotting their faces out of affectation of a mole, to set off their beauty such as Venus had; and it is well if one black patch will serve to make their faces remarkable, for some fill their faces full of them, varied into all manner of shapes.

Patches remained popular well into George III's day, receiving further impetus from their association with the practice of powdering the hair. Despite the long life of this fashion, McClellan asserts that its more extreme manifestations, as described by Bulwer, were not likely seen in the Colonies:

> Her patches are of every cut,
> For pimples or for scars.
> Here's all the wandering planets' signs
> And some of the fixed stars;
> Already gummed to make them stick
> They need no other sky.

In fact, such satirical lines may well have reflected the beginnings of a large-scale public reaction against the patches vogue.

BIBLIOGRAPHY

McClellan, Elizabeth. *History of American Costume, 1607-1870*. New York: Tudor, 1937. il.

The Perky Girl

The "perky girl" persona dominated the first half of the 1960s, those euphoric Kennedy years when the world appeared awash with possibilities. She symbolized what being young, vibrant, and female were all about at the time. Jane and Michael Stern made the following assessment of her impact upon American society:

> She seems so frivolous now, when most people think of the sixties as a time of civil-rights protests and Vietnam anguish and LSD hallucinations. Unless you catch a television rerun of Marlo Thomas in "That Girl" or pick up a mid-sixties issue of *Cosmopolitan*, it is easy to forget how much her flibbertigibbet disposition defined an ideal of young womanhood back then. But the perky girl's influence on history cannot be dismissed. Although she quickly seemed obsolete in a decade that yearned for *issues*, her vigor got things off to a running start. The perky girl was proof that a new decade had begun.

In her heyday, the perky girl was everywhere. Combining the physical image of youth and diminutive beauty with an irresistible zest for life, she was in TV sitcoms (e.g., Mary Tyler Moore in both *The Dick Van Dyke Show* and *The Mary Tyler Moore Show*, Sally Field in both *Gidget* and *The Flying Nun*), films (e.g., Goldie Hawn in *Cactus Flower*, Jane Fonda in *Barefoot in the Park*, Audrey Hepburn in *Breakfast at Tiffany's*), fashion magazines (models like Jean Shrimpton and Twiggy), planes (stewardesses were generally chosen according to criteria epitomizing the perky girl profile), the toy industry (the Barbie doll may have been the perkiest character of all), and the radio (singers like Joanie Sommers and Shelley Fabares).*

---

*Ironically enough, perhaps the best proponent of perkiness within the music field, Cyndi Lauper, came along some 20 years later, incorporating just enough of the street-smart punk ethic to appear contemporary.

Based upon these models, a number of indicators emerged to help define perky girl status. These included:

- the hairstyle of choice being either "the bubble" (lightly teased to achieve a roundish effect) or "the flip" (hair cut all one length with ends flipped up evenly all around the circumference);
- a lemon scent;
- large, false eyelashes;
- "lively legs" panty hose with patterns and textures;
- mini skirts;
- bikinis;
- costume jewelry; and
- the pill.

In order to achieve the look and spirit of perkiness, girls of the time had the perfect guidebook, Helen Gurley Brown's *Sex and the Single Girl*, published in 1962. An international best-seller, later made into a film starring Natalie Wood and Tony Curtis, it helped create the new feminine ideal of the young, freewheeling girl who mesmerized men with her uninhibited antics. When Brown assumed editorship of the formerly staid *Cosmopolitan*, she continued her proselytizing for the perky sensibility.

While the growing inclination of Americans toward more topical forms of popular culture helped date the perky girl, she appears to have been a victim of her own successful formula. As noted by Sterns, perkiness came more and more to signify abnormality (e.g., flying nuns; witchy housewives as in the TV show, *Bewitched*; genies such as the one played by Barbara Eden in *I Dream of Jeannie*): "As the sixties got freakier and extravagant behavior became more common (among hippies, for instance), ordinary perky girls were ever more limited in their ability to turn heads." To this day, the excesses of this persona taint efforts at appreciating any of its positive qualities (witness Sally Fields' "you like me" address upon receipt of her second Oscar for Best Actress).

BIBLIOGRAPHY

Stern, Jane, and Michael Stern. "Perky Girls," In: *Sixties People*. New York: Knopf, 1990. pp. 6-33. il.

Field, Sally
Rollin, B. "TV's Sally Field: The Flying Nun," *Look.* 31 (November 14, 1967)
M18-20ff. il.

Moore, Mary Tyler
Bowers, J. "From TV to Tiffany's in One Wild Leap," *Saturday Evening Post.*
239 (November 19, 1966) 97-101. il.
Gordon, S. "America's Favorite TV Wife," *Look.* 28 (April 21, 1964) M9-M10ff. il.
"Personality Girl," *Newsweek.* 68 (August 1, 1966) 78. il.

Thomas, Marlo
Rollin, B. "Marlo Thomas: That Girl is Some Girl," *Look.* 31 (October 17, 1967)
124ff. il.

Pet Rocks

Pet rocks grew out of a barroom joke in 1975. After listening to friends complain about dogs that soiled the carpet, cats that clawed upholstery, and gerbils that simply reproduced out of control, Gary Dahl, then a 38-year-old Los Gatos, California-based adman, retorted, "I have a pet rock." The ensuing verbal sparring inspired Dahl to try out his idea on the gift market.

The rocks–approximately the size and shape of large eggs–were framed in excelsior inside cardboard carrying cases and retailed for four dollars apiece. Dahl purchased two and one-half tons of them from a Mexican beach and by November 1975 was sending 3,000 to 6,000 units daily to prestigious outlets throughout the U.S., including Macy's, Lord & Taylor, Liberty House, and Bloomingdale's. John Giesecke, a buyer for Nieman-Marcus in Dallas, noted at the time: "It's been a spectacular item. [Because we sold out the first day they went on sale] we've been flying them in from California."

According to *Newsweek*, the rocks' success owed much to the witty care-and-training manual which Dahl wrote and included in each package. Excerpts included:

- If the rock seems excited on first being introduced to a new home, "place it on some old newspapers. The rock will know what the paper is for and will require no further instruction."
- Information on teaching the rock to roll over (hills make good training sites), come to heel, and play dead.
- Advice that rocks are particularly good at sitting, lying, and playing dead, but that shaking hands is out.
- Rocks can be given attack training. In a mugging, "Reach into your pocket or purse, as though you were going to comply with the mugger's demands. Extract your pet rock. Shout the command, ATTACK. And bash the mugger's head in."

The pet rock continued to sell through the Christmas season and into early 1976. By spring, however, its momentum was spent and it disappeared into oblivion.

BIBLIOGRAPHY

"Hot Rocks," *Newsweek.* 86 (November 10, 1975) 95. il.

The Philly Cut

The Philly cut was a descendant of a 1930s style called the tapered cut. First employed by Philadelphia Black Muslims, it evolved into two lengths during the 1960s–a high "English" (high taper) and a low "English" (low taper)–both of which approximated the black crew cut, a style also popular at the time with non-Muslim blacks. The name was applied by Washington D.C. blacks who frequently visited the City of Brotherly Love for purposes of both work and play.

In the 1970s, the style took on more accentuated characteristics such as sharp edges and high tops. It became associated with Go-Go groups centered in D.C. during the 1980s. When this percussive brand of dance funk attained worldwide popularity due to the recordings of Trouble Funk, Chuck Brown & The Soul Searchers, Redds & The Boys, and other bands, the Philly cut reached a wider audience.

In recent years, the Philly has permutated into many forms, including a skinhead cut which has grown out on top and a sculpted Afro (e.g., Grace Jones). Urban black youth have popularized special touches such as long tapered V's at the back of the head and many parallel cuts shaved into the hair just above the ears. The style continues to remain in favor thanks to the visibility provided by college basketball players, pop musicians, and notable celebrities like Olympian Carl Lewis and heavyweight boxing champ Mike Tyson.

BIBLIOGRAPHY

Jones, Dylan. "The Philly Cut," In: *Haircults: Fifty Years of Styles and Cuts.* New York: Thames and Hudson, 1990. p. 109. il.

Go-Go (music genre)
Barol, Bruce. "Going Crazy Over Go-Go" *Newsweek.* 105 (June 17, 1985) 77. il.
Fricke, David. "Go-Go!" *Rolling Stone.* (June 20, 1985) 12ff. il.

Pierced Ears

Pierced Ears for wearing earrings caught on in a big way during the 1960s. Piercing was actually in vogue during the nineteenth century in America. The practice became rare, however, following the invention of clip-on and screw-type earrings around the turn of the century. The 1950s saw a moderate return to piercing, and it began making a significant impact in the fashion world in 1963. By 1965, pierced ears had become a full-fledged style explosion, filtering down from the college-age set to younger teens.

Testaments to the popularity of pierced ears could be found everywhere:

- In 1963, Beverly Hills jeweler Marvin Hime was lucky to unload ten pairs of pierced earrings per week; two years later, the number soared to over 100.
- At a Houston high school, a mere handful of girls had punctured lobes in spring 1965; by fall, 30 percent had them.
- Griffith Jewelers, based in Providence, Rhode Island, enjoyed steady, albeit modest, sales of quality pierced earrings dating back to the Civil War era. Sales were averaging $250,000 a year in 1962 when a market survey of colleges alerted the company to the potential of piercing. As a result of aggressive marketing, its sales reached $1 1/4 million in 1966.
- Wells, Inc., of Attleboro, Massachusetts sold its first earrings in 1960, adding a line of the pierced variety three years later. By 1967, the latter accounted for 20 percent of its annual overall sales of ten million dollars and were available in 700 different styles.

Pierced ears, and the earrings made for them, offered a variety of attractions to users–and potential users. College girls–credited by some for bringing the fad back from Europe as a result of junior-year-abroad programs–considered the custom, as well as its hard-ware, to be erotic. It also represented an assertion of individuality and an escape from confining conventionality for young girls. One female noted, "It started with kids away at school as a kind of rebellion that wouldn't be allowed at home. All the upperclassmen had pierced ears. So when you arrived, you did it, too." For some, this rebelliousness was somewhat muted. A secretary noted in *Business Week*, "They have such cute earrings for pierced ears. They're daintier. Besides, I want to be a little bit different."

Perhaps most significant of all, the pierced style made possible a greater number of choices than clip-ons or screw-ons. A pair could be constructed from a bit of wire and any small bangle, bead, etc. Many boutiques made their own to capitalize on shifting consumer tastes. Jewelers also could convert clip-ons and screw-ons into the pierced type.

Consumers also found that they were harder to lose. Pierced earrings couldn't be knocked off and the inconvenience of taking them off–combined with the fact that they were more comfortable to wear–precluded leaving them behind in phone booths, public restrooms, etc.

Jewelers were quick to respond to heightened interest in pierced earrings. One noted, "They're definitely the hottest thing. Girls are not satisfied with one, two, three pairs. They keep building up. It's been a gold mine for us." Many stores began offering free ear piercing (others provided it along with a purchase of earrings). They also sold "sleepers," tiny gold hooplike wires that pierce the lobe gradually if worn approximately one week. Soon teenagers began bringing their mothers and grandmothers in to get their ears pierced.

The custom has remained highly popular up to the present day. Pierced earrings began turning up in other mainstream retail outlets by the late 1960s; e.g., shoe stores, bookstores, museum gift shops. As women became more involved in strenuous physical activities, they saw further practical benefits to pierced earrings. The jewelry industry, anxious to maintain its hegemony in the market, began upgrading them into the higher-priced areas formerly dominated by watches and engagement rings. The practice received yet another boost with the dawn of new wave fashions as youthful males began reviving the ancient tradition (best remembered in old pirate films) of piercing one ear.

BIBLIOGRAPHY

"Airy Lobes," *Time*. (October 15, 1965) 70. il.
"Pierced Ears Thrill Girls and Jewelers," *Business Week*. (June 3, 1967) 100-101. il.
"Remarkable Return of Pierced Ears," *Changing Times*. 20 (January 1966) 30. il.

Pigs

In the early 1980s, the farmyard pig *(Sus domestica)* seemed to be displacing the cat as a national object of attention. Retailers across the nation–including specialty shops like Hog Wild in Boston, the Hogography chain in Arkansas and Hogs & Kisses in San Francisco–offered a vast array of merchandise concerned with the porker, such as greeting cards, books, posters, clothes, games, stuffed toys, jewelry, office accessories (e.g., oinkwells), and bumper stickers (e.g., Have you hugged a pig today?). Charlotte Iwata at Homeworks in Santa Monica, California noted, "Cats were in for a long time. Then there was a rush for penguins and polar bears. Alligators came and went, thank God. Unicorns still have a small contingent. But pigs are in the lead." Bill Zwecker, owner of a Chicago gift shop, Animal Accents, concurred, "Pigs, like owls, will be a long-term thing."

Greeting and invitation cards were by far the most pervasive form of pigophilia. The leader in this field was the American Postcard Co., whose Pig Line depicted preening porkers in human clothing and human situations. Featuring characters such as the Easter Pig, the Ballerina Pig, and Calvin Swine (in designer jeans), the cards had sold over three million by mid-1982.

Pig books also sold very well. Notable examples included *Pigs: A Troughful of Treasures* (by Lucinda Vardey and Sarah Bowman; published by Macmillan) and *Pigs in Love* (Clarkson N. Potter), a racy paperback cartoon book by Revilo about Porkov and Daisy, whose amours were described as "an adult love story for pigs and sows everywhere." Another popular work was *The Pig-Out Diet Book* (Bacon Printing Co.) by two New England doctors who prescribed a regimen of no breakfast or lunch followed by a "pig-out" dinner.

Fans included Betty Talmadge, ex-wife of former Georgia Senator Herman Talmadge and author of *How to Cook a Pig*; Charles

Braverman, a Chicago commodities trader who had collected such items as a $2,000 brass pig dinner bell, a $2,400 pig ashtray and a 100-pound lead pig located in front of his home; and David Mercer, owner of Hog Wild!, who mailed the *Hogalog* catalogue advertising his "Pork Avenue Collection" to 30,000 subscribers at one dollar apiece.

The pig wasn't always so popular, and–in many cultures–remains associated with greed, stupidity, fascism, and filth. On the other hand, the boar was once regarded as a symbol of strength and the sow as the embodiment of fertility. Writers like Shelley and Dr. Johnson have praised the species. The animal's more recent vogue– which began in the 1970s–appeared harder to ascertain. Some of the testimonials from the period offered a few clues:

- Sarah Bowman: "The love of pigs is an inborn thing. I have always thought the wallowing was a nice quality."
- Revilo: "Pigs really know how to live."
- William Hedgepath, author of *The Hog Book*: "Perhaps, say some, the hog artfully mirrors the pathos of the country itself: huge, heroic, maladroit, and always straining toward some elusive dream underneath yet another clod of dirt."

Whatever the reasons, the appeal of pigs has proved to be long-lasting. They have remained a staple subject in souvenir shops, bookstores, and show business (e.g., Miss Piggy of the Muppets) up to the present day.

BIBLIOGRAPHY

Demarest, M. "Getting High on the Hog," *Time*. 119 (May 24, 1982) 69. il.

The Pill

In the early 1960s, birth control pills became so popular that *Newsweek* dubbed that period the "Age of the Pill." Following their introduction into the marketplace in 1961, the number of U.S. women taking the oral contraceptives at a rate of 20 pills a month had risen to approximately five million in 1965 (see Figure 1).

FIGURE 1. U.S. Women Using the Pill*

1961	500,000
1962	1,000,000
1963	2,000,000
1964	4,000,000
1965	5,000,000
1966	6,000,000

*Figures represent rough approximations

The eight competing brands on the market by the mid-1960s–Enovid, Ovulen, Ortho-Novum, Norlestrin, Dracon, Norinyl, Provest, and C-Quens–all offered the following advantages to users:

1. convenience;
2. relative effectiveness (99 to 100 percent) in preventing pregnancy; and
3. positive side effects for some (e.g., weight gains, clearing up of skin).

Nevertheless, concerns over the safety of the pill continued to linger, despite the release of a 21-page report by the Food and Drug Administration's Advisory Committee on Obstetrics and Gynecology in mid-1966 which found no adequate scientific data proving it dangerous to human health. Critics noted defects in the report:

1. Some drug companies had made detailed investigations of alleged side effects, others had not.
2. The committee was hampered by inaccurate estimates of the disease rates among the general population which were used to compare with rates among women taking the pills.
3. The drugs had not been in use long enough to tell whether they had any long-range side effects.

In addition, various temporary conditions–reversible when use of the pill was stopped–had been documented by doctors in some patients; e.g., abnormal liver functions, acne, hirsutism. The pill also was found to aggravate migraine headaches.

Given the cautious optimism of most doctors and the FDA, more and more women began using the pill, leading in no small part to the much ballyhooed sexual revolution as well as a full-fledged media bonanza. Movies, television programs, publications, and popular songs appeared in the late 1960s and early 1970s which documented the social impact of the pill. As medical evidence continued to surface attesting to its overall safety–combined with gradually changing cultural mores–the pill became the birth control instrument of choice among American women. Despite the peripheral use of various alternative methods of birth control (e.g., vasectomies, the diaphragm), the preeminence of the pill appeared unchallenged well into the 1990s.

BIBLIOGRAPHY

"Birth-Control Pills; Safe, But–," *U.S. News & World Report.* 67 (September 15, 1969) 10.
"Doubts About the Pill," *Newsweek.* 73 (May 19, 1969) 118. il.
"Freedom from Fear; the Pill," *Time.* 89 (April 7, 1967) 78-80ff. il.
"Pill: Cloudy Verdict; FDA Report," *Newsweek.* 74 (September 15, 1969) 90.
"Pill for Men?" *Newsweek.* 74 (July 14, 1969) 62. il.
"Popular, Effective, Safe," *Newsweek.* 68 (August 22, 1966) 92. il.
"Pros and Cons of the Pill" *Time.* 93 (May 2, 1969) 58ff. il.

Plugging Products on the Silver Screen

The memorable scene from *E.T.*, in which the lovable alien followed a line of Reese's Pieces laid down by the film's young hero–causing sales of the candy to leap 66 percent in three months during 1982–almost singlehandedly rendered movie pitches a lucrative field. Giving products visibility on the big screen is hardly a new development. As noted by J. D. Reed, "Joan Crawford knocked back Jack Daniel's in *Mildred Pierce*, and Rosalind Russell dabbed on Charles of the Ritz perfume in *Auntie Mame* (1958)." Following *E.T.*, however, show business and big business appeared equally inclined to place brand names on the big screen.

A dozen or so agencies have sprung up to help companies find scenes for their products in suitable upcoming films, charging stiff fees upwards of $50,000. "A movie goes from theaters to TV to the video marketplace which makes it far more profitable than a one-shot on *Dynasty*," argued Cliff McMullen of UPP Entertainment Marketing in late 1988. The eagerness of companies to go this route appeared to support McMullen's contention. Everyone wished to repeat the success enjoyed by Ray-Ban, whose classic Wayfarer model sunglasses had a 300 percent jump in sales on the heels of Tom Cruise's shaded performance in *Risky Business*; the company's Aviator line then went on to experience a 40 percent increase in sales during the seven months after Cruise wore them in *Top Gun*.

Cost-conscious movie studios in turn created licensing and merchandising departments to facilitate such deals. Director John Badham, who incorporated Alaska Airlines, Apple computers, Bounty paper towels, and Ore-Ida frozen french fries into his film, *Short Circuit*, noted, "If we can help each other, and it doesn't intrude on the movie, it's fine." He added, "Movie budgets have become unreasonably high, so we're always looking to maximize the money available."

Given these budgeting constraints, it appeared likely that the studios would continue to be receptive to plugging products for some time to come. In 1989, for instance, James Bond fans were treated to the spectacle of their hero driving a Lincoln Continental Mark VII rather than his famous Aston Martin in the latest installment of the long running series, *License to Kill*.

BIBLIOGRAPHY

Reed, J. D., and Elaine Dutka. "Plugging Away in Hollywood," *Time*. (January 2, 1989) 103. il.

Ponytails for Men

Ponytails on men, thanks to the long-established Puritan moral aesthetic,* could never be viewed in America as a routine fashion trend. As noted by John Berendt, "They are highly charged symbols, and the men who wear them are trying to tell us something. . . . The one thing they all have in common is that they confront a basically hostile world."

The practice of wearing a ponytail evolved out of the long-hair-for-men movement of the 1960s. It certainly had its practical side; that is, keeping one's hair out of the way due to reasons of hygiene (e.g., food preparation), comfort (e.g., hot weather), aesthetics (to instantly achieve a different look), etc. From a gesture of radical chic among maturing hippies–and later, laid-back rednecks–in the 1970s, its appeal spread to ever-widening sectors of the male population during the following decade. Teenagers adopted the look because it struck them as a rebellion against adult standards; in reality, however, it was a gesture of conformity in that its universal popularity rendered them one of the crowd. For middle-aged males, it took on the role of low-keyed nonconformity. Without actively sending out a message, they revealed a willingness to appear a bit different from the rank and file.

Berendt noted an interesting spinoff of the latter group, the disillusioned yuppie, as personified by their cultural icon, Kevin Costner.

> Head-on, they appear to be the clean-cut Babbitts they've always been; it's when they turn to leave that you notice the ponytail. They are informing you discreetly that they are not

---

*The Puritan roots were established in large part by Elizabethan pamphleteer William Prynne, who in *The Unlovelinesse of Love-Lockes,* damned long hair as unnatural for men and blamed it on "this Vaine, Fantastique, Idle, Proud, Effeminate, and wanton age."

Gordon Gekko anymore, that part of them really does care, deeply–about the ecology, about the homeless, about Native Americans. They can't quite get it together to do anything about these concerns, but at least they've got the outfit.

By the 1990s, the trend had reached truly faddish proportions, stoked by an endless parade of movie stars and fashion magazine ads with megastars such as Sean Connery, Robert DeNiro, and Marlon Brando sporting ponytails. Men wore ponytails as a means of looking hipper or attempting to recapture their youth (i.e., a ponytail in back as compensation for the loss of hair on top). By 1991, wigmaker Louis Feder had even introduced clip-on ponytails for the impatient or fainthearted interested in weekend nonconformity from within the privacy of their own homes. More than ever before, the practice appeared on the brink of losing credibility among its original constituency, thereby consigning it to an inevitable oblivion.

BIBLIOGRAPHY

Berendt, John. "Ponytails and Earrings," *Esquire.* 116:3 (September 1991) 57-59. il.
Mitchell, E. "The Long and Short of It," *Time.* 136 (December 10, 1990) 74. il.

Prince Charles Cut

By the early 1960s, an increasing number of mothers had become less enamored of the crewcut look which had dominated the previous decade and opted for a shaggier style for their young boys. The most preferred cut of the day was modeled after the hair style worn by the just-turned-teenager Prince Charles of Great Britain. It feature a forward-oblique movement of the hair that fell over (and midway down) the forehead. It was several inches long on top while tapering into the barest trace of a ducktail in back. Barbers–eschewing clippers in the cutting process–created a feathered effect over the ears and allowed the sideburns to become rather full.

Many barbers of that era questioned naming it the "Prince Charles Cut." Tristan of Hollywood termed it "only a variation on the Buster Brown Cut and the style I myself invented for Edd [Kookie] Byrnes." Michael Fiscella, proprietor of Michael's Children's Hair Cutting Salon (New York City), noted, "I gave my first Prince Charles Cut over 30 years before the royal young gentleman was born. It was called the 'French Cut' then but the new name is just as apt." F. B. Hollett, owner of a barber school in Washington, D.C., argued that it should be called the "Ivy League Cut" and credited then President Kennedy with inspiring it.

Whatever its origins, the style remained highly fashionable up to 1964. *Newsweek* noted that half the boys' haircuts given to five-year-olds and under at San Francisco's Hotel Mark Hopkins by late 1962 were Prince Charles Cuts. However, the rise of Beatlemania hastened the style's fall from favor as youths of all ages begged and cajoled their parents to permit them to imitate the luxuriant moptops worn by the Fab Four.

BIBLIOGRAPHY

"Hair Apparent," *Newsweek.* 60 (December 3, 1962) 62-63. il.

Raggedy Ann and Raggedy Andy

Raggedy Ann and Raggedy Andy are the most popular rag dolls ever. Their look has not changed in any discernable way over three generations: the shoe-button eyes, wide smiles, ragged red yarn hair, red- and white-striped socks, and the little red heart which bears the printing, "I Love You." Likewise, Ann still wears a blue and white print dress and Andy a checked shirt and blue cotton trousers.

Their creator, Johnny Gruelle, started out as a political cartoonist in 1889. Years later he found a badly worn rag doll–its face obliterated–in the attic. He sketched on a new face and gave the doll to his young daughter, calling it Raggedy Ann after the poem, Little Orphan Annie, by his friend James Whitcomb Riley. When entreated to make a companion for Ann, Riley's "Raggedy Man" provided the impetus for the name, Raggedy Andy.

Gruelle utilized the name and character of Raggedy Ann in a cartoon he drew for the *New York World*. At this time, in 1918, his book, *Raggedy Ann Stories*, was published. Its great success led to *Raggedy Andy Stories* (1920) and 20-odd other books in the series which together sold more than 10 million copies prior to Gruelle's death in 1938.

The early volumes spurred the mass production of the two dolls. Like the later Cabbage Patch phenomenon, the ease in constructing them caused a good many Raggedy Anns and Andys to be made at home by mothers and grandmothers as well. The twosome have remained big sellers into the present decade even though they exhibit none of the state-of-the-art features typifying more recently created competitors.

BIBLIOGRAPHY

Hudson, Patricia L. "Still Smiling at Seventy-Five: What a Doll! For Her Diamond Jubilee, Raggedy Ann and Creator Johnny Gruelle Have Earned a Rousing Hoosier Salute," *Americana*. 18 (December 1990) 52ff. il. Includes a related article on Raggedy Ann memorabilia.

Jailer, Mildred. "Happy Birthday Raggedy Ann & Andy," *Antiques & Collecting Hobbies*. 93 (December 1988) 51ff. il.

"Raggedy Ann; Still Flouncy at Fifty," *Life*. 57 (December 18, 1968) 4. il.

Young, Helen. "Fabric Dolls," In: *The Complete Book of Doll Collecting*. New York: Putnam, 1967. pp. 41-54. il.

The Rice Diet

The Rice Diet ran contrary to the traditional rules governing food and weight reduction; i.e., it was a high-carbohydrate, low-protein diet. The diet was developed in the late 1930s and early 1940s by Walter Kempner, M.D., then a member of the Duke University School of Medicine faculty, with the aim of assisting patients suffering from critical kidney disease. The menu of cooked rice, fruit, sugar, and tea provided patients with a minimum of protein and salt to process. Test results reported by Kempner in the *North Carolina Medical Journal* in April 1944 indicated that the blood pressure of patients employing the diet dropped to normal, and electrocardiograms revealed that their hearts had returned to normal size and functioning as well.

As early as 1945, Kempner–noting the side benefit of weight loss on such a diet–started utilizing it with obese individuals solely to help them thin down. Results proved spectacularly successful in this respect. Folk singer-actor Burl Ives went to Duke twice in four years and lost 80 pounds each time; the high-protein diets he had tried prior to that time had produced weak results.

Success stories such as this led to many popularizations of the rice diet. A typical version, which ran in the summer 1973 issue of *Epicure*, went as follows:

> Each meal consists of: 8 ounces of fruit juice (minus sugar); 3 ounces fruit (raw, baked, canned, stewed, from a selected list); and 1/3 of a pound (raw weight) rice, cooked. Three meals can be divided into six. Mustard, herbs, horseradish, and pepper are allowed for seasoning. But absolutely *no* salt.

The rice diet had the advantage of being easy to prepare. In addition, its blandness tended to work in its favor by discouraging overeating. Those using the diet also reported that it kept down hunger pangs as the next mealtime rolled around. The medical fraternity was favorably disposed because of the "protein-sparing effect of carbohydrates."

On the other hand, the aforementioned blandness required a great deal of willpower in order to stay with the diet for the long haul. Nevertheless, it has remained popular into the 1990s, aided by the fact that rice has become far more familiar to Americans as a starch substitute than was the case immediately following World War II.

BIBLIOGRAPHY

Bulletin of the Walter Kempner Foundation. Durham, North Carolina. 4:1 (June 1972) entire issue.

Kempner, Walter. "Radical Dietary Treatment of Hypertensive and Arteriosclerotic Vascular Disease, Heart and Kidney Disease, and Vascular Retinopathy," *GP.* 9 (March 1954) 71-93.

Kidwell, Claudia Brush, and Valerie Steele. *Men and Women; Dressing the Part.* Washington: Smithsonian Institution, 1989.

"McCall's Diet of the Month. April: Remember the Rice Diet?" *McCall's.* 97 (April 1970) 32-34. il.

"A Mini-Dictionary of Diets," *Epicure.* (Summer 1973) 56.

Rollerblades

At the onset of the 1990s, Rollerblades were the bright new hope for future growth in the sporting-goods industry. Industry experts predicted that blades would soon overtake the $350 million alpine-ski-boot market. Unlike conventional skates, with their side-by-side wheel configuration, "in-line" blades feature a single row of polyure-thane rollers. Handling more like ice skates than the rigid, clunky design of traditional roller skates, the blades proved to be faster and more maneuverable.

The Rollerblade concept originated in the Netherlands for racing on land. It was then adapted for summer hockey training in the U.S. by two former high school players based in Minneapolis, Scott and Brennan Olson. Their company, started in a garage in 1980, ulti-mately became Rollerblade Inc.

In 1987, Rollerblade Inc. decided there was a market for skates as a fitness product. The blades were slimmed down and painted a fashionable neon. The company next launched a secret marketing strategy; in view of the fact that trends frequently started and spread quickly in California, it gave away large numbers of Rollerblades to skate-rental shops along the beach in Los Angeles.

The gambit proved successful. Blading took off in California (Rollerblade Inc. still does about 25 percent of its business there) and quickly spread across the country. Rosa Hallowell noted in 1990, "The whole lakefront in Chicago is covered with Roller-blades. Every weekend it's a battle between the cyclists and the bladers." By the early 1990s, Rollerblade Inc. controlled more than 70 percent of the market, with sales having zoomed from three million dollars in 1987 to a projected 40 million dollars in 1990. Other leading manufacturers included Vermont-based Canstar, which marketed the Bauer brand, and Minnesota's First Team Sports, the maker of Ultra Wheels.

Thomas Doyle, research director for the National Sporting

Goods Association, noted two reasons for the popularity of blading: "It's a natural fitness activity, and the price is right." (The cost, as of 1990, varied from $100 for basic in-line skates to $330 for pump-up Racerblades, which had five wheels rather than the usual four.) In addition, the activity–unlike male-dominated sports such as bicycle racing and skateboarding–was popular among women. The appeal of blading to females included its sociability, its toning qualities for the lower body, and the likelihood of fewer injuries due to lessened pounding (compared to traditional skates, jogging, etc.). The activity's primary hazards–stopping at high speeds and impact injuries–were at least partially alleviated by the presence of rear-mounted brakes (which required lots of practice to use) and by wearing protective clothing (e.g., helmets, hand and knee guards).

The growing popularity of the sport had also given rise to a new subculture by the 1990s, complete with its own slang vocabulary. David Gross observed that "Bladers hang out with rollerbuddies (friends) who prowl the asphalt in an eternal quest for greased turf (smooth pavement) and try to avoid rollerblood (injuries) at all costs."

BIBLIOGRAPHY

Graver, F. "My Life as a Trend," *Esquire*. 116 (July 1991) 54ff. il.

Gross, David M. "Zipping Along in Asphalt Heaven," *Time*. 136 (August 13, 1990) 56. il.

"In-Line Skates: They Aren't Just For Kids," *Consumer Reports*. 56 (August 1991) 515. il.

Mitchell, E. "Whiz! Zoom! Crash! Ouch!" *Time*. 137 (June 10, 1991) 75.

Therrien, L. "Rollerblade is Skating in Heavier Traffic," *Business Week*. (June 24, 1991) 114-115. il.

"Wheels in Line and on a Roll," *National Geographic World*. 188 (April 1991) 4-8. il.

Rompers

Rompers or creepers–a one-piece garment with gathered leg openings and buttons or snaps closing the crotch–became the status quo in infant wear, particularly as daytime play outfits, in the early twentieth century. Originally introduced in the 1890s as playclothing for older children, they soon were made available for babies as well.

Rompers represented a departure from traditional infants' clothing–most notably dresses, which from then on would be employed only for formal occasions–in two key respects: (1) they were bifurcated, and (2) they were usually constructed out of colored fabrics (e.g., solid blues and reds, gingham checks in pink, red, and blue, and blue or gray ticking stripes). These characteristics were in keeping with the times in that they signaled the acceptance of the concept of infants' individuality and allowed parents to dress their babies in costumes regarded as appropriate to each child's personality and activities.

Rompers also played an important role in terminating the centuries-old tradition of genderless costumes for babies. While the garment was initially unisex in nature, each sex wore it for different reasons: little boys because their parents considered dresses unmanly, and little girls because they needed a practical alternative for play. By mid-century, however, modern sexual conventions for baby clothes had taken hold (e.g., pink for girls, blue for boys, differentiated pictorial motifs and trim such as baseballs for boys and lace embroidery for girls); rompers led the way in reflecting this trend.

Despite the ubiquitousness of rompers, dresses remained a staple item in infant wardrobes well into the twentieth century. As late as the early 1950s, infant boys still wore them, although rompers–as well as competing forms of clothing like overalls and footed sleepers–were far more common. Given the modern day emphasis upon

variety and practicality in baby clothing, rompers are likely to remain a fixture for many years to come.

BIBLIOGRAPHY

Kidwell, Claudia Brash, and Valerie Steele, editors. *Men and Women; Dressing the Part*. Washington: Smithsonian Institution, 1989.

Rubik's Cube

By late 1981, Rubik's Cube was being hailed as one of the most popular, albeit infuriating, playthings ever marketed. In just seven years–it was developed in 1974 by Erno Rubik, a Hungarian architecture professor, to provide his students greater experience in dealing with three-dimensional objects–sales surpassed 30 million worldwide. A vice president for the Ideal Toy Corp., which made the item under an agreement with a Hungarian manufacturing company, exclaimed at the time, "It's phenomenal. Every month we pinch ourselves and say it won't last, but the cube is still selling like nothing else." A senior buyer for FAO Schwarz, the Manhattan toy emporium, noted that it had become "the world's most asked-for plaything."

Described in *Time* magazine as "a brightly colored plastic widget that could have been designed by Mondrian," it had six sides, each with a different bright color. Each side was divided into three rows, and each row into three smaller cubes ("cubies"). Each row could be made to rotate 360 degrees so as to enable the user to manipulate the cube from top to bottom or from side to side. When the three-by-three-by-three cube was first purchased, all nine squares on each face were aligned to make a solid color–one red, one yellow, etc. The aim was to scramble the colors and then to manipulate them back the way they were. The number of potential color patterns was 43,252,003,274,489,856,000, and it was estimated that the most advanced computer of the time would take 1.4 million years to figure out all the possible combinations. Some competitors sought to realign the puzzle in a minimum of moves (most notably, scientists), others–particularly young users–went for speed records (one high school student was alleged to have solved the puzzle in a mere 28 seconds).

The appeal of the cube appeared to lie in the challenge posed by attempting to unscramble it; some, however, argued that it could lead to obsessive behavior. One woman, who gave her husband the puzzle for Christmas, sought a divorce because he ended up spending all of his time with it. No matter, Rubik's Cube proved so successful that it spawned a bountiful and profitable array of sequels, spinoffs, and literary works. Ideal itself capitalized on the cube's success with the following spinoffs:

- Rubik's Revenge, which has 16 tiles on a side, instead of nine.
- Rubik's Pocket Cube, a simpler version aimed at children.
- Rubik's World, a globe made of 26 sections that twisted apart.
- Rubik's Game, a three-dimensional pegboard.
- Rubik's Race, a two-player game in which the multicolored tiles must duplicate various patterns.
- Calendar Cube, which required manipulating the tiles every day to form the correct date.

Rubik also came out with Son of Cube, a three-dimensional twister called the Magic Snake, which could assume the shape of a swan, saxophone, or steamroller. F.A.O. Schwarz sold out its initial shipment of almost 1,000 in a week. Other companies manufactured and distributed versions in the shape of pyramids, octagons, cylinders, etc., while pirated editions turned up in places like Taiwan and Hong Kong as well as in some American cities.

Within the publishing realm, there were also countless success stories. *The Simple Solution to Rubik's Cube*, a 64-page booklet authored by Stamford chemist James Nourse, became the fastest-selling title in the history of Bantam Books with more than seven million copies sold, topping the best-seller lists in the U.S. and around the world. Penguin Books sold 1.2 million copies of Patrick Bossert's *You Can Do the Cube*. Bossert also released a half-hour video cassette that demonstrated his cube-twirling technique. Ideal's solution booklet was also a big seller as was the Cambridge University Press's *Conquer That Cube*. David Singmaster's *Notes on Rubik's "Magic Cube"* went into five editions, becoming an unofficial repository of the puzzle's lore.

Books fueling the inevitable cube backlash also did well, including Ballantine's *Not Another Cube Book* (in which Steven and Roger Hill tell readers "How to Live with a Cubaholic" and "How to Kick the Habit"), *You Can Kick the Cube* and Tor's *101 Uses for a Dead Cube.* Bookseller John May noted, "The cube phenomenon is the biggest thing of its kind we have ever experienced. Books on the cube are selling like mad."

Rubik himself took a leave of absence from his teaching post to help Ideal organize a world cube-twisting championship which took place in spring 1982. However, the puzzle's popularity had peaked by this time. A victim of overexposure, the cube had receded into the background by late 1982. It has yet to be revived to any notable degree up to the present day.

BIBLIOGRAPHY

"Hot-Selling Hungarian Horror," *Time.* 117 (March 23, 1981) 83. il.

Hauptfuhrer, F. "Obscure Hungarian Professor Transforms America into a Nation of Cubic Rubes," *People Weekly.* 16 (September 28, 1981) 30-33. il.

Keerdoja, E. "Rubikmania: Lots of New Twists," *Newsweek.* 99 (April 19, 1982) 16ff. il.

"A Patent Puzzle Over Rubik's Cube," *Business Week.* (August 2, 1982) 26. il.

"Rubikmania," *Time.* 118 (December 7, 1981) 62. il.

Warshofsky, F. "Rubik's Cube: Madness for Millions," *Readers' Digest.* 118 (May 1981) 137-140. il.

Saddle Shoes

Saddle shoes were first manufactured by Spalding in 1906 as an accessory for tennis and squash. The saddle was not initially conceived of with style in mind; it functioned as an orthopedic girdle that reinforced the instep and held the shoe together against the strain of fast starts and jolting stops. Tennis and squash players did not take to the shoe, however, in part, it appeared, due to the lurid color combination–mauve and red.

Saddle shoes finally caught on in the 1920s as a result of Spalding's decision to outfit the bottom with spikes and go after the golf market. Golfers at all levels–from duffers up to the likes of Bobby Jones–loved them. From there, they became the footwear of choice at the Ivy League colleges–now in the brown-and-white and black-and-white configurations. Irving Press, of J. Press clothiers, then a Yale undergraduate, recalled that saddle shoes were de rigueur, along with raccoon coats and white flannel trousers. "Saddle shoes were the forerunner of white bucks and dirty bucks. You didn't have to keep them terribly clean, but you *had* to have a pair."

Saddle shoes peaked in popularity during the 1930s and 1940s. Since then, however, they have had their ups and downs. But they remain a fixture on golf courses, particularly with the country club set.

BIBLIOGRAPHY

Berendt, John. "The Saddle Shoe," *Esquire*. (October 1988) 56. il.

The Vidal Sassoon Haircut

Swinging London–which dominated many facets of popular culture in the 1960s with Beatlemania, miniskirts, bell-bottoms, etc.–was the scene of one of the truly revolutionary developments in modern hair styling, the Vidal Sassoon haircut. His sculpted, chunky, blunt cut–boyishly short all over, exposing the nape of the neck, with sideburns sometimes forming points in front of the ears, occasionally asymmetrical (short and square on one side and long on the other)–was originally conceived for mannequins rather than people in 1961 as a result of Mary Quant's request that he fix their hair so it wouldn't interfere with the high collars she was showing in the dress shop Bazaar.

Sassoon's style caught on with those seeking the aura of the mod set without a great deal of expense or embarrassment (e.g., exposing heavy legs in a miniskirt). Nevertheless, the cut required perfectly straight hair, flawless bone structure, and firm facial muscles in order to flatter the wearer. Enough women on both sides of the Atlantic liked what they saw to enable Sassoon to open a chain of beauty parlors.

In this respect Sassoon was also a visionary. Whereas hair styling salons for women used to be hushed sanctuaries where attendants scurried about ministering to the rituals of glamour in a manner aimed to relax patrons, Sassoon made his salons mod, emulating discothèques in their hipness and sexiness. Good-looking, clearly heterosexual, male hairdressers in hip-hugger pants toted blow driers from their belts like six-guns, keeping in time to the best of contemporary rock hits while punctuating their routine with occasional caresses for the client such as a kiss on the neck or a squeeze on the thigh.

From here, Sassoon found success with his own lines of hair care accessories and beauty products. Despite his humble Cockney beginnings, Sassoon's name has come to embody the sort of mystique attained by only a select handful of figures in the fashion world.

BIBLIOGRAPHY

"Sassoon and His Scissors," *Life*. 59 (July 9, 1965) 67-68. il.
Stern, Jane, and Michael Stern. "I'm English," In: *Sixties People*. New York: Knopf, 1990. pp. 122-145. il.

The Scarsdale Medical Diet

The Scarsdale Medical Diet arose out of Dr. Herman Tarnower's involvement over the years in counseling patients to eat and drink sensibly as a means of weight control. He eventually had his suggestions typed up and mimeographed so as to save time. Ultimately, word of mouth awareness of the program was picked up by the mass media; newspaper and magazine articles spurred thousands of people to call or write Tarnower asking for information about the diet.

By the early 1960s, the Scarsdale Medical Diet was a nationwide phenomenon. Teachers in physical fitness classes distributed its essentials to students. Jogging groups took it up. Many restaurants began making the Diet a menu feature.

Testimonials sprang up everywhere:

- Alexandra Penney stated in *The New York Times*, "A vice president of Bloomingdale's was shown the printed diet by the owner of a fish restaurant, decided to try it, lost 20 pounds in 14 days and claims he was never hungry and never tired. . . ."
- *Westchester Magazine* ran an item on it noting, "A Diet People Are Talking About . . . 'as much as a twenty pound loss in two weeks is not unusual' . . . those who have tried it insist it's the only one that works."
- Anthony Dias Blue, in a report for *Sunday Woman*, termed it "The Ultimate Diet."

Tarnower eventually elaborated upon his ideas in a book, *The Complete Scarsdale Medical Diet Plus Dr. Tarnower's Lifetime Keep-Slim Program* (1978), in response to popular demand.

The Scarsdale Medical Diet contained six basic qualities considered by Tarnower to be most essential to success for the dieter:

1. safe nutritional balance;
2. rapid weight loss;
3. tasty, varied, and filling food choices;
4. simplicity and ease of understanding and preparation;
5. the beginning of behavior modification (i.e., learning good eating habits by following simple eating instructions); and
6. a practical diet flexible enough to allow for eating out in restaurants, other people's homes, etc.

The program consisted of two distinct stages: (1) the Scarsdale Medical Diet (SMD), which set forth a basic weight loss plan for adults (the cornerstone being the alteration of the typical American intake with respect to proteins–more than tripled to 43 percent; fats–cut almost in half; and carbohydrates–cut approximately 25 percent); and (2) the Keep-Trim Program (KTP), which provided for the maintenance of weight loss with a greatly expanded list of foods to choose from relative to the SMD. Tarnower advocated a Two-On-Two-Off system (i.e., two weeks on the SMD, followed by two on the KTP) with as many repetitions in the cycle as deemed necessary in order to achieve one's goal regarding weight loss.

Tarnower supplemented his various menus with some basic rules regarding the application of the diet.

1. Eat exactly what is assigned. No substitutions.
2. Don't drink any alcoholic beverages.
3. Between meals you eat only carrots and celery, but you may have as much as you wish.
4. The only beverages allowed are regular or decaffeinated coffee, black; tea; club sodas in all flavors. You may drink as often as you wish.
5. Prepare all salads without oil, mayonnaise, or other rich dressings. Use only lemon and vinegar, specified vinaigrette or mustard dressings, etc.
6. Eat vegetables without butter, margarine, or other fat; lemon may be used.
7. All meat should be very lean; remove all visible fat before eating. Remove skin and fat from chicken and turkey before eating.

8. It is not necessary to eat everything listed, but don't substitute or add. Indicated combinations should be observed.
9. Never overload your stomach. When you feel full, STOP!
10. Don't stay on the Diet more than fourteen days.

Unlike many popular diets, the Scarsdale program was generally accepted–if not wildly supported on the basis of its more inflated claims–by medical and dietary professionals due to its sound, reasoned advice, based upon time-honored nutritional concepts, as well as Tarnower's solid credentials. As a result, its popularity continued for decades.

The Diet attained further publicity, albeit of a notorious bent, when Tarnower was murdered in early 1980 by his former lover and research assistant, Jean Harris. In view of the doctor's alleged peccadillos, Harris elicited considerable public sympathy; nevertheless, she received a 15-year sentence following a lengthy court trial.

BIBLIOGRAPHY

The Scarsdale Diet

DeMoss, Virginia. "The Fad Diet Guide," *Runner's World.* 16 (May 1981) 41ff. il.
Tarnower, Herman, and Samm Sinclair Baker. *The Complete Scarsdale Medical Diet Plus Dr. Tarnower's Lifetime Keep-Slim Program.* New York: Rawson, Wade, 1978. il.

Death of Dr. Tarnower

Alexander, Shana. "Jean Harris's Defense Was Bungled, the Author Says, and Her 15-Year Sentence Was a Miscarriage of Justice," *Life.* 6 (March 1983) 64ff. il. Excerpted from *Very Much a Lady.*
Alexander, Shana. "The Ordeal of Jean Harris: A Matter of Integrity," *People Weekly.* 15 (March 9, 1981) 90ff. il.
Bernays, Anne. "Cad and Mouse," *The New Republic.* 184 (March 7, 1981) 9ff.
"Death of the Diet Doctor," *Time.* 115 (March 24, 1980) 27. il.
Haden-Guest, Anthony. "The Headmistress and the Diet Doctor," *New York.* 13 (March 31, 1980) 36ff. il.
"Harris: 'I Only Want to Die,' " *Newsweek.* 97 (March 9, 1981) 28. il.
" 'Integrity Jean' on Trial," *Newsweek.* 96 (December 8, 1980) 34ff. il.
Isaacson, Walter. "Murder With Intent to Love," *Time.* 117 (March 9, 1981) 20ff. il.
Isaacson, Walter. "The Things She Did For Love," *Time.* 117 (February 9, 1981) 29. il.

Langdon, Dolly, Patricia Reilly, and Martha Smilgis. "The Killing of Scarsdale Diet Doctor Herman Tarnower Leaves a Single Haunting Question: Why?" *People Weekly.* 13 (March 31, 1980) 40ff. il.

The Shapka

The streets of big cities north of the Mason-Dixon line were liberally interspersed with a new form of headgear during the winter months of 1961-1962: shapkas, or fur hats worn throughout Scandinavia and the former U.S.S.R. It became fashionable on a minor scale as far back as 1959, when Great Britain's Prime Minister was photographed wearing a white lamb's-wool version during a state visit to Moscow. Others were won over by actor Yul Brynner's use of a shapka in *The Brothers Karamazov*.

By now more venturesome Americans discovered that the shapka had some notable advantages over standard-issue felt hats: it was warm and comfortable. In addition, it was shapely and exuded a rather sophisticated air. Eventually, even men who were notoriously conservative about clothing had become convinced that the hat was acceptable despite its lingering associations with Communism and the cold war.

Committed to prolonging the boomlet, importers and U.S. manufacturers began supplying a wide array of styles, typically in greys, blacks, and browns, ranging in price from $3.95 for a bargain-basement ersatz fur to $85 for a karakul number. Popular versions included the cuffless Macmillan (also known as the Ambassador and the Astrakhan), the cuffed Alaskan (sometimes called the Troika and the Stockholm), and the round Pillbox (also known as the Detroit and the Arctic).

Women also followed suit; the most conspicuous new hat style on female heads that year was a high-fashion version of the shapka. Less squat and masculine than the styles worn by men, it looked like a furry coal scuttle.

The hat suffered a lapse in popularity the following year on the heels of the bad feelings toward all things Russian engendered by the Cuban missile crisis. Nevertheless, it has remained a relatively visible form of alternative headgear for men in the Northern states, particularly in wintertime, up to the present day.

BIBLIOGRAPHY

"The Shapka," *Time*. 79 (February 16, 1962) 55. il.

Short Shorts

By summer 1956 the wearing of shorts in public–not only by teenagers, but also by many thousands of older females–had become a permanent, accepted (and generally welcome) part of the American landscape. The phenomenon appeared to be the result of the growing informality of suburban living in an age increasingly preoccupied with leisure and play.

After years of limited popularity, short shorts were in high demand. Their acceptance derived from the vogue for knee-length Bermuda shorts, by then regarded by many women as a kind of "classic" that essentially served the same purpose as slacks. Short shorts also gained favor due to their comfort and because longer variants (e.g., the Jamaica and Bermuda styles) tended to emphasize the least attractive part of the legs–the knee and calf. They made such an impact that the Royal Teens' tribute song, "Short Shorts" (ABC-Paramount) became a Top Ten smash in early 1957.

While short shorts were worn virtually everywhere in America, some cities evoked ages-old ordinances governing what clothes females could wear in public places. Ordinance No. 36, "Proper Attire," in Southampton, Long Island–which was rigidly enforced–stated:

> No person shall walk or ride in any vehicle upon or along the public streets of the Village in any bathing suit, shorts, trunks or other apparel which does not cover properly the body and limbs from midway between the knees and hips to and including the shoulders.
>
> Any person who violates thus ordinance shall be liable to a penalty of not more than TEN DOLLARS ($10.00) for each offense to be recovered by the Village of Southampton and such violation shall constitute disorderly conduct and such person shall be a disorderly person.

Nearby Westhampton Beach proved closer to mainstream American attitudes in this respect, however, as reflected in the following notice issued by its Board of Trustees:

> The Village Board has been asked to take action regarding the increasing number of improperly attired people appearing on the streets each summer.
>
> It will avoid embarrassment to yourself and your neighbors and will be appreciated by the undersigned if, in your public appearances, particularly in the shopping district, you will wear clothes that are generally considered appropriate for the occasion.

As daring as short shorts may have appeared to some at the time, fashion statements in the 1960s (e.g., the bikini, miniskirts, the topless bathing suit) and 1970s (e.g., hot pants) rendered it seemingly pale by comparison. Shorn of their original moniker various spinoffs of short shorts have remained a part of the feminine wardrobe up to the present day.

BIBLIOGRAPHY

"Short Shorts Become Permanent in U.S. Scene," *Life*. 41 (September 10, 1956) 49-54. il.
"Short Shorts Story," *Newsweek*. 46 (August 1, 1955) 29.

Silly Putty

In 1944, General Electric announced the invention of silicone, a freak substance its chemists had produced while conducting experiments aimed at turning out synthetic rubber. Demonstrations revealed that it could bounce like a rubber ball, stretch like taffy, and break into a hundred pieces when hit by a hammer (and then go right back together again). Called "bouncing putty" by GE, it quickly disappeared from a public mind preoccupied with more important things.

Then, in 1949, Peter Hodgson happened upon a blob of silicone that a chemist had left at a friend's home. Fascinated by its possibilities, Hodgson had some chemical engineers in Schenectady, New York produce a few trial batches. When he got what he was looking for, Hodgson patented the name "Silly Putty" and began supplying it to retailers.

The gooey, pink-colored material was promoted on a purely recreational basis. It not only bounced when rolled into a ball and stretched like taffy as did its predecessor, but could be modeled into various non-permanent shapes, and if pressed against comic strips, would pick up the pictures, in color. It was marketed in plastic containers the size and shape of eggs. The shell came in two equal sections of different colors, with various combinations available. Hodgson utilized the egg-style container because his invention began appearing in stores around Eastertime 1950. "Easter eggs being so unimaginative, I decided to combine my putty with Easter and give them both a lift."

The appeal of Silly Putty appeared to cut across demographic lines. Adults not only appreciated the fact that it was non-toxic for children who got it in their hair or swallowed it, but enjoyed playing with it themselves. Hodgson noted,

> It means five minutes of escape from neurosis. It means not having to worry about Korea or family difficulties. And it

appeals to people of superior intellect; the inherent ridiculousness of the material acts as an emotional release to hard-pressed adults.

For whatever reason, the item made a great impression upon the public. Mr. Lee Weber, manager of the Doubleday bookshop in New York City, called Silly Putty the "most terrific item the Doubleday shops have been privileged to handle since *Forever Amber.*" He considered it the biggest novelty of 1950. By August 1950, Hodgson had received orders for a quarter-million units; over a million eggs were sold that year.

Silly Putty continued to sell well over the next 40 years in its trademark container, particularly to a new wave of baby boomers in the early 1960s. During the summer months of 1991, Binney & Smith successfully marketed a phosphorescent version through such giant retail chains as Wal-Mart.

BIBLIOGRAPHY

"Here to Stay," *New Yorker.* (August 26, 1950) 19-20.

The Simpsons

The Simpsons, a leading proponent of the adult cartoon wave on television in 1989-1990, was a product of the warped genius of Matt Groening. Following in the footsteps of his father, who was a cartoonist and filmmaker, Groening began drawing cartoons himself during grade school classes; a practice, he observes, which resulted in occasional visits to the principal's office.

After graduating from Evergreen State College in Olympia, Washington, Groening relocated to Los Angeles, where he found a job with an alternative weekly, the *Los Angeles Reader*. His *Life In Hell*–a comic strip dedicated to the proposition that "hell is the here and now," debuted in that publication in 1980. He also met his wife at the paper's advertising department and by 1984 they'd set out on their own to market *Life In Hell* in a number of guises–syndicated strip, T-shirt, coffee mug, etc.

By 1988, Groening's strip was appearing in 105 mainstream papers (up to 140 by late 1989) and had also been issued in several paperback editions: *Work Is Hell*, *School Is Hell*, *Love Is Hell*, and *Childhood Is Hell*. He then developed an animated cartoon, *The Simpsons*, which appeared in 15 to 25 second vignettes on the Fox Network's *The Tracy Ullman Show*. That program's executive producer, on the lookout for animated segments to integrate into the series, thought of Groening while looking at a *Life In Hell* cartoon on his wall.

Groening, who is said to be extremely close to his family, evidently used them as the inspiration for the characters in *The Simpsons*: his father (Homer), mother (Margaret), and sisters (Lisa and Maggie) have the same names as the Simpson clan members. Only Bart (an anagram for "brat") varied from this formula. Groening's own description of this constantly bickering family possessed of bulging eyes and overbites was "lovable–in a mutant sort of way. [They reflect] the normal American family in all its beauty and all its horror." According to Groening, they appealed particularly to children because they "are unrepressed and do naughty things."

Despite critics of his work–ranging from those put off by the lack of respect shown authority figures to the religious fanatics complaining about the casual use of the "H-word"–Groening was awarded a 30-minute slot in the Fox lineup for *The Simpsons*. The expanded program premiered on December 17, 1989 with the airing of "The Simpsons Roasting on an Open Fire." Videotaped editions of the program began appearing in 1990; in addition, Simpsons shorts prefaced various motion pictures in the video format by 1990. Countless merchandizing spinoffs were also produced, ranging from clothing to marbles. A rock/rap album, *The Simpsons Sing the Blues*, complete with the characters' trademark voices, also reached the Top Ten album charts during 1990-1991.

BIBLIOGRAPHY

"Eat My Shorts! Pesky Bart Simpson Tees Off a California Principal–and Gets Kicked Out of School for Swearing," *People Weekly.* 33 (May 21, 1990) 130. il. Re. the Cambridge Elementary School in Orange.

Feldman, Gayle. " 'Simpson' Creator Groening Moves From Pantheon to Harper," *Publishers Weekly.* 237 (May 4, 1990) 33-34. il.

Flint, Joe. "Burger King–'Simpsons' Ad May Not Air on NBC, ABC," *Broadcasting.* 118 (June 11, 1990) 80.

Gordon, Mary Ellen. "The Simpsons Arrive on SA," *Women's Wear Daily.* 159 (May 9, 1990) 10. il. JouJou gets license to use Simpsons characters on girl's jeanswear.

Grimm, Matthew. "A Smash Cartoon Hit Called 'The Simpsons' Hits Licensing Paydirt; With 100 Offers Coming in Daily, the Offbeat Show is Turning Suitors Away," *Adweek's Marketing Week.* 31 (March 5, 1990) 17. il.

Horton, Liz. "The Simpsons Turns to Print," *Folio: the Magazine for Magazine Management.* 20 (May 1, 1991) 57-58. il.

Kaufman, Joanne, and Cindy Yorks. "Life in Hell's Matt Groening Goes Overboard to Make *The Simpsons* the First Family of TV 'Toons," *People Weekly.* (December 18, 1989) 108-110. il.

McConnell, Frank. " 'Real' Cartoon Characters: 'The Simpsons,' " *Commonweal.* 117 (June 15, 1990) 389-390.

Morris, Chris. "Simpsons' TV Power Has Everyone Doing the 'Bartman,' " *Billboard.* 103 (January 12, 1991) 4-5.

Rebeck, Victoria A. "Recognizing Ourselves in the Simpsons," *The Christian Century.* 107 (June 27, 1990) 622. Editorial.

Reese, Michael. "A Mutant 'Ozzie and Harriet,' " *Newsweek.* 114 (December 25, 1989) 70. il.

Zoglin, Richard. "Home Is Where the Venom Is; Domestic Life Takes a Drubbing in TV's Anti-Family Sitcoms," *Time.* 135 (April 16, 1990) 85-86. il.

Sleex

In 1950, Sleex appeared poised to relegate traditional trousers to the attic. Sleex were a beltless pair of pants which featured a waistband split on each side with zippers, thereby allowing adjustment for variations in girth and in the seat. A rubberized ring around the inside of the waistband ensured a snug fit and held the wearer's shirt in place.

When Sleex were test-marketed in 50 cities in fall 1949, demand ran "far beyond expectations." Its manufacturer, the Esquire Sportswear Co., then introduced them to the mass market in May 1950. The firm turned out 150,000 pairs during the remainder of the year, roughly one-third of its total sportswear production.

The product failed to make a lasting impact on the nation's fashion scene. However, variations on the beltless idea have continued to garner a healthy portion of the men's pants industry, sans side zippers.

BIBLIOGRAPHY

"Sleex Instead of Slacks," *Newsweek.* 35 (May 29, 1950) 60. il.

The Slinky

The Slinky was a coil of spring steel approximately three inches in diameter, two inches high, containing 87 feet of flat-rolled wire which fascinated post-World War II Americans with its undulations and lifelike motions (most notably, coiling and uncoiling down steps).

Its inventor, Richard T. James, got the idea as a shipbuilder during World War II when a spring he was working on made a curious slithering movement. When one of the gadgets he developed made a hit with a bedridden boy, James decided to commercialize it.

After being turned down by Woolworth's and other major department stores in the Philadelphia area, he got a toy outlet to take four dozen Slinkies on consignment in early November 1945; the entire batch sold out immediately. Quitting his job as an air conditioner salesman, James located a piston-ring manufacturer capable of mass-producing the toy and set up a demonstration at Gimbels in Philadelphia. Gimbels sold 21,000 Slinkies at one dollar apiece in the three weeks following his appearance, and the other department outlets in the area began carrying them as well. Within two months of his first sale, James had sold over 50,000 Slinkies and grossed $30,000 (half of which was net profit).

As sales for the toy continued to rise into the 1950s, James was beset by numerous difficulties such as patent infringements by copy-cat firms, the bankruptcy of his sole distributor in 1947 (from that point onward, he divided his distribution among six outfits), a steel shortage in 1948, and a grievance against local building inspectors which required legal intervention. Nevertheless, James's operation progressed to where six million Slinkies had been sold by mid-1953; at that time, 7,000 units were being turned out daily.

In 1950 he began diversifying in other areas, supplying industrial springs to major electronics firms and manufacturing a children's game utilizing two miniature Slinkies. Several years later he set up another company to flat-roll his own steel wire. Still, the continued sales of the Slinky alone well into the 1960s were sufficient to make James a very wealthy man.

BIBLIOGRAPHY

"The Case of the Slithering Slinky," *Fortune.* 48 (August 1953) 148. il.
Yoder, R. M. "Up Bounced a Business," *Saturday Evening Post.* 219 (December 21, 1946) 6. il.

Slot Car Racing

Slot cars–miniature vehicles whose electric motors draw juice from an electrified slot, or busbar, embedded in the track–were wildly successful during the 1960s. In 1963, the cars surpassed model trains in sales. By 1965, they had become the second biggest product in the toy business (behind dolls), reaching retail sales of around $150 million at 20 to 60 dollars a set. One slot racing expert observed, "I could take a pencil, put it in a plastic bag, print 'Slot Racing Equipment' on the label, and sell thousands."

The genre originated with tinkerers racing homemade cars in basements and clubhouses. As the cars rapidly made inroads into the home market, the business took on a new dimension in 1962 with the rise of the so-called slot store. These establishments sold racing time by the hour on steeply banked, eight-lane tracks as long as 200 feet. They boasted wall-to-wall carpeting and were organized in the fashion of big-time bowling centers (e.g., competition leagues, trophies). The outlets began in California and spread eastward–there were an estimated 2,000 in the United States by late 1965.

The underlying reason for the appeal of slot cars was the obsession of American youth with the automobile. James B. Russell, a former racing driver who founded American Russ-Kit in 1962, also noted, "It's the best thing to satisfy a Walter Mitty complex. You can be a terror of the track." The model cars were most heavily supported by the 10-to17-year-old age group. Interest would generally wane after the teenager obtained a driver's license; the hard core hobbyists would then return to model cars after marriage and the establishment of a career track.

While the bulk of slot car sales–approximately 70 percent–was for the simple track layouts of the low budget home sets (sized in the tiny HO, 1/87, scale), the older enthusiasts were more inclined to patronize the commercial racing centers, built for cars several times larger. Many slot car manufacturers banked upon the widespread growth of these centers, including the following:

- Aurora Plastics Corp., dominant in the HO-scale home market, opened a fancy slot store on Long Island in summer 1965. In 1964, it had begun putting its name on cars and equipment in the larger scales.
- Eldon Industries, Inc., also a home racing giant, jumped into the sports arena with a complete line of products, as well as setting up a test center in Riverside, California where fans could race for prizes and see experimental products fresh off the company drawing board. Eldon also sponsored a club with over 45,000 and published a promotional quarterly bulletin, *The Pit Pass*.
- Revell, which began with high-performance parts and build-it-yourself kits for the hobbyist, introduced a home line in 1964 in 1/32 scale, a compromise size suitable for both markets. In 1965, it opened a showcase racing center in California and purchased International Raceways, Inc., a small builder of commercial track installations.
- Strombecker Corp., based in Chicago, a pioneer in the home market (having started in 1959, selling 700,000-odd sets in 1965), geared up for rapid expansion into the racing centers sector, particularly in the largely untouched eastern portion of the U.S.

In addition, hundreds of small companies worked out of converted garages to supply components to retailers. Many specialized in one particular component such as tires, frames, or electrical pickups.

Beginning in the 1970s, the market leveled off, due to both external factors such as increased competition from other electronic toys (e.g., video games) and internal problems, most notably the lack of standardization of cars and equipment. As a result, the hobby now belongs primarily to the hard-core enthusiasts, who find many of the high performance features now available for home use.

BIBLIOGRAPHY

"Slot Car Racing Fad Gets on a Faster Track," *Business Week.* (November 13, 1965) 190-192.

Sock Shops

The late 1980s witnessed the rise of hundreds of quick-stop sock emporiums across the United States as well as abroad. These outlets proved superior to department store layouts in that they offered (1) attentive service; (2) an eccentric inventory designed to appeal to hip tastes (patterns popular in early 1989 included world maps, tie-dye configurations, jack-o'-lanterns, happy faces, and Scottie-dog appliques); and (3) rapid turnovers in stock in order to keep up with ever-changing consumer demands.

One of the field's prime success stories, the Sock Express chain in Manhattan, utilized its own factory so as to ensure an innovative product. Because the company specialized in socks with rhine-stones, zippers, and buttons–all of which would be difficult for a mass manufacturer to produce–28 skilled costume builders were employed to cut fabrics and assemble the final product. Founder Barton Weiss boasted, "I can have an idea tonight and have it in the stores tomorrow."

The originator of the stockings-on-the-run concept was Sophie Mirman, an ex-secretary in London, who opened her first Sock Shop in 1983 at the busy Knightsbridge Underground station. Mirman's operating philosophy, "Socks should be as easy to buy as a newspaper," propelled her business into the big leagues. By early 1989, the chain had expanded to 118 outlets spanning Great Britain, France, Belgium, and the U.S.

In the 1990s, however, the trend appeared to have lost some of its momentum as mainstream clothing and department stores began offering a more souped-up array of hosiery for customers.

BIBLIOGRAPHY

"Sock It to Me!" *Time*. (March 6, 1989) 52. il.

Sports Sandals

Sports sandals–described in one source as a cross between a dime-store thong and a ripped-up, stripped-down running shoe–were conceived in 1983 by Mark Thatcher, a Colorado river outfitter. He was seeking an alternative to athletic footwear which he considered too slippery and spongelike for use on white-water rafting trips. After several years of unspectacular sales, centered primarily in the Western mountain region, sports sandals took off in popularity during 1991. *Time* magazine noted,

> Once the uncelebrated darling of Western college students, they are the coolest thing under your feet since Air Jordans and can cost nearly as much. Sports sandals, this summer's must-have shoe, are now standard equipment for hikers, mountain climbers and even some skydivers.

The appeal of the sandal was based on several factors:

1. Comfort. They were quick-drying and fitted with a variable web of beltings, tethers, and buckles that snugly gripped the toes and the ankle while keeping the foot from sliding back and forth.
2. Durability. The tough rubber sole and high arch could take the off-road punishment expected by hikers and mountain climbers.
3. Attractiveness. Hot colors and a high-tech look attracted consumers with a yen for the back-to-nature aura.
4. Versatility. One Montana outfitter, Dale Covington, stated, "They're all I wear when it's warm. When it cools off, I wear them with socks."

The bestselling brand, Teva, manufactured by Deckers Corp. of Santa Barbara, California, was available in 30 different styles and cost from 35 to 80 dollars. One executive for the company predicted that revenues from the sandal would double in 1991 to 12 million dollars, and likely double once more the following year.

BIBLIOGRAPHY

"Tarsorial Splendor: Attention, Footwear Fetishists! Sports Sandals are Hip Soles for Hip Souls," *Time*. 138:4 (July 29, 1991) 61. il.

Spring Breaks on the Florida Beaches

Starting in 1938, when the Fort Lauderdale Chamber of Commerce staged a "Swimming Forum" to attract collegians during Easter vacation, Florida beaches steadily gained popularity as a place to let off some steam. In 1959, 20,000 students descended upon Fort Lauderdale. *Time* noted that "the townspeople regard the invasion with edgy amusement: student-watching has become a local sport."

The article's quote of one coed explaining why she was drawn there–"This is where the boys are"–was appreciated by Glendon Swarthout as the title of a 1959 novel describing the spring break phenomenon. The film adaptation of *Where the Boys Are* (1960) is credited with projecting such an alluring image of Florida beaches that the number of visiting students doubled. Jane and Michael Stern state,

> Despite its moralistic overlay, *Where the Boys Are* was an inspiration to millions of restless American students, who embraced it as a sympathetic image of young people having fun; Connie Francis's moaning rendition of the title song became an anthem of youth's vague, still-unfocused longing for liberation, sex, and euphoria.

When Fort Lauderdale authorities attempted to diffuse the 1961 onslaught by closing the bars and beaches, students rioted, chanting "We want beer!" Eight hundred people were arrested in the melee. The following year, Daytona Beach made a move to increase its share of the partying tourists, welcoming the students turned away by Fort Lauderdale. The latter city–spearheaded by its business elements–recognized the error of its ways and encouraged the spring break vacationers to return. The tradition has continued to grow in popularity over the past three decades, embracing other sunbelt locales as well, including the Padre Islands of South Texas and Palm Springs, California.

BIBLIOGRAPHY

Stern, Jane, and Michael Stern. "Party Animals," In: *Sixties People*. New York: Knopf, 1990. pp. 95-101. il.
"Teen Travel Talk," *Seventeen*. 27 (April 28, 1968) 268. il.

Where the Boys Are **(1960 film)**

[Where the Boys Are], *Newsweek*. 57 (January 23, 1961) 84.
[Where the Boys Are], *Time*. 77 (January 20, 1961) 72. il.

Stick-on Initials

For six years, from 1953 to 1959, the National Key Company of Cleveland turned a modest profit manufacturing stick-on initials for key chains. Beginning in September 1959, however, sales underwent a sharp increase. Department chains, drug stores, and supermarkets clamored for more and more of the product, of which there were a dozen types ranging in price from a dime to a quarter. Altogether, ten million initials were purchased during 1959.

Looking into the matter, the company discovered that the upsurge in demand had resulted from teenagers utilizing the initials in myriad unorthodox ways, including:

- identification on eyeglasses, button earrings, earmuffs, bicycles, guitars, sweat shirts, hair bands, checkers, and dog collars;
- autographs on items such on plaster casts; and
- humorous assessments of others (e.g., *Life* published a photograph of one girl adhering the letters "M-A-D" to the back of the sweater of a boy whose hobbies were taxidermy and short-wave radio broadcasting).

Shortly thereafter, sales of the initials returned to the less spectacular levels of years past. It would appear to have been no coincidence that monogrammed items of a personal nature–e.g., coffee mugs, sweat shirts, key chains, pens–became a staple in countless retail outlets from that point onward.

BIBLIOGRAPHY

"A Non Belles-Lettres Fad," *Life*. 48 (March 28, 1960) 73-74. il.

The Straw Boater

The straw boater–flat as a saucer and shellacked to a board-hard stiffness–was in vogue from 1870, when machines capable of sewing straw were invented, until 1926, when *Blackwood's Magazine* administered the symbolic death knell, referring to it as "that horrible and obsolete form of headgear." The hat reached its peak of popularity between 1880-1900. During that time, the boater eclipsed all other forms of male headgear, including business wardrobes.

The straw boater was best known, however, as the ultimate leisure hat. As the working class acquired sufficient leisure time in the late nineteenth century via mechanization to discover the simple pleasures of boating, tennis, and lounging at sidewalk cafes, the inexpensive, machine-made boaters came to symbolize their newfound emancipation. The hat popped up continually in magazine illustrations and Impressionist paintings of the common man at play.

The popularity of boaters owed as much to their evocation of supreme lightness–they floated rather than fitting snugly on the head–as to their low cost. In addition, one of the era's most charismatic entertainers, Maurice Chevalier, made the hat his own; its lighthearted appearance combined with his unshakably sunny disposition proved to be the perfect match.

Once the boater slipped out of fashion–its playful character seemed out of place during the Depression and World War II, not to mention the frenetic pace of the post-war era–nothing could revive it. The hat was relegated to the status of a costume piece, worn by Venetian gondoliers, the Princeton marching band, various college alumni classes at reunions, and the like.

BIBLIOGRAPHY

Berendt, John. "The Straw Boater," *Esquire*. (August 1988) 24. il.

McClure, W. F. "Manufacture of Straw Hats," *Scientific American*. 90 (June 4, 1904) 440-441. il.

"Straw Hats and Dignity," *Spectator*. 73 (July 14, 1894) 43-44.

Stuffed Pandas

The U.S. toy industry rode the crest of a full-fledged boom in stuffed pandas in 1972 as a result of President Richard Nixon's diplomatic visit to the People's Republic of China. Raymond S. Reed, president of the nation's most prestigious toy chain, F.A.O. Schwarz, noted, "Stuffed pandas had always been a staple, but the market was very quiet." When Chinese leader Chou En-lai gave Nixon a present of two live giant pandas, however, the rage for the stuffed version started.

Those companies anticipating the demand for pandas realized the greatest profits. Good Manufacturing of New York brought out a line of pandas to show at the New York Toy Fair, which happened to coincide with the visit. Its president reported that the production of stuffed pandas was 70 percent higher than the previous year. Pascal Kamar, a West Coast toy distributor, put in large orders for pandas with Japanese and U.S. manufacturers. F.A.O. Schwarz took the first batch and, after selling them in three days, contracted for all the pandas Kamar could supply through the summer and early fall of 1972.

In all, some 15 million stuffed pandas were estimated to have been sold in the U.S. in 1972. Retailing between $2 and $40 each, the boom played a major role in lifting the toy industry out of the doldrums ensuing from a bad year in 1971.

BIBLIOGRAPHY

"The Panda Boom," *Forbes*. 110 (July 1, 1972) 27. il.

"Panda-monium Again," *Life*. 72 (March 24, 1972) 42ff. il.

Reed, T. H. "What's Black and White and Loved All Over?" *National Geographic*. 142 (December 1972) 803-815. il.

Sunglasses

Sunglasses go back as far as the ancient Chinese, who, it has been passed down, shielded their eyes from the sun with tea crystals. The next notable advance came when British opticians began making a primitive version out of green glass in the sixteenth century. During the twentieth century, lenses were refined to such a degree that they were capable of blocking out harmful ultraviolet rays without distorting perception of the overall color spectrum.

The industry reached a major turning point with the development of the green Ray-Ban aviator sunglasses by Bausch & Lomb in the 1920s in response to the request of the U.S. Army Air Corps for fliers' goggles that would absorb the glare of the sun. The aviators–whose free-form lens configuration traced the outline of the wearer's peripheral vision–became a classic, the most-imitated style in the world.

The aviators represented more than mere quality performance; they ultimately became an item of fashion. They helped turn sunglasses into a 25-million-dollar-a-year industry in 1965; by the late 1980s the annual figure had soared to over a billion dollars with unit sales of about 200 million pairs.

The Hollywood film industry played a key role in glamorizing sunglasses. In addition to providing protection from the bright southern California sun, shades enabled well-known stars like Greta Garbo, Katharine Hepburn, and Gary Cooper avoid eye contact with or recognition by an adoring public. Despite the rudeness and even hostility often implied by using them in order to place a barrier between the wearer and others, sunglasses took on an aura of "cool" that evidently appealed to millions of Americans.

The plastic-framed Wayfarer model proved to be the hottest performer of the 1980s. Brought out by Ray-Ban in 1952, they were on the verge of being discontinued in 1981 following years of meager sales (i.e., 18,000 per year). When they suddenly appeared on the likes of Tom Cruise (in the film *Risky Business*), and Don Johnson (in the TV drama *Miami Vice*), sales soared to two million pairs a year.

The future remains bright for sunglasses. They continue to be a popular fashion accessory no longer necessarily tied to the purpose for which they were originally created. As documented by modern-day observer/rock star Corey Hart, "I wear my sunglasses at night."

BIBLIOGRAPHY

Berendt, John. "Sunglasses," *Esquire*. (July 1988) 27. il.

Day, B. "Living in Shadow; Sunglasses Stand for Glamour & Social Status," *New York Times Magazine*. (April 12, 1964) 42ff. il.

Rudolph, B. "Shades of Discontent," *Forbes*. 132 (July 18, 1983) 50. il.

Stengel, R. "Status in the Shading Game," *Time*. 124 (July 23, 1984) 87-88. il.

"Throw Away Your Aviators; Today's Stylemakers are Ready for Risky Business in '50s Shades," *People Weekly*. 20 (October 4, 1983) 121-122.

Super Ball

By early fall 1965, over six million Super Balls were bouncing around America; not only children played with them but adults as well. Cabinet member McGeorge Bundy had five dozen shipped to the White House. Brokers on the Pacific Stock Exchange tossed them about during slack hours. Manhattan executives dribbled them on their desks.

The key to the ball's appeal was its resiliency–looking like a handball and made from an elastic compound called Zectron, it was capable of bouncing 92 percent as high as the level from which it was dropped. Dropped on a hard floor from shoulder level, it would continue bouncing for a full minute (a tennis ball's bounce lasts only ten seconds).

Super Ball came about almost by accident. Norman Stingley, a chemist for Bettis Rubber Co. in Whittier, California, was experimenting with high-resiliency synthetic rubber, when he discovered that a crude ball formed by compressing the goo under some 3,500 pounds of pressure per square inch had a fantastic bounce. Bettis wasn't interested, mostly because the ball tended to fall apart within minutes, so Stingley offered it to Wham-O Manufacturing Co. in San Gabriel, California, famous for the Frisbee and the Hula-Hoop. Stingley and Wham-O spent a year making the ball more durable (the finished product was still apt to chip or shatter on rough surfaces), then dyed it purple, gave it a 98-cent price tag, and released it in early summer 1965.

One reason for the ball's astounding success was the ingenuity exhibited by fans in inventing games for it. Young girls used it for jacks, skate-boarders bounced it as they rolled along, and office workers placed bets to see who could bounce it into a wastepaper basket. Another popular application consisted of giving the ball lots of spin, bouncing it against the wall, and seeing how many times it would bounce back to the wall without stopping (*Time* reported the unofficial record at five hits).

Well aware of the short life span experienced by most fads, Wham-O executives waxed philosophical about its prospects. Executive Vice President Richard P. Knerr commented, "Each Super Ball bounce is 92% as high as the last. If our sales don't come down any faster than that, we've got it made." And President Arthur Melin quipped, "Super Ball is better than sucking your thumb."

BIBLIOGRAPHY

"A Boom With a Bounce," *Life*. 59 (December 3, 1965) 69-70ff.
" 'It's a Bird, It's a Plane . . . ,' " *Time*. 86 (October 22, 1965) 69-70. il.
"Way the Ball Bounces; Super Ball, Success of Wham-O Manufacturing Co.," *Newsweek*. 66 (November 29, 1965) 80. il.

The Swinging London Look

The swinging London look had its genesis in the opening of Bazaar in 1955, a boutique owned by Mary Quant and her husband, Alexander Plunket Greene. Because Quant disliked the clothing being manufactured at the time, she started designing her own. Jane and Michael Stern noted that she was an original in a land used to French imports, creating

> cheap-to-make (and to buy), ready-to-wear, exuberant outfits made for the irreverent, the young, and the slim. Her fashions combined severe tweeds with laces, riotous stripes with bold checks; she designed rib-tight poor-boy sweaters and vests made out of knotted string, shiny plastic raincoats, fishnet gloves, foolish patterned stockings, and great fox-fur hats in the style of the cossacks.

In 1961, Quant's creations were introduced to Americans through *Seventeen*'s spring fashion issue. The following year her designs were marketed by the JCPenney chain in order to give it a youthful image; Quant in fact owed much of her success to the fact that she was selling youth. In her own words,

> There was a time when every girl under 20 yearned to look like an experienced, sophisticated 30; when round-faced teen-agers practiced sucking in their cheeks to achieve interesting hollows; when every girl dreamed of a slinky black dress worn with high heels. All this is in reverse now. Suddenly, every girl with a hope of getting away with it is aiming to look not only under voting age but under the age of consent. . . . Their aim is to look childishly young, naively unsophisticated.

American manufacturers tooled up to produce merchandise in the Quant mold in record time. The mod mystique was employed to sell

The mid-60s brought Carnaby Street style direct from London to America. Short skirts for women and bold-pattern attire for men made for the best in imported hippness.

everything from Scotch tape fashion accessories (e.g., colored plastic raindrops to be applied to raincoats, eyelashes for sunglasses) to sanitary napkins. By 1966, with the myth of swinging London at its peak, Quant caught fire once more with the pantsuit concept (originally presented in 1962 as the trouser suit).

Men's fashions were also heavily influenced by the mod revolution. Here, the major force was John Stephen, who opened a shop in 1962 at the age of 24 selling tight, hip-hugging trousers. The site of his outlet–Carnaby Street–became an international symbol of the movement. According to the Sterns, the Carnaby Street fashions were even more fickle than women's:

> Mod style for men omnivorously grew to include a dandyish Lord Fauntleroy look in the form of Edwardian suits and shirts cascading with lace at the collars and cuffs, or floppy bows tied at the throat. Mod came to mean almost anything op, pop, or foppish, from Regency ruffles and nineteenth-century frock coats to silver lame capes and gorilla-like fur crests.

Stephen's fashions proved just as irresistible to Americans as had those introduced by Quant. A show of his clothes at Stern Brothers department store in New York City in 1966 resulted in a mob scene. Chicago retailer Cesar Rotondi expressed amazement that schoolboys there were paying up to $150 a month to outfit themselves in high-heeled boots, broad belts and flared-bottom trousers. Fashion shows helped turn on their audiences via liberal dosages of British beat music and (often bogus) British accents.

By 1967, however, the mod movement was on the wane. Carnaby merchants were being accused of hucksterism, and the look, in that it was by definition "instant and disposable" and therefore cheap and mass-produced, was all too easy to imitate badly. The appearance of the hippie ethic and its focus on a more "natural" look helped to bring down swinging London. Still, elements of the look–such as an inclination toward bright colors and cuts which favored youth and slim figures–remained in the fashion mainstream for years to come.

BIBLIOGRAPHY

Halasz, Piri. *A Swinger's Guide to London.* Coward-McCann, 1968. il.
Stern, Jane, and Michael Stern. "I'm English," In: *Sixties People.* New York: Knopf, 1990. pp. 122-145. il.
Zimmermann, G. "London: The Cutting Edge," *Look.* 30 (September 20, 1966) 82-84. il.

Carnaby Street

Littler, F. "Carnaby Street," *Saturday Review.* 52 (October 25, 1969) 6-7.
"Whither Carnaby Street?" *Newsweek.* 72 (July 1, 1968) 76.

Quant, Mary

"Chez Mlle: Mary Quant at Home; excerpts from interview by E. Blair," *Mademoiselle.* 65 (September 1967) 824ff.
"Name That Spells Mod Fashions," *Business Week.* (June 8, 1968) 118-119ff. il.

Synthetics in Clothes

The early 1950s saw a substantial rise in the use of synthetic fabrics for clothing. Men's summer suits made of new materials such as Dacron and dynel progressed from novelty status in 1951, when they were first introduced in limited quantities, to bonafide best-seller status. As noted by *Time*, "merchants, whose clothing business had been in a marked slump, found customers crowding their stores with a curiosity faintly reminiscent of the one-time rush for ballpoint pens."

The snappy sales figures for synthetics belied their high price. For example, men accustomed to paying about 20 dollars for a cotton seersucker or 50 dollars for a light worsted, were being asked to ante up $82.50 for a 100% Dacron suit at New York's Witty Bros. Nevertheless, the outlet sold some 16,000 such suits in 1952, plugging the fact that they were washable. Some merchants offered blends of synthetics and less expensive yarns (e.g., John David's, Brooks Brothers, Hart Schaffner & Mark). Chicago's Lytton's store sold 1,000 suits made of a blend of dynel, acetate, and rayon in a fortnight.

In fall 1952, Deering, Milliken & Co., Inc.–reading the market indicators–introduced "Lorette," made of a 55 percent Orlon-45 percent wool blend, which was used for women's sportswear and suits. DuPont, Union Carbide, and other large chemical companies announced plans to build big new plants so as to permit still further expansion in the production of synthetics. *Time* noted in its May 12, 1952 issue that the wool industry, "already quaking, [would] have to look sharp lest it go the way of silk."

In retrospect, while the glory years of synthetics were still ahead, the 1980s saw a retrenchment back to the greater use of natural fibers (e.g., cotton, wool) in clothing. Synthetic/natural blends have remained a fixture up to the present, requiring minimal maintenance to look good and often combining the best features of the 100%

natural or 100% synthetic alternatives. However, the preponderance of all-synthetic clothing–which peaked in the late 1970s (remember disco fashions?)–receded as the public became better informed about the advantages of natural fibers such as durability and comfort. Ironically, by the 1980s all-natural clothes had become the prestigious, premium-priced alternative.

BIBLIOGRAPHY

Block, J. "Rush to S-t-r-e-t-c-h," *Readers' Digest.* 82 (January 1963) 199-200ff. il.

Eklund, C. S. "Now Polyester Wants to be Asked to the High-Fashion Ball," *Business Week.* (March 4, 1985) 116-117. il.

Gander, R. "Wash and Wear," *Newsweek.* 53 (June 8, 1959) 79-80. il.

Haynes, K. "The Comeback of Polyester," *Working Woman.* 10 (August 1985) 50ff. il.

"Revolution in Fit and Comfort: Stretch Fabrics and Expandable Fashions," *Good Housekeeping.* 160 (May 1965) 102-103ff. il.

"Stretch Clothes," *Look.* 27 (May 21, 1963) 45-46. il.

"Synthetic Surge," *Time.* 59 (May 12, 1952) 96-97. il.

Sports Clothing

Walzer, W. "Dressed for Chill," *Health.* 22 (November 1990) 53-55. il.

Wolkomir, R. "High Tech Materials Blaze Urban Trail for Outdoorsy Duds," *Smithsonian.* 15 (January 1985) 122-126ff. il.

T-Shirts

Since its days as regulation issue for sailors, the T-shirt–known during World War II as the skivvy shirt–has been a fixture on the American scene. Its popularity reached new heights when Marlon Brando wore one in *A Streetcar Named Desire* in 1947.

By the mid-1970s, however, the T-shirt evolved beyond old mainstays such as advertising slogans, iron-on glitter, tie-dye designs, and clever one-liners to embrace a dazzling array of new concepts. Visually arresting creations included the T-shirt as a tuxedo jacket, a simulated blazer and bow tie number complete with a flower on a lapel; and the Body Language series (e.g., the depiction of shapely legs draped over the shoulders, appearing as if someone were riding piggyback). Also available was the Shirt-O-Gram, which depicted a Western Union-style message in large capital letters. Yet another novelty were the Smellies shirts in which microscopic capsules containing odoriferous oils–depicting everything from pizza to burnt rubber–were embedded in the fabric; by scratching the shirt, the wearer broke the capsules and released a particular fragrance. From late 1974 to early 1976, the Miami-based company, Smell It Like It Is, Inc., alone sold (or supplied the fragrance for) four million shirts.

The insatiable demand for T-shirts of every strip appeared to owe much to their low cost (often as low as three dollars apiece) as well as their compatibility with jeans. Larry Farrell, a Cal-Berkeley student, provided another reason: "It's a more graphic way of displaying your feelings." Anthropologist Alan Dundes posited, "People want to be different, unique, departing from the norm–so they buy an anti-Establishment shirt. But then everybody ends up wearing the same thing." Whether going to department stores, fashion boutiques, music outlets, or flea markets, enough people have continued to buy T-shirts to enable them to remain one of the most successful subsectors of the apparel industry up to the present day.

BIBLIOGRAPHY

Burgess, A. "T-Shirt Makes the Man," *Saturday Review.* 7 (June 1980) 16.

"Dozen Ways to Trim a T-Shirt," *Good Housekeeping.* 190 (May 1980) 92ff. il. Re. women's shirts.

Howrey, J. "Dealers, Bootleggers Step Up T-Shirt Wars," *Rolling Stones.* (October 16, 1980) 36.

Swanbow, D. "Talking T-Shirts: America's Raunchy New Ritual," *Human Behavior.* 8 (March 1979) 12-13.

"The T-Shirt: A Startling Evolution," *Time.* 107 (March 1, 1976) 48-50. il.

Tailfins on Cars

The years 1957-1959 represented the golden age of automobile tailfins. Notable proponents included the 1958 Chrysler Imperial, the 1959 Chevy Impala, and the 1959 Cadillac Fleetwood. The style has been generally attributed to the growing fascination by both automotive engineers and the general public with outer space propulsion, fostered by the testing of supersonic jets and the imminent space race between the U.S. and Soviet Union.

Tailfins seemed to inspire strong reactions from virtually all Americans, whether of a positive or negative nature. *Newsweek* noted that no adornment related to motor vehicles had been so caricatured. Unfortunately for the long-term prospects of the tailfin, many prominent observers tended to take a dim view of their inherent value. These critics included:

- Sumner Slichter, Harvard University Economist: "One trouble with the auto industry . . . [is] the weird collection of headlights, fins, tails, wings, etc., that is called an automobile in 1958."
- Walter Reuther, Labor Leader: "[Cars have gotten] sillier and bigger . . . I think the auto industry should make a car which can at least be parked in a single block."
- An editorial in the New Haven, Connecticut *Journal-Courier*: "Obviously a mistake has been made in gauging the public's taste in automobiles. Yet the industry's leaders still go on insisting that the size, overpowered motor capacity and pretentious fin-like protrusions of today's monsters of the highway are predetermined by public desire and not arbitrarily by the manufacturers. But mistakes have been made before in adjudging public wants. Actually, the turn by so many toward the tiny cars from Europe should have brought the truth home to an alert industry."

One significant face among the apologists for tailfins, however, was a German scientist, Dr. Wunibald Kamm, who had created them in about 1935. Then in charge of the Automotive Research Institute in Stuttgart, he saw tailfins as the means of concentrating all the wind forces which act on a car at a focus between the center of gravity and the midpoint of the vehicle, thereby achieving directional stability. Mathematical analysis as well as wind-tunnel and towing-tank tests all supported the need for such a device. He argued that the tailfins appearing on American cars as of mid-1958 were in fact not large enough to achieve the desired effect. Despite this argument and the open admiration of various car buffs, the early 1960s swing by car makers in the direction of down-sized, more fuel-efficient designs sealed the fate of tailfins.

BIBLIOGRAPHY

Keats, J. "Rise and Fall of Symbol: the Fin," *New York Times Magazine.* (March 25, 1962) 63-64. il.
"Now Even Mercedes Has Tail Fins," *Popular Science.* 175 (December 1959) 76-77. il.
"The Sense in Tailfins," *Newsweek.* 52 (July 14, 1958) 81. il.
"Weird Collection," *Time.* 71 (April 28, 1958) 88.

The Teenage Mutant Ninja Turtles

While everyone seemed to be talking about the Teenage Mutant Ninja Turtles at the tail end of the 1980s–they were even interviewed by Barbara Walters for ABC's Academy Award Night special on March 25, 1990–the characters were hardly an overnight success. They first appeared in a black-and-white alternative comic book in 1983. Their creators, Peter Laird and Kevin Eastman, (then 29 and 20 years old, respectively), were teamed together by the editor of a local comic publication. Laird had been drawing for the gardening page of a Northampton, Massachusetts newspaper and Eastman was employed as a short-order cook when they came up with the idea of slow-moving turtles in the role of quick, battle-hardened ninja warriors–the concept a humorous take-off on two of the more popular themes within the comic book industry at the time, mutants and ninjas.

The plot line consists of four very average turtles who accidently fell through a manhole into a sewer, where a radioactive goo caused them to attain human size as well as the power to speak. They were adopted by Splinter, a similarly altered rat who had been the pet of a ninja warrior. Splinter taught them the martial arts and named them after his favorite Renaissance artists, Leonardo (the leader), Raphael (the rebel), Michelangelo (the jokester) and Donatello (the technical whiz).

The characters did not attract much attention until New York licensing agent Mark Freedman signed to market them. Freedman worked out a merchandizing deal with Playmates Toys, Inc., who, in turn, sponsored the initial television episodes of the characters' syndicated cartoon series. They debuted in 1988 and became the biggest animated adventure act in that medium since the Ghostbusters cartoons. By early 1990, the show was appearing daily on 130 TV stations, and three videotape collections culled from it were among the Top Ten videos for children.

The TV series also stimulated success in other sectors of the entertainment field. Playmates' action figures of the foursome were the third biggest-selling toy during the 1989 Christmas season (behind Barbie and Nintendo machines). Three hundred-odd merchandising spinoffs, including breakfast cereals, skateboards, trading cards, lunch boxes, and T-shirts, registered $100 million in sales during 1989. Lynn Kejtmanek, the director of marketing for Ultra Software Corporation, which sold 1.4 million copies of a Ninja Turtles game for Nintendo, noted at the time, "They have just taken over the toy and entertainment industry."

The TV series also modified the characters' persona to some extent, most notably providing their passion for pizza, the much imitated "Hey, Dude" lingo and the oft-criticized tendency for the punks and villains with whom they did battle to fit within racial stereotypes. Nevertheless, youth were attracted to their hip sense of humor, daring–albeit absurd–feats, and interminable squabbling.

Success peaked with the release of their 12 million dollar feature film debut, *Teenage Mutant Ninja Turtles*, in the spring of 1990. Portrayed by actors outfitted in high-tech turtle costumes (Jim Henson's Creature Shop designed the computerized masks which utilized remote control to change facial expressions) and accompanied by a rap-music soundtrack, the movie was extremely popular in both its theatrical and videotape (late 1990) releases. With a sequel available on videotape and the foursome's likeness spread throughout the shelves of retail outlets, the Ninja Turtles still appeared to be cresting as of late 1991.

BIBLIOGRAPHY

"Don't Believe the Hype," *Rolling Stone.* (December 13/27, 1990) 70. il.

Hammer, J., and A. Miller. "Ninja Turtle Power," *Newsweek.* 115 (April 16, 1990) 60-61. il.

Schneider, K. S. "Cowabunga! Unshelled, These Teenage Mutant Ninja Actors Kick Off the 1990 Silly Season," *People Weekly.* 33 (April 23, 1990) 44-46ff. il.

Simpson, Janice C. "Lean, Green and on the Screen; the Teenage Mutant Ninja Turtles Go Hollywood," *Time.* 135:14 (April 2, 1990) 59. il.

Walters, Barbara. "Pizza, Ooze, and Success: Talking Turkey With the Turtles," *TV Guide.* 39:11 (March 16, 1991) 3, 7. il. Cover story.

Wloszczyna, S. "Cowabunga, Dude! Here Come the Turtles," *TV Guide.* 38 (September 29/October 5, 1990) 24ff. il.

Tie-Dye Fashions

The tie-dye phenomenon had its roots in the centuries-old practice in which Nigerian women tied cotton fabrics into knots, dipped them into dyes, and produced materials ablaze with splotches of color. No one seems to know how knowledge of the process spread to the U.S.; however, by the late 1960s, "hip" fashion boutiques were buying one dollar white cotton T-shirts, tie-dying them, and selling the rainbow-hued products for up to six dollars apiece.

The process hit the mainstream where Best Foods, whose Rit dye dominated (i.e., 75 percent or more) a retail market worth 24 million dollars per annum, mailed out 500,000 instruction booklets on tie-dying, thereby enabling 1969 sales of liquid Rit to jump 35 percent over the previous year's figure. The company joined forces with Van Raalte Co. and Arrow Co. to package ready-to-dye garments with bottles of Rit in "tie-dye kits." Soon department stores were sponsoring "tie-dye parties in which youthful consumers could learn how to turn a pair of blue jeans into "an original work of art," or convert ordinary bedsheets into "a light show on cloth." Even high-priced designers got into the act, concocting tie-dyed fashions for well-heeled clients.

The hippie capitalists, however, remained in the vanguard of the movements. Up Tied co-owner, Eileen Richardson, whose expertise with 79-cent bottles of Rit enabled her to transform two-dollar-a-yard velvets into 20-dollar-a-yard fabrics, exhibited the insight into the counterculture ethics of her consumers necessary to remain successful. Her statement, "[tie-dye fashions are] all part of the youthful trend away from rigidity and conformity," spoke volumes regarding her commitment to the movement. Other counterculture entrepreneurs chose to enter the mainstream as in the case of Smooth Tooth, Inc., co-owned by a drop-out stockbroker, which mass-produced some 50 dozen tie-dye items daily for the likes of Christian Dior, Jonathan Logan, and Stiletto, Inc., a wholesaler whose 65-dollars-and-up dresses were sold to high-end retailers. Head shops and boutiques also continued to sell tie-dye apparel by the truckload even after its appeal had diminished among mainstream customers. The market for tie-dye clothing began to flatten out by the mid-1970s. However, it has remained a marginally popular youth fashion, particularly as a do-it-yourself practice.

BIBLIOGRAPHY

David, S. M. "We Tied and Dyed," *School Arts.* 68 (May 1969) 18-19. il.
Peterson, P. "Tie It and Dye It," *New York Times Magazine.* (September 7, 1969) 104-105. il.
"Profit Hint: Always Say Dye," *Business Week.* (January 24, 1970) 71. il.

Tights

Originally the uniform of ballet dancers (who wore the genuine, torso-covering article), leotards were renamed "stretch tights" and sold in department stores as an undergarment beginning in the late 1950s. They first caught on with college girls as an accessory for tartan skirts. Although not considered particularly proper, tights proved exceedingly practical; no girdle or garter belt was needed, and slips appeared on the way out as tights were warmer and less bulky.

Beatniks also picked up on the stockings (in black only) as the perfect complement to their heavy black turtleneck sweaters. For this reason alone, mainstream American females steered clear of tights.

Eventually, however, mothers began dressing their children in red, blue, and green versions as a means of coping with winter days. Next, suburbanites started wearing them to shopping centers, bowling alleys, restaurants, and other typical haunts. By 1962, the remaining holdouts–office workers, grandes dames, dowdy matrons–took to wearing tights in order to ward off the cold.

Tights also appealed because they had a way of making almost any shape look more shapely and because, in the private reflection of her bedroom mirror, their wearer was the sexiest thing going. These pluses–combined with the fitness craze of the 1980s–have rendered the garment a fixture on the fashion scene up to the present.

BIBLIOGRAPHY

O'Gorman, M. V. "First Leotard," *Sports Illustrated.* 14 (May 15, 1961) E7-E12. il.
"Warm & Tight," *Time.* 81 (January 4, 1963) 48. il.

Top Hats

The top hat appeared on the scene in the waning years of the eighteenth century. During the first 40 years of the nineteenth century, it held absolute sway over men's daytime headgear.

This dominance was characterized by some degree of variety, as noted by Fiona Clark:

> . . . up to 1810 crowns and brims both tended to be broad, while the "Wellington" shape with concave sides to the crown was popular in the 1820s and 1830s when its curves echoed the rounded lapels and padded "pouter pigeon" chests of the currently fashionable frock coat. In the 1930s, the "Cumberland," tall and narrowing towards the top, resembled the tapered crowns of women's hats and bonnets in this decade. A very short version was worn throughout this period and became identified with the yeoman farmer . . .

A collapsible form of the top hat was introduced in 1812, later modified by various patents for "elastic" hats, culminating in the "gibus" of 1840. These and the regular rigid form of the top hat made inroads into the realm of evening wear. Even small boys, aged three or four, wore them in the early decades of the century. Their versions had a leather peak and sometimes a tassel.

The heyday of the top hat in the 1840s and early 1850s saw it reach its most extreme form, the crown becoming higher than ever before and the brim its narrowest, thereby emphasizing its vertical character. Clark observed,

> A variety with totally straight sides was given the name of "Stove pipe" while that with slightly convex sides was known as the "chimney pot." During the early part of the century beaver felt had gradually been superseded by silk "hatter's

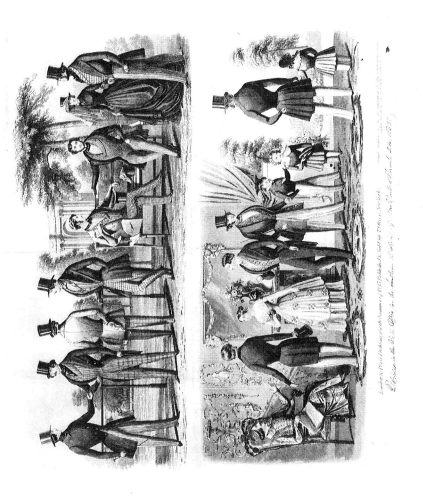

These continental gentlemen proudly display fine silk top hats for gauche Americans who were used to wearing beaver felt models to gawk at. Abraham Lincoln, who hardly needed to add height to his torso, helped popularize the cruder stove pipe top hat. 1860s.

plush" as the chief material for the top hat, so that by 1850 its dark lustrous surface symbolized the respect in which it was held.

During mid-century, the top hat evolved from a fashion into a symbol, coming to represent urban respectability. The lower classes would hire toppers, buy used ones or even cheap versions made of materials such as papier-mâché so as to give the appearance of gentility. With industrial prosperity bringing fashionable clothing within the reach of a much wider cross section of society, most members of the professional class took to wearing top hats on the job as well as for formal occasions.

At its peak in popularity, however, a reaction against the fashion had already begun, led in large part by artists and intellectuals. In addition, by the 1860s an increased variety of informal headgear–e.g., the straw hats such as the wide-brimmed "Jim Crow" and the soft felt hat–emerged to challenge its hegemony in the marketplace. Nevertheless, the top hat continued to be used in modified form until the end of the nineteenth century for more formal activities, particularly in the evening.

BIBLIOGRAPHY

Clark, Fiona. *Hats*. New York: Drama, 1982. Also published in London by Batsford/Anchor in 1982. il.

Johnston, C. "Evolution of the Top Hat," *Cosmopolitan*. 29 (August 1900) 427-428. il.

"Top Hat Mind," *Living Age*. 280 (March 14, 1914) 701-703.

Toy Giveaways at Fast-Food Restaurants

Fast-food restaurants have found premiums to be an effective means of attracting impulse buyers for over a generation; however, the late 1980s brought a new wrinkle to the practice–toys, particularly those of the stuffed variety. In December 1988, McDonald's offered Christmas-tree ornaments based on the Disney film *Oliver & Company,* Wendy's sold tiny safari animals, and Burger King peddled the Purrtender, a stuffed animal that could be transformed from a cat into various other cuddly critters. Hardee's "California Raisin" series proved to be a particularly big hit, fueling the following developments:

- In a Charlotte, N.C., restaurant, two customers reportedly exchanged punches after one purchased the last figurine.
- In an Orlando, Florida, outlet, raisin supplies ran out so quickly that the corporate offices had to airlift in thousands of them to meet demand.
- In Atlanta, phone calls from raisin fanatics were so frequent that the company decided to set up a 24-hour hot line.

The phenomenon seemed attributable to several interrelated factors: (1) the market was saturated with hamburger chains, (2) low inflation had put a ceiling on price increases, and (3) the health-conscious "thirtysomething generation" had begun to shy away from fat-and-sodium laden fast-food fare. The final impetus was provided by the chains' marketing departments; they found that kids account for much of their sales. For instance, a Wendy's study revealed that 83 percent of parents are influenced by their children in deciding what restaurants the family patronizes–and premiums were said to greatly influence those selections. Accordingly, the company more than quadrupled its budget for toy premiums. Other chains were thinking along the same lines, and the strategy appeared to be working. According to *Newsweek,*

263

Selling about 40 million California Raisins helped boost Hardee's revenues to an expected $3.3 billion [in 1988], up from about $2.7 in 1986. Led by Jack Laughery and William Prather, the company has become the third biggest selling chain, behind McDonald's and Burger King but ahead of Wendy's. Despite its problems, Wendy's has also benefitted from the toy strategy: after losing $4.9 million in 1986, the chain earned $22 million in the first nine months of 1988.

Many industry observers felt that toy giveaways would ultimately prove to be a negative force. Richard Simon, an analyst for Goldman, Sachs, considered it detrimental to long-term customer loyalty. "I think it's bad for the industry," he stated in late 1988. "People bounce around from promotion to promotion." The likelihood of consumer backlash was another pitfall. Rob Densen, a Summit, New Jersey father, was a case in point. Noting that two children drove him crazy with their lust for the giveaway, he stated, "I'll go anywhere where I don't have to buy a toy with my burger."

BIBLIOGRAPHY

Miller, Annetta, with Howard Mandy and Elisa Williams. "Toys in Hamburgerland," *Newsweek*. (December 12, 1988) 50. il.

The Trilby

The trilby is a slightly rumpled fedora accented by a tapered crown. Due to its usually being unlined and constructed of very lightweight felt, the trilby is not as stiff as the traditional fedora. It can be molded into any shape or even rolled up and stuffed into a small pocket.

The name came from George du Maurier's novel, *Trilby*, which was dramatized in 1895. The play set into motion an enormous Trilby craze. As a result, many things–soaps, taffy, cigars, societies, etc.–were named Trilby. Countless baby girls were christened Trilby, and pets, particularly cats, were named for her hypnotizing husband-mentor, Svengali. Film versions of the story also appeared, most notably *Svengali*, starring John Barrymore.

The origin of the hat itself was explained by a reporter for the *Bradford Daily Argus* in November 1895:

> I have been puzzling my head to account for the reason of so many soft hats being worn at present, and at last hit it. It is another phase of the "Trilby" complaint. In one of the illustrations of the book, "Trilby" wears a hat of this description, so it has been seized upon by those worshipers at the shrine of Trilby whom nature will not assist in the cultivation of a Svengali beard.

The trilby is supposed to have had a deeper psychological significance as well. Historian James Laver attributed a sexual symbolism to men's hats, noting that men have worn high hats during periods of male dominance whereas:

> With the advent of the New Woman in the 1880s many men adopted the boater, which might be thought of as a very truncated top hat. And toward the end of the century men began to

wear, so to speak, the very symbol of their bashed-in authority: the trilby hat.

Others have stuck to a more aesthetic perspective regarding the hat's virtues. "The trilby is the most expressive hat a man can wear. It can be jaunty, sedate, or sporty," noted Arthur Grodd of Paul Stuart, which had continued to sell hundreds of trilbies annually up through the late 1980s.

BIBLIOGRAPHY

Berendt, John. "The Trilby," *Esquire*. (November 1988) 46. il.

The Turtleneck

The turtleneck first appeared as a sportswear staple shortly before the turn of the century. When Noel Coward began wearing colored turtle-necked jerseys in the mid-1920s, the garment took on a new role; i.e., acting as a formal substitute for the shirt and tie. In effect, Coward fired the opening salvo in what has become an ongoing struggle against the tyranny of neckties.

The turtleneck enjoyed a major resurgence in the 1960s. The beatniks and folkies bequeathed the look to the flower generation, and, from there, it filtered down to the mainstream. By early 1967 they were being worn with blazers and sports coats to the office. At small Manhattan parties, half the men were then showing up in turtlenecks. Bonwit Teller repeatedly sold out its Pierre Cardin version, priced from 30 dollars to $37.50, to such customers as Steve McQueen, Jason Robards Jr., and Paul Newman. Some of the fiercest conflicts regarding its use took place in upscale restaurants. One of the maître d's who stood firm against the turtleneck was 21's Walter Weiss, as chronicled by *Esquire*:

> "Forgive me," Walter would say politely, "but our dress code is jackets and ties. Do let me offer you one of these." Walter would hand the gentleman a perfectly hideous, brightly-colored tie to wear over his turtleneck. The look in Walter's eye foreclosed all possibility of argument.
>
> "They either left the premises or put the tie on and felt ridiculous," he says. Whatever they did, they never tried it again."

Many have testified to the garment's appeal over the years. John Berendt noted,

> . . . the turtleneck was the boldest of all the affronts to the status quo. It was the picture of masculine poise and arro-

gance, redolent of athletes, sportsmen, even U-boat commanders. The simplicity of its design made neckties seem fussy and superfluous by comparison.

The designer Halston argued,

Turtlenecks are the most comfortable garment you can wear. They move with the body, and they're flattering too, because they accentuate the face and elongate the figure. They make life so easy: you can wear a turtleneck to work and then afterwards throw on a jacket, and it becomes very dressy. You can go anywhere you like.

In the 1980s, the turtleneck successfully established itself as a "crossover" item of apparel. Whether made of silk, cashmere, acrylic blends, wool, or cotton, the garment appeared likely to be a fixture in the fashion world for many years to come.

BIBLIOGRAPHY

Berendt, John. "The Turtleneck," *Esquire*. 111 (March 1989) 48. il.
"Flashback!" *Redbook*. 166 (November 1985) 124ff. il. Reports that turtleneck sweaters, once popularized by Audrey Hepburn, are back in style again.
"Making the Turtles Move; Can Turtlenecks Replace the Button-Down Shirts?" *Business Week*. (November 11, 1967) 152. il.
"Many-Layered Golf; Golfers Prefer Turtleneck Sweaters," *Sports Illustrated*. 22 (April 12, 1965) 72.
"Turtleneck," *Newsweek*. 70 (November 27, 1967) 86. il.
"Turtlenecks for Men," *Time*. 89 (March 3, 1967) 59. il.

Tutus for Young Girls

Tutus–that warhorse of classical ballet productions–became extremely popular as a form of leisure wear for young girls two through eight years of age in 1990. Leslie Sexer of the bodywear company Jacques Moret noted, "Our sales have increased 300 to 400 percent in the first three months of [1990]."

Priced from 12 to 15 dollars by Moret, the tutu seems to have reached its audience via television commercials for products such as Cheer detergent and Flintstones vitamins. In addition, the increasing popularity of bodywear departments made them readily accessible. Beth Karten of Karten for Kids backed up this point, stating "When mothers go to buy leggings, their daughters point to the tutus and say, 'Mommy, that's real pretty.' "

Whether or not the tutu will retain this level of popularity remains to be seen; however, its high pedigree and appeal to ever present youthful desires to dress up would appear to bode well for the future.

BIBLIOGRAPHY

Sporkin, Elizabeth. "Style Watch: Tutu Much," *People Weekly.* (1990) 36. il.

Twiggy

Twiggy, born Leslie Hornby in London in 1949, came to represent fashion chic to Americans in the mid-1960s with its emphasis on youth, ambition, and self-image. After some false starts, her career began its rapid ascent when her boyfriend, entrepreneur Justin de Villeneuve, helped her secure a contract with the British fashion magazine, *Woman's Mirror*, in 1966. She was immediately sent to Leonard in Mayfair's Upper Grosvenor Street to have her hair cut. After eight hours of cutting, tinting, highlighting, and drying, the trademark Twiggy style emerged. As Twiggy recalled,

> They kept drying it to see if it fell right. Those short haircuts have to be absolutely precise. The back was just an inch long, with a little tail, and the front very smooth. I thought it was marvelous.

Shortly thereafter, photographer Barry Lategan worked with her. One of his prints caught the eye of *Daily Express* fashion editor Dierdre McSharry. The paper dubbed her "The Face of 1966." Wearing Mary Quant miniskirted ensembles set off by her close-cropped light brown hair and big, Bambi eyes, Twiggy found the U.S. (still in the midst of the British Invasion of rock music) extremely receptive to her look. *Newsweek* termed her hairstyle "the year's most radiant and evocative new image."

Twiggy's time in the spotlight was short-lived in duration. The flower power movement of the following year rendered her Swinging London persona passé. Twiggy turned from modeling to films and a singing career; however, she experienced little success in these and other ventures.

BIBLIOGRAPHY

"Arrival of Twiggy," *Life*. 62 (February 3, 1967) 33-34ff. il.

"Cockney Kid," *Time*. 88 (November 11, 1966) 49. il.

Is It a Girl? Is It a Boy? No, It's Twiggy," *Look*. 31 (April 4, 1967) 84-86ff. il.

Jones, Dylan. "Twiggy," In *Haircults*, New York: Thames and Hudson, 1990. pp. 47ff. il.

Kerr, J. "Twiggy Who?" *McCalls*. 94 (July 1967) 62-63ff. il.

"Twig," *Newsweek*. 69 (April 3, 1967) 62. il.

"Twiggy; Click! Click!," *Newsweek*. 69 (April 10, 1967) 62-66. il.

"Twiggy Talks About the Twiggy Look," *Ladies Home Journal*. 84 (June 1967) 62. il.

"Whatever Happened to . . . ," *Look*. 32 (August 6, 1968) 78ff. il.

The Tylenol Scare

In early October 1982, seven Chicago-area residents died from taking capsules of Extra-Strength Tylenol laced with cyanide, a poison capable of killing within minutes of ingestion. According to *Newsweek*, news of the related deaths triggered "the biggest consumer alert in memory and a public-health drama more gripping than any episode of 'Quincy.'" The victims–Mary Kellerman, Paula Prince, Mary Reiner, Stanley Janus and his wife Theresa, Adam Janus, and Mary McFarland–were linked together by a combination of luck and diligent medical sleuthing. Initially, the deaths appeared unrelated. Doctors believed that 12-year-old Kellerman, the first to die, had had a stroke, and that Adam Janus, the second victim, had succumbed to a massive heart attack. However, Dr. Thomas Kim at Northwest Community Hospital in Arlington Heights became suspicious when Janus's brother and sister-in-law were admitted with dilated pupils and very low blood pressure that did not respond to treatment. Consultation with the Rocky Mountain Poison Center led to the determination that cyanide had precipitated the death.

The Tylenol link was established by two off-duty firefighters at the same point in time. Philip Cappitelli, the son-in-law of a friend of Kellerman's mother, was told by a fellow firefighter, Richard Keyworth, "This is a wild stab–maybe it's the Tylenol [known to have been taken by Kellerman before collapsing]." Cappitelli then checked with Arlington Heights paramedics and learned that the Janus family had taken the same product. The bottles retrieved from the two homes (Stanley and Theresa Janus had shared the Tylenol found in his brother Adam's house) both bore the manufacturer's lot number MC2 880.

The discovery of yet another contaminated batch led Tylenol's manufacturer, Johnson & Johnson subsidiary McNeil Consumer Products Co., to recall some 264,400 bottles of the medication nationwide. The U.S. Food and Drug Administration warned Americans not to take *any* Extra-Strength Tylenol capsules until the mystery was solved. Some state health departments went even further, banning sales of all Tylenol products, including tablets and liquids. Some retailers removed only the suspect lots of Extra-Strength Tylenol from their shelves while others stopped sales of the product in all forms.

With the threat seemingly centered in Chicago, the health and law-enforcement officials there took extraordinary steps to spread the warning. Police cruised neighborhoods, shouting over bullhorns. Boy Scouts knocked on doors and church groups manned telephones to try to reach those not tuned in to radio and TV warnings. Schools, buses, and trains also helped to spread the word.

Elsewhere around the country officials were besieged by false alarms. A 72-year-old man who died shortly after consuming Extra-Strength Tylenol was determined by the autopsy to have had a stroke. A Cleveland-area woman who'd taken the product was treated for low-level cyanide poisoning; however, no poison could be found in her remaining capsules and health officials were quick to note that minute traces of cyanide can be ingested by eating some types of fish or unwashed fruit. *Newsweek* noted that "at Georgia's Regional Poison Control Center in Atlanta, Fred Graves became so weary of dispelling fears about minor physical complaints that he began asking callers why they had taken Extra-Strength Tylenol in the first place. 'Invariably,' he said, 'the answer came that they were already sick.' "

In the meantime, investigators from 15 federal, state, and local law-enforcement agencies searched the various links of the Tylenol supply chain: the manufacturing plants in Ft. Washington, Pennsylvania, and Round Rock, Texas from where the contaminated batches originated, the delivery apparatus, wholesalers, and the retailers where the victims' bottles had been purchased. Experts noted that the culprit–or culprits–could be virtually anyone: a psychopath, a disgruntled employee of McNeil or Johnson & Johnson, or even an overzealous competitor, given the fact that aspirin manufacturers, trailing Tylenol in the marketplace and recently hurt by government studies suggesting a connection with Reye's syndrome, had much to gain from such a scare. A resolution to the case, however, was never found.

As time passed, the damage to Johnson & Johnson slowed. Company stock rebounded following a brief drop and the Tylenol brand returned to the shelves (albeit with improved tamper-resistant packaging) and a leading market share. In the wake of the company's estimated losses of 50 million dollars and widespread consumer fears, government authorities pressed for laws requiring all over-the-counter medicines to be individually sealed at the factory to guard against undetected tampering. Chicago Mayor Jane Byrne proposed a city ordinance requiring all OTC medicines sold there to carry protective seals. The major companies producing OTC medicines, vitamins, and other drug-related products–ever mindful of the PR factor–didn't bother to wait for legislature directives. In short order, protective packaging became the standard within the pharmaceutical industry and has remained so up to the present day.

BIBLIOGRAPHY

"After Its Recovery, New Headaches for Tylenol," *Business Week*. (May 14, 1984) 137.

Beck, Melinda, and others. "The Tylenol Scare," *Newsweek*. 100 (October 11, 1982) 32-36. il. Includes sidebars: "In Search of a Madman," by Peter McGrath and others, and "The 15-Minute Killer" (i.e., cyanide).

"Booked," *Time*. 120 (December 27, 1982) 19. Re. suspect J. W. Lewis.

Church, G. J. "Copycats are on the Prowl," *Time*. 120 (November 8, 1982) 27. il.

"J & J Will Pay Dearly to Cure Tylenol," *Business Week*. (November 29, 1982) 37. il.

"Package Safety a Year After the Tylenol Scare," *Changing Times*. 37 (September 1983) 10. il.

Trafford, A. "Lessons That Emerge from Tylenol Disaster," *U.S. News & World Report*. 93 (October 18, 1982) 67-68. il.

"Tylenol's 'Miracle' Comeback," *Time*. 122 (October 17, 1983) 67. il.

Unisex

In the mid-1960s, Great Britain was responsible for exporting more than beat revival music (as manifested in chart-topping recordings by the Beatles, the Rolling Stones, and others) to the United States. Originating in London, unisex–a teen fashion exhibiting a distinctly androgynous look–was very much in vogue by early 1966, particularly with the "switched-on urban kids" who act as tastemakers for youth in the "provinces" (i.e., rural areas and the Midwest and South in general). The look, according to *Life and Leisure* editor Harry F. Waters, set off "a wave of mistaken-identity cases among parents, teachers, store clerks, waiters, policemen, and, on occasion, even the kids themselves." A Detroit girl noted at the time, "The boys I know dress more like girls than the girls I know. And they fuss so before mirrors."

The look–which had antecedents in the "His" and "Hers" fad of 1951 set off by photographs of socially prominent married couples in *Vogue*–included hair styling (long, with scented hair sprays and perms), clothes (e.g., high-heeled boots, hip-huggers, ring belts, ruffled shirts in bright–often with floral patterns–colors, Liverpool caps), toiletries (Dana Perfumes Corp. found that 20 percent of the users of its Canoe men's cologne were teenage girls and that one of the most potent new sellers was a "His-Her" cologne advertised as the "scent of togetherness"), and even dancing, with youth performing the same moves out on the floor (as opposed to the traditional leading role assumed by men in more traditional steps).

Many considered pop music stars (Mick Jagger of the Rolling Stones and a host of other long-haired, slim-figured male stars, not to overlook the assertive stage presence of females such as Grace Slick of The Jefferson Airplane and Janis Joplin of Big Brother and the Holding Company) and fashion kings (e.g., Pierre Cardin's spring 1966 line had two girl models strutting about in black leather motorcycle jackets and long stockings while the boys wore suede) to be largely responsible for this trend. Some professional observers offered deeper interpretations of the causal factors at work with unisex:

- Dr. Bruce Buchenholz of New York's Psychiatric Treatment Center: "It alleviates their anxiety. They can say he/she is not that different from me and thus it becomes easier for them to establish a relationship."
- Dr. Ralph Greenson, a clinical professor of psychiatry at UCLA: "[It's] just another form of the teenagers' rebellion against what their parents stand for."
- Others have noted what seems to be a reversal of teenage roles; the assistant manager of a Boston clothing store noted, "The girl tells the boy everything. She picks out the style and color for him. He just looks and listens."
- Most psychologists blame the new docility of the teenage male on mom. According to *Newsweek*,

In the absence of a strong masculine influence during the day, the average boy may decide that it is the mother who is the real center of power and initiative in the family. Once this occurs, the male may naturally come to accept female direction–in fact even seek it out–in his adolescent companions. At the same time other observers have perceived an extension of the nature of Momism. As they see it, the matriarchal, overly protective mother has been replaced by the type who competes with her children at everything from skateboarding to the Jerk. "In the 1960s," says one psychiatrist, "Jewish mothers are out. Now it's Momma a Go-Go."

Unisex continued in one guise or another as a popular form of expression up through the late 1970s. However, the movement lost its impetus with the rise of the conservative Reagan agenda in the 1980s.

BIBLIOGRAPHY

Anspach, Karlyne. *The Why of Fashion*. Ames, Iowa: Iowa State University Press, 1969 (©1967). il.
"Uni-sex," *Newsweek*. 67 (February 14, 1966) 59-60. il.

The Velcro Ball and Mitt Set

The hottest toy during the summer of 1991 was known variously as "Magic Mitts," "Scatch," "Katch-a-Roo," and "Super Grip Ball." It consisted of stick-to-itself Velcro covering a tennis ball-sized sphere and two disks, the latter of which strapped across the back to allow use as a mitt. Regarding its use, *Newsweek* observed,

> On streets, playgrounds and at the beach, players have added their own fancy moves, twisting into pretzel shapes to make behind-the-back catches, or getting a grip on the ball while doing a high-kick. Another trick: strapping a mitt on each hand to grab two balls at once. In short, the new adhesive playthings do what the Frisbee used to do, with less effort.

The popularity of the toy can be attributed to a number of factors:

1. The prices, ranging from 13 to 20 dollars for the various three-piece sets, were within the means of most Americans.
2. Even beginners looked good playing with it. Ashley Petrus, 12, of Columbia, South Carolina, noted, "You really get into it. The best part is the feeling of pride when you catch." Her brother Brad, nine, added, "You don't have to be exact. If the ball hits on the mitt's side, it sticks."
3. Its availability in splashy, neon colors.
4. The currently depressed state of business in most parts of the nation. Stephen Sandberg, owner of the Sanco Toy Co., in Foxboro, Massachusetts, observed at the time, "When the economy gets tough, you need a diversion. You look for something simple to do. You use your imagination, and make up your own rules."
5. Aggressive marketing.

Mark Paliafito, co-founder of Paliafito America Inc., agreed to spend at least one million dollars in advertising after obtaining the

U.S. marketing rights to a South Korean-made set which had been a big hit with the young players of a baseball league he'd been coaching in the fall of 1990. The company handed out hundreds of its balls and mitts, called Super Grip Ball, to college students on Florida and Texas beaches during the 1991 spring break. The game caught on quickly; within a few months Paliafito America had sold 650,000 units and taken orders for almost one million more. It was popular in the 75-store Sharper Image chain, whose typical customer was described as a middle-aged male, as well as with toy stores. Sanco also shipped 100,000 of its version called Scatch.

As the summer began to fade, the game appeared likely to be around for some time to come. Paliafito America had begun lining up commercial sponsors to stamp their logos on the Super Grip Ball. In addition, the company was planning to manufacture disks seven feet in diameter for use in team play. Five more versions of the game were anticipated to be on the market by 1992.

BIBLIOGRAPHY

Mitchell, Emily, with Dan Cray and Elizabeth Rudolph. "The (Sticky) Fad of Summer," *Time*. (July 29, 1991) 61. il.
"One for the Gripper," *People Weekly*. 36 (August 19, 1991) 95-96. il.

Video Cassette Recorders

Billboard, in its January 6, 1990 issue, dubbed the 1980s "the video decade." During that decade, the majority of American families acquired a video cassette recorder. While the majority of consumers may have considered broadcast recording (usually in the form of time-shifting; i.e., taping television programs via automatic commands for playback at a more convenient time) the prime reason for VCR ownership at the outset, by the mid-1980s, the growing number of available titles on tape had become a powerful lure. In 1978, prerecorded cassette sales were estimated to be in the 33 to 44 million dollar range. Within two years the figure had increased approximately tenfold; by the late 1980s, tapes (sales and rentals) accounted for more than ten billion dollars annually.

Hollywood films became the backbone of the prerecorded cassette market from the outset, when Twentieth Century-Fox leased 50 titles to Magnetic Video in 1977. Despite their early reservations (selling titles in mass quantities opened the door to piracy and other unauthorized activities), the film studios ultimately reaped a financial bonanza as home video revenues grew to twice that of theaters by 1990. Industry insiders supported this view. Producer Herbert Ross (*Airport*, *The Poseidon Adventure*, etc.) noted, "I think of home video as movies premiering all over again. It's the most exciting thing that's ever happened to the motion picture industry." Producer Jerry Bruckheimer (*Top Gun*) added, "Home video has brought back a dormant audience to movie theaters."

The appeal to consumers of being able to watch *what* one wanted, *when* one wanted provided the impetus for the rise of countless video store-franchise dealers, "mom and pop" outlets, departments within supermarkets, drug stores, department stores, and audio shops, etc. It is estimated that about 3,000 specialty operations started up in 1980 alone, at a time when less than 1,000 titles existed in the video market. In the early years, the high sale price (i.e., usually 59 dollars and up) of prerecorded cassettes acted as an obstacle to the growth of the industry. Exchange and rental programs sprang up as a means of getting around this problem.

The film studios, zealously trying to protect what they perceived to be their copyright prerogatives, sought to control the rental process (i.e., either disallowing it or insisting on a portion of the profits above and beyond the initial sale of the tapes). A concerted effort on the part of video retailers–already a powerful lobbying force by the early 1980s–helped defeat attempts at repealing the right of first sale.

The intelligence–and sanity–of the film industry was also subject to question in the landmark *Universal v. Sony* case in which Universal and Disney sued Sony for breach of copyright. Winding its way up to the Supreme Court, the justices ruled on January 17, 1984 that it was entirely lawful to copy a program for later viewing as well as to sell machines making such copying possible. Once the pall of a possible lawsuit was removed from the horizon, home video entrepreneurs and film industry insiders alike seemed to heave a collective sigh of relief and commit themselves wholly to the VCR and prerecorded cassettes.

The remaining obstacle to VCR growth–that of format compatibility–proved somewhat harder to overcome. Sony, the early leader in the VCR sweepstakes, had committed itself in the 1/3-inch Beta standard, whereas the majority of its Japanese competitors (most notably Matsushita/JVC, Mitsubishi, and Hitachi) developed hardware for the 1/2-inch VHS format. Following an early lead ensuing from its reaching the marketplace first with SL-7300 Betamax deck in February 1976, Sony steadily lost ground; as early as mid-1979 VHS models were outselling Beta by two to one in the U.S. Despite the appearance of yet another format in the mid-1980s (8mm), which was closely tied to the home movie market, VHS continued to maintain a strong lead into the 1990s. In fact, its future hegemony within the prerecorded programming sector appeared likely to come from the laser videodisk rather than tape.

Despite the importance of the Hollywood film to the VCR industry, many other forms of programming arose and prospered, including TV shows, kid vid, exercise videos, instructional tapes, documentaries, and live dramatic/musical productions. In fact, the VCR proved capable of transmitting any form of video material, no matter what the source–films, television, home movies, computer graphics, etc. This diversity of programming–able to reflect the needs and interests of virtually everyone–assured the long-term success of the medium. At the outset of the 1990s, it appeared likely that the VCR–or some close descendant–would occupy a primary place in the American lifestyle for generations to come.

TABLE 1. A VCR Chronology

April 1956

Ampex gives the first exhibition of its videotape recorder at the National Association of Radio Broadcasters. The company would go on to control the VTR business for years to come.

Fall 1969

Sony produces the U-matic recorder which uses 3/4-inch-wide tape within a cassette shell. It goes on the market in 1971. Being too big and too expensive for ordinary consumers, its use is confined largely to educational, industrial, and professional customers.

February 1976

Sony puts the Betamax on the market.

1977

VHS recorders are introduced into the U.S. By March 1978, Americans are buying more RCA SelectaVisions (made by Matsushita) than Betamaxes, due to their better styling and longer playing time.

February 1980

CBS establishes its Video Enterprises Division to manufacture and market video software.

March 1980

RIAA/Video is established to handle video rights and represent companies involved in videocassettes and videodisks.

September 1980

WEA and Warner Home Video scuttle their video software sales policy in favor of a lease-to-dealer for-rental-only program.

October 19, 1981

The San Francisco Referral Appeals Court rules that copying television programs off the air with a VCR is an illegal infringement of copyright law.

October 20, 1981

Congress offers a flurry of legislative proposals to amend the 1976 Copyright Act to exclude private home videotaping from copyright infringement violations, in reaction to the 9th Circuit Court of Appeals decision on the 19th.

January 1982

Warner Home Video radically modifies its controversial rental-only plan in response to strong negative dealer reaction. Beginning in March, the company will allow sale of the bulk of its titles.

March 1982

Sony Corp. of America files a petition for the Supreme Court to reverse the 9th Circuit Court of Appeals decision in the "Betamax Case."

September 1982

Paramount announces plans to release *Star Trek II: The Wrath of Khan* in November at $39.95, a new low for a major motion picture. By early 1983, the price had become a reference point for the home video market.

December 1983

New pricing strategies, further home penetration of VCRs, and a surging economy place the year's sales of prerecorded home videos at double that of 1982.

January 1984

The Supreme Court, in a five to four vote, rules in the so-called "Betamax Case" that noncommercial, private home videotaping of off-the-air copyrighted programs is legal and does not constitute copyright infringement.

May 1984

The home video industry is threatened by the specter of governmental regulation. Two states have already passed laws turning the Motion Picture Association of America's voluntary ratings system into full-scale legal requirements, and two other states are considering similar laws.

June 1984

Media Home Entertainment slashes home video price levels to a never-before-reached low with the release of 20 titles at $19.95.

September 1984

Paramount Home Video and Warner Home Video give the low-priced prerecorded video market a major boost by releasing and re-releasing a large number of major titles at less than 30 dollars.

January 1985

Videocassette recorder sales soar to new heights, with volume at wholesale hitting a pace of 12 million machines per year, according to the EIA/CEG.

March 1985

Industry observers note that major motion picture studios are substantially shortening home video release windows, making recent feature film titles available on a regular basis to the home video sales/rental market as early as four months after theatrical release.

June 1985

Paramount Home Video announces plans to release 30 titles over the summer with list prices ranging from $16.95 to $29.95, thereby establishing new lows.

July 21, 1985

Five companies release the first mainstream product (e.g., Hollywood films) in the 8mm format appearing anywhere in the world.

February 1986

Family Home Entertainment becomes the first significant home video independent to crack the $10-suggested-list-price barrier with popular children's category titles.

May 1986

The U.S. Supreme Court's decision on the 22nd to allow states to legally seize allegedly obscene videos following the issuance of a "probable cause" warrant will have "a chilling effect" on the nation's video stores, according to the top lawyer for the VSDA (Video Service Dealers Association).

August 1987

A VSDA study reveals that when consumers have a head-to-head choice between renting a title and watching it on pay-per-view, rental activity falls off 40 to 60 percent.

September 1987

The move to an $89.95 list price on most major video titles may have angered some video retailers; however, distributors say that they'd never know it from the amount of titles being ordered.

October 1987

In an effort to arouse interest in the floundering Beta format, Paramount Home Video says that all new Beta releases will be list-priced no higher that $29.95, regardless of VHS pricing. By the end of the decade, though, Beta has ceased to be a factor within the home video industry.

December 1988

Orion Home Video and Hitachi join in a campaign to promote Super VHS VCR sales that make 30 Orion and 10 Nelson S-VHS movie titles available to Hitachi hardware customers for a limited time.

October 1989

The runaway success of releases such as *The Land Before Time* and *Bambi*, in the estimation of many, created an excessively hit-oriented market. According to rackjobbers, program suppliers, and retailers at a Paul Kagan Seminar held in New York, however, the sell-through business (retail sales of a new product) is extremely broad-based.

BIBLIOGRAPHY

Lardner, James. *Fast Forward*. New York: Norton, 1987.
"1980-1990: The Video Decade," with an Introduction by Jim McCullaugh, *Billboard*. (January 6, 1990) V1ff. (special section)

The Watchman

Sony Corp.'s Watchman–the first pocket television set, released in 1982–was the hottest novelty product during that year's Christmas season. Margot Rogoff, a spokeswoman for New York's Bloomingdale's, noted, "It's been the most talked-about item in the store. It's a total, total sellout." In fact, Sony had trouble keeping many retailers supplied with the item, all the while fielding angry calls from disappointed customers who had found the product sold out.

Only eight inches long, 1.4 inches thick, and 3 1/2 inches wide–about the size of a box of Cracker Jack–the Watchman fit easily into a coat pocket. At a retail price of $350, it produced a two-inch picture that strained even the sharpest eye and sported sound which was a trifle on the tinny side (although the earphone accompanying it boosted audio quality somewhat). In addition, the Watchman could only pull in signals in metropolitan areas which had broadcasting stations in the nearby vicinity.

The set's diminutive size was the result of a technological breakthrough at Sony. In conventional TV sets, an electron beam is bounced directly onto the video screen from the tube behind it, thereby necessitating that set designers build models with plenty of depth. Sony engineers, however, worked out a means of bouncing the electron beam so that it struck the screen from the side, permitting a significant reduction in size.

Despite its initial success, the Watchman–and a host of models issued shortly thereafter by competitors–failed to equal the popularity of its antecedent in the audio field, the Walkman cassette player. Unlike the Walkman and other portable cassette machines, the Watchman did not complement such activities as walking, running, bicycling, or driving. It has found a stable niche, nevertheless, providing a quick fix for television junkies who could never be far away from a video screen for long.

BIBLIOGRAPHY

"A Watchman for TV Junkies," *Newsweek.* 100 (December 20, 1982) 75. il.

Wigs for Men

Following the European example, American men in the eighteenth century took to wearing wigs. Fashionable boys began wearing them at the age of seven. Even house slaves were required to wear white goat's hair or horsehair wigs by many owners. While the majority were American-made, the upper class imported theirs from England. Only in rural areas, particularly the South, could a preponderance of men be found who displayed their own hair in public.

Well-made wigs were expensive; they cost as much as a complete outfit of clothes. Dressing and caring for them also cost a great deal; most barbers were paid an annual fee to dress a Colonial male's wig as well as keep him clean-shaven.

Styles continued to be dictated by the British. Bill Severn notes,

> When Englishmen shortened them, so did the colonials. Later in the century, they even imitated London's Macaroni dandies, with less extravagance but with hair looped up and pinned in place with a comb. Yankee Doodle wasn't the only wig-sporty American who hoped to be taken for a Macaroni.

The American Revolution served to turn many against wigs. New England patriots, although wigged themselves, showed contempt for the elaborate wigs worn by Tories by ripping some of them from their heads. The majority of men continued to wear them, however; illustrations of the signing of the Declaration of Independence, for instance, show a substantial number of elaborately wigged individuals. Wigs remained fashionable in the U.S. until European men began going without them after the French Revolution. Many were timid at first, given the long reign of wigs, and combed and powdered their hair to imitate a wig. But, in time, more and more men came to appreciate the comfort (e.g., cool, no itching) of going without one and overlooked the boorish connotations of appearing in public wigless.

BIBLIOGRAPHY

Severn, Bill. *The Long and Short of It: Five Thousand Years of Fun and Fury Over Hair.* New York: David McKay, 1971. il.

Women's Adoption of Men's Clothing

In 1836, Lucretia Mott founded the American feminist movement in reaction to a society where many rights–to vote, hold certain jobs, engage in certain leisure-time activities, etc.–were denied women. Many proponents wore adaptations of masculine attire to make their point. In 1849, the daughter of a New York Congressman, Mrs. Elizabeth Smith Miller, began wearing an unconventional costume consisting of a skirt which extended barely beyond the knee with full baggy trousers of broadcloth gathered together at the ankle with an elastic band underneath. Mrs. Dexter Bloomer immediately launched a campaign of reform in women's dress based on the outfit in her journal, *The Lily*; the ensuing notoriety caused them to become known as "Bloomers." The fight to reform dress was never won, and women stopped wearing the garment due to the ridicule it caused (Mrs. Bloomer held on for eight years, perhaps longer than any of her followers) until the style was revived as an accepted form of girls' gym suits in the early years of the twentieth century.

For the duration of the nineteenth century, however, women remained slaves to specialization in dress. A woman of even modest means might make ten or more wardrobe changes per day: a morning dress for receiving callers or housekeeping dress for doing chores, a walking costume or tailor-made outfit for church or travel, a carriage dress for display while riding, an opera dress for a matinee, a dinner gown which had to be changed for a ball gown at ten o'clock, etc.

The rise of sporting activities played a key role in enabling women to adopt a freer form of dress. Women attending the beach in the 1920s and 1930s began dressing for the demands of the sport rather than paying attention to the "taboos of an outworn prudery." The true beginning of the era of slacks and shorts for all originated with lounging pajamas for the beach during the 1920s and 1930s.

Marlene Dietrich, the internationally renowned German actress, furthered the trend by covering her legendary legs in a mannish slack suit.

The feminine trend toward adopting men's wardrobe items became a necessity—as opposed to a fashion whim—when women were called to replace men in factory jobs during World War II. The demands for safety led to the introduction of items such as the one-piece slack suit, designed by the U.S. Bureau of Home Economics, with plenty of room for movement but with no extra fullness to get snagged on moving machine parts.

The use of slacks spread still further to other spheres of feminine living such as a leisurely evening at home. The *New York Times Magazine*, March 1, 1942, observed,

> Right now it is a matter of comfort—being able to move around without worrying about pulling your dress down, being warm, being crisp and efficient looking, and also being economical because slacks cut down on stockings, dry cleaners and laundry bills.

Karlyne Anspach notes that during 1942, Filenes in Boston installed three "Slack Bars," and Marshall Field's, the Fair, and Goldblatt Brothers in Chicago reported trouser sales five to ten times greater than the previous year.

Women continued wearing pants—as well as other male clothing such as blazers, ties, and boots—during the increasingly more permissive years following the war. Some 150 years after Mrs. Bloomer's social transgressions, traditionally male-oriented articles of dress—most notably, pants—are no longer considered "special items" but are parts of the basic stock in retail stores because of their widespread acceptance, particularly by the more educated and urbanized sectors of the female population.

BIBLIOGRAPHY

Anspach, Karlyne. *The Why of Fashion.* Ames, Iowa: Iowa State University Press, 1969 (©1967). il.

Young Vulgarians

The Young Vulgarians, street-smart teenagers growing up in Northern urban centers, dominated the youth subculture in the early 1960s, influencing mainstream tastes in the process. Jane and Michael Stern succinctly captured the visual essence of the movement in the following passage:

> Unburdened by middle-class rules of good taste, young vulgarians positively dripped with splendiferous cheapness. If you want a quick mental picture of what they looked like, think of Priscilla Presley in 1963, when Elvis acted as her personal cosmetology consultant; or remember the sassy kids in John Waters's movie *Hairspray*; or flash back to continental doo-woppers such as Dion and the Belmonts. Young vulgarians flaunted huge bouffants, heavy eyeliner, pounds of Vitalis, and black leather coats over sharkskin trousers.

There was more to the movement, however, than a hoodlum baroque look. At its core, its practitioners/exponents expressed a turgid universe of teenage passion and despair. The young vulgarian ethic found its most expressive voice via the Girl Group phenomenon which peaked during this era.

TABLE 1. Leading Girl Groups and Their Major Hits

The Cookies	Chains (1962-1963)
	Don't Say Nothin' Bad (About My Baby) (1963)
The Crystals	Uptown (1962)
	He's a Rebel (1962)

	He's Sure the Boy I Love (1962-1963)
	Da Doo Ron Ron (1963)
	Then He Kissed Me (1963)
The Jelly Beans	I Wanna Love Him So Bad (1964)
The Ronettes	Be My Baby (1963)
	Baby, I Love You (1963-1964)
	(The Best Part Of) Breakin' Up (1964)
	Do I Love You? (1964)
	Walking in the Rain (1964)
The Shangri-Las	Remember (Walkin' in the Sand) (1964)
	Leader of the Pack (1964)
	Give Him a Great Big Kiss (1964-1965)
	Give Us Your Blessings (1965)
	I Can Never Go Home Anymore (1965)
The Shirelles	Dedicated to the One I Love (1959; 1961)
	Will You Love Me Tomorrow (1960-1961)
	Mama Said (1961)
	Baby It's You (1961-1962)
	Soldier Boy (1962)
	Foolish Little Girl (1963)

The boys had a new generation of cool urban crooners to emulate such as Bobby Darin, Frankie Avalon, Dion DiMucci, Fabian, and Bobby Rydell.

These artists catered to a teenage world left largely untouched by major merchandisers and adults in general. The relative isolation in which teens operated at the time enabled them to develop their own sense of style, one based upon the resources and raw materials available. A random listing of accessories for young vulgarians included the following:

For guys:

• wraparound sunglasses.
• tight sharkskin suits.
• three-quarter length leather raincoats.

For girls:

- pancake makeup for a colorless opaque skin.
- dead-white lipstick.
- black liquid eyeliner and black eyebrow pencil.
- pointy padded bras (often black).
- white nylon "pussycat" blouses.
- boyfriend's oversized ID bracelets, made of thick, coarse, silver links.
- lockets with pictures of fave singers.
- ankle bracelets, worn under nylons.
- short, tight black skirts.
- elastic black belts with gold buckles.
- sheer black nylons.
- black shoes–with pointy toes and curvy Cuban heels an inch high–made of Leatherette.
- sneakers (not athletic type but rather pointy-toed in purple leopard skin, etc.) and "poodle socks."
- huge cable-stitched mohair cardigans in pinky peach or turquoise blue.
- high-school jacket with white Leatherette sleeves and name of school in felt letters on the back (and breast pocket, in loopy white letters, with owner's name embroidered).
- copious handbag slung over shoulder.

The crowning glory of the style, however, was the hair. For girls–particularly in 1962-1963–this meant the beehive. Despite its having a stiff, impervious look, the beehive was, in fact, extremely unstable, taking hours to create and demanding constant care and attention to maintain. The hair-styling books of the time included the following procedures for its construction:

When construction begins, the first task is overcoming the hair's cleanliness. Just-washed hair is limp, and so it must be slathered immediately with setting gel to give it body and texture. While damp and still tacky from the gel, the hair is rolled onto big plastic rollers (preferably pink) covered with a triangular hair net.

Now the hairdo is dried. While its owner reads a fan magazine in a chair, the curled and wrapped coiffure on her head is snuggled into a giant metal-domed hair dryer and baked with currents of hot air for about as long as it takes to cook a chicken. When thoroughly dry, it is ready to be combed out.

Shaping begins. Section by section, using a rat-tail comb, the hair is cordoned off and back-combed mercilessly, tuft by tuft, until it becomes a dozen or more weedy clumps standing out from the head. Each matted clump is saturated with a heavy-duty spray such as Aqua Net until it is as malleable as a bundle of solder wires. As the clumps dry, more back-combing further fluffs out any hair that might have wilted under the salvos of spray.

Now a hairbrush is used to gingerly create the familiar beehive or keg shape, then even more carefully arrange the uppermost layers of the tangle into a halo as delicate as spun sugar. The spire is then sprayed once more to make certain it keeps its place.

Boys had almost as hard a time of it creating their hair style. Hair was worn long and secured with large amounts of grease (brands preferred included Brylcreem, Dixie Peach, and Pomatex). The grease was applied to achieve the look of comb tracks in perfect, parallel relief. The back of the head often consisted of hair criss-crossed in an overlapping pattern from nape to top of head. The top might consist of either Edd "Kookie" Byrnes's "unitary look" or fashioning a wave curling over the front of the head and jutting out as far as possible. Rather than old-fashioned fenders on the sides (combed as a separate entity), a completely integrated look was sought.

Main venues for displaying the look and lifestyle to the world included holiday shows emceed by personality deejays such as Murray the K (later to jump on the British Invasion bandwagon as the "Fifth Beatle"), record company artwork and recordings, and most notably, Dick Clark's *American Bandstand*, with its cast of trend-setting South Philly teenagers. The young vulgarian survived into the mid-1960s despite the inroads made by other styles such as those of London's Carnaby Street. It was finally swept aside by the carefree lifestyle ethic and natural look spearheaded by West Coast bohemians, both of the surfing and flower power variety.

BIBLIOGRAPHY

Stern, Jane, and Michael Stern. "Young Vulgarians," In: *Sixties People*. New York: Knopf, 1990. pp. 58-77. il.
"Up in the Hair; Skyscraping New Hair Styles," *Newsweek*. 60 (October 29, 1962) 54. il.

Yuppies

Newsweek labeled 1984 the "year of the yuppie" in its December 13, 1984 issue, citing that group's increasingly higher visibility in politics and the marketplace. The magazine provided several criteria typifying Yuppies (the acronym for "young urban professional"):

- age; they were among the 60 million baby-boom Americans born between 1946 and 1964.
- income; some four million Americans between 25 and 39 earned more than $40,000 per annum.
- environment; of the above groups of well-to-do youth, 1.2 million lived in cities.
- a broader view would encompass all baby boomers who went to college or work in white collar or technical jobs (i.e., around 20 million people).

Perhaps most notable of all, however, Yuppies represented a marketing executive's dream; i.e., they were consumers with a vengeance. The mass media flooded the public with observations on this characteristic of Yuppiedom. Tom Overton, a reporter for the *Houston Post*, noted, "[for Yuppies] the name of the game is THE BEST–buying it, owning it, using it, eating it, watching it, wearing it, growing it, cooking it, driving it, doing whatever with it."

The phenomenon also spawned a variety of reference/coffee table compendiums, including *Yuppie Handbook, The State-of-the-Art Manual for Young Urban Professionals*, probably the ultimate source of information about Yuppies. The book included the following insights:

1. A Yuppie is usually a WASP (White, Anglo-Saxon, Protestant); however, there are numerous variations, such as the

Guppie (Gay Urban Professional); Buppie (Black Urban Professional), and Huppie (Hispanic Urban Professional).

2. A Yuppie will never eat or drink anything instant, wear permanent press garments or clothes made of synthetic fibers, pay cash, or cancel an hour of reserved court time.

3. Yuppies speak the same language, frequently using words like "minimalism," "menu driven," "world class," "disc (i.e., julienne, floppy, and digital)," "mesquite," "postmodern," "wraparound mortgage," and "beta endorphine."

4. Yuppies have their own Ten Commandments, such as:
   - Thou shalt take unto thee only designer labels.
   - Thou shalt speak the name of thy wine merchant and the name of thy cleaning person with reverence.
   - Honor thy investment banker and thy real estate agent.
   - Thou shalt not kill whales or baby seals (save murder for the stock market).
   - Thou shalt not steal. Your lawyer's a pro at it–that's why you have one.
   - Thou shalt not wear false materials, neither polyester nor vinyl; nor serve false consumables, neither Cool Whip nor Tang.

5. Yuppies are likely to eat the following for lunch:
   - Tuna Sashimi
   - Hunan Chicken
   - Tortellini Salad
   - Empañadas
   - Pâté
   - Chef's Salad
   They don't eat:
   - Tuna on White
   - Chicken Pot Pie
   - Bologna
   - Chef Boy-ar-dee Ravioli

While the "Yuppie" label certainly oversimplified the behavioral characteristics of many purported to fall within that grouping–some even chafed at being so designated–it made sense (real "dollars and cents"!) to merchandisers attempting to get a handle on consumers possessing these particular demographic features. From the perspective of the confluence of such criteria as high income, professional occupation, early adulthood, and higher education, the Yuppie profile has always existed. The post-World War II generation was unique, however, given its proportionately substantial numbers and the healthy state of the American economy in general. The group will likely lose its current image as members gradually become senior citizens; the elderly are decidedly not heavy consumers. And succeeding generations of young professionals may find their consuming style cramped somewhat by recessionary trends, diminished resources, and changing fashions (e.g., conspicuous consumption is out).

BIBLIOGRAPHY

"Arise, Ye Yuppies!" *New Republic.* 191 (July 9, 1984) 44ff.
Bruning, F. "The Yuppie Generation," *Macleans.* 97 (October 22, 1984) 13. il.
"Here Come the Yuppies!" *Time.* 123 (January 9, 1984) 66. il.
"Onward and Yupward," *People Weekly.* 21 (January 9, 1984) 46-48ff. il.
Overton, Tom. "Yuppies: Beyond the Preppie," *Houston Post.* (January 8, 1984) 3G.
Piesman, Marissa, and Marilee Hartley. *Yuppie Handbook, The State-of-the-Art Manual for Young Urban Professionals.* Produced by Connie Berman and Roseann Hirsch; illustrated by Lonni Sue Johnson. New York: Pocket Books, 1984.
"Upscale Anxiety," *Harpers Bazaar.* 117 (September 1984) 243-246ff. il. Special Edition.

The Zipper

The zipper, according to John Berendt, is commonly considered one of the most brilliant of all American inventions. Its immediate forerunner, the "clasp locker," consisted of two chainlike rows of hooks and eyes that were fastened and unfastened with the aid of a sliding guide. The brainchild of Chicagoan Whitcomb L. Judson in 1891, it had the unfortunate propensity for continually falling apart.

Early in the twentieth century, another inventor, Gideon Sundback, succeeded in perfecting the mechanism by eliminating the hooks and eyes and creating the now-classic design: two rows of tiny metal scoops mounted face-to-face on cloth tapes. The zipper worked by means of the ball of one scoop fitting snugly into the socket of the next so that when closed it formed a firm but flexible seam of interlocking scoops.

In 1913, Sundback and his partners bought out Judson and established the Hookless Fastener Co. in Meadville, Pennsylvania, servicing manufacturers of corsets, gloves, sleeping bags, money belts, and tobacco pouches. The market for the "slide fastener" began to expand in the early 1920s when B. F. Goodrich decided to use it in rubber boots. In seeking a name for the boot, the company's president, Bertram G. Work, reportedly said, "What we need is an action word–something that will dramatize the way the thing zips up. Why not call it the zipper?"

Despite the huge success of the Zipper Boot and other products employing the device, men's trousers remained off limits. The conquest of that industry–which assured the long-term ubiquity of the zipper–was outlined by Berendt:

> Custom tailors disdained zippered flies as vulgar, and mass manufacturers claimed they were too expensive–a zipper added a dollar to the cost of a pair of trousers; buttons cost only two cents. That's where matters stood until 1934, when the

Prince of Wales, the Duke of York, and their second cousin "Dickie" Mountbatten suddenly started wearing zippered flies. It wasn't something they flaunted, obviously, but word got around anyhow. The zippered fly was finally respectable.

Today, only a few holdouts remain: e.g., a small fraction of the customers for tailored clothes, Levi's classic 501 blue jeans with the trademark riveted metal buttons, and U.S. Army combat uniforms (an Army spokesman noted that, given zipper failure, "You can't fix a zipper in the field, but you can always sew on a button."). Despite recent inroads made by velcro, the zipper–on pants as well as a host of other garments–has moved on to institutional status within the clothing industry.

BIBLIOGRAPHY

Anspach, Karlyne. *The Why of Fashion.* Ames, Iowa: Iowa State University Press, 1969 (©1967). il.

Berendt, John. "The Zipper," *Esquire.* (May 1989) 42. il.

Jones, S. V. "Fifty Years of Zip," *New York Times Magazine.* (April 28, 1963) 108-109. il.

Wharton, D. "Zip Goes the Hookless Wonder," *Readers' Digest.* 83 (November 1963) 168C-168Dff.

Zoot-Suits

The zoot-suit–which includes an oversized jacket and baggy pants–arose among urban youth as the preferred mode of dress when frequenting jitterbug dance venues with featured big band swing music.

However, by 1943, it had become associated with sporadic episodes of violence across the nation. According to Dr. Fritz Redl, then affiliated with Wayne University's School of Public Affairs and Social Work, the zoot-suit had evolved from an informal uniform of the youth subculture to "a symbolic expression of potential unity of attack." He added,

> The original basis of dance enjoyment seems to be brushed aside by an interest in tough-guy behavior, in alcoholic excesses, in rebelliously manifested freedom of inhibition in social relations with the other sex.

Cities experiencing the greatest degree of disturbances at the time were Los Angeles, New York, Washington, D.C., and Detroit. Redl and his associates noted in a report of the "Subcommittee on the Study of the Zoot-Suit Movement" that Zoot-Suiters, in addition to such seemingly harmless activities as the development of their own brand of double-talk language, have exhibited an inclination

> . . . toward disturbance of the establishment they enter, and of immediate cohesion when attacked, toward violence and destruction on a large scale (tearing up plush seats, etc.) and toward the provocation of closed fights with local boys, bouncers, and police.

Speaking for his colleagues, Redl noted further that not all wearers of the zoot-suit were delinquents or criminals; three different groups, hard for the outsider to discern, affected this form of dress:

1. Enthusiastic jitterbugs who find the orgies of this wild form of dancing a release for restless emotions.
2. Those wearing the clothing as a chronic sort of irritation in the age-old friction between youth and adult; they viewed the zoot-suit merely as a clothing fad.
3. Those engaging in delinquent gang activities under cover of the zoot-suit.

Citing the special needs of youth from a particular socio-economic background whose needs weren't being met by any of the official adult-dominated youth organization and agencies, Redl counseled against overly dramatizing the phenomenon. His points, viewed in retrospect, appear well-taken. The zoot-suit movement did, in fact, lose its momentum during the war years.

While the growing generation gap between youth and authority figures continued to dominate the mass media in the post-World War II period, the focal point shifted to new media and youthful infatuations (e.g., comic books, rock 'n' roll, greaser fashions).

BIBLIOGRAPHY

"Zoot-Suit Epidemic," *Science News Letter.* (June 19, 1943) 388.

Zubaz

In 1991, Zubaz were termed "the hottest sports fashion since neon jams." They were designed in 1989 by two men, Bob Truax and Dan Stock, who owned a weight-lifting gym, in order to accommodate the bulging legs of their clients. Shortly thereafter, JCPenney introduced them onto the commercial market. Then the National Football League licensed them in all 28 team colors and, as of early 1991, deals were being finalized with the professional baseball, basketball, and hockey leagues. Miami Dolphins quarterback Dan Marino and German model Claudia Schiffer donned them in ads. Truax and Stock expected sales of $100 million for 1991 and had by that year expanded their line to include caps, shirts, knee-length shorts, and diapers as well as long pants. They came in classic zebra and an eye-catching array of florals, geometrics, reptile, and the ever-popular barbed-wire pattern–53 designs in all. The caps sold for about 15 dollars and the legwear from 32 to 38 dollars.

The name derived from "zuba," which in Minneapolis slang meant "in your face." Stock noted, "You wear these pants, you're saying you really don't care what anybody thinks." The loud abstract designs–replete with bright, day-glo colors and a baggy cut–certainly indicated some degree of individuality regarding fashion.

The garments were initially sewn by women prisoners at a Minnesota correctional institution as a result of friends Stock had within the system. When demand exploded, manufacturing was relocated to factories in Orlando, Florida and North Carolina. With Zubaz poised to infiltrate the leisure wear market by early 1992, the growth potential of the line appeared unlimited.

BIBLIOGRAPHY

Brecker, Elinor J. "Zubaz: New Athletic-Inspired Pants Sell Well," *Corpus Christi Caller Times.* (January 17, 1991) il. (Knight-Ridder News Service)

Index